Finding Arthur

The True Origins of the Once and Future King

ADAM ARDREY

OVERLOOK DUCKWORTH
NEW YORK • LONDON

This edition first published in paperback in the United States and the United Kingdom in 2014 by Overlook Duckworth, Peter Mayer Publishers, Inc.

NEW YORK
141 Wooster Street
New York, NY 10012
www.overlookpress.com
For bulk and special sales, please contact sales@overlookny.com,
or write us at the above address.

LONDON
30 Calvin Street
London E1 6NW
info@duckworth-publishers.co.uk
www.ducknet.co.uk

Library of Congress Cataloging-in-Publication Data
Ardrey, Adam.
Finding Arthur : the true origins of the once and future king / Adam Ardrey.
    pages cm
    Summary: "The legend of King Arthur has been told and retold for centuries. As the king who united a nation, his is the story of England itself. But what if Arthur wasn't English at all? As writer and activist Adam Ardrey discovered, the reason historians have had little success identifying the historical Arthur may be incredibly simple: He wasn't an Englishman at all. He was from Scotland. Finding Arthur chronicles Ardrey's unlikely quest to uncover the secret of Scotland's greatest king and conqueror, which has been hidden in plain sight for centuries. His research began as a simple exploration of a notable Scottish clan, but quickly it became clear that many of the familiar symbols of Arthurian legend—the Round Table, the Sword in the Stone, the Lady of the Lake—are based on very real and still accessible places in the Scottish Highlands. Sure to be controversial, Finding Arthur rewrites the legend of King Arthur for a new age."— Provided by publisher.

Includes bibliographical references and index.

    1. Arthur, King. 2. Britons—Kings and rulers—Historiography.
    3. Scotland—History—To 1057. 4. Scotland—Antiquities.
    5. Great Britain—Antiquities, Celtic. 6. Arthurian romances—Sources. I. Title.
    DA152.5.A7A75 2013   942.01'4—dc23   2013030939
A catalogue record for this book is available from the British Library.

Book design and typeformatting by Bernard Schleifer
Manufactured in the United States of America
ISBN US: 978-1-4683-0941-6
ISBN UK: 978-0-7156-5049-3
10 9 8 7 6 5 4 3 2

Finding Arthur

ALSO BY ADAM ARDREY

Finding Merlin:
  The Truth Behind the Legend of the Great Arthurian Mage

For Dorothy-Anne, Claudia, Kay, and Eliot

Contents

Argyll, Scotland

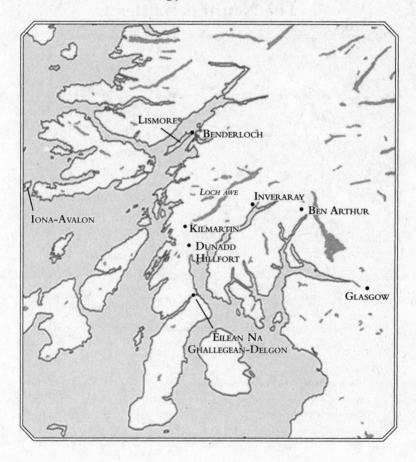

The Nennius Battles

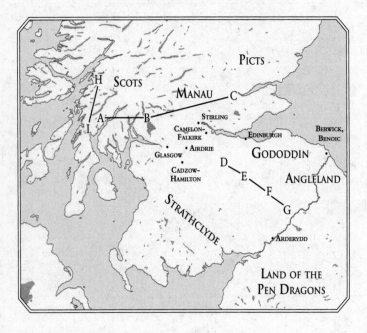

A. **GLEIN** (ARGYLL)

B. **THE FOUR BATTLES OF DOUGLAS** (LOCH LOMOND)

C. **BASSAS** (CIRCENN-CHIRCHIND-CARPOW)

D. **CALEDONIAN WOOD**

E. **GUINNION** (STOW)

F. **CITY OF THE LEGIONS** (TRIMONTIUM, MELROSE)

G. **TRIBRUIT** (RIVER TEVIOT)

H. **BREGUION / AGNED** (BENDERLOCH)

I. **BADON'S** (BADDEN, ARGYLL)

Chronology

410	The Romans leave Britain.
c. 475 to c. 548	The traditional time of Arthur.
c. 500	Fergus Mor Mac Erc, Arthur's great-great-grandfather, invades Argyll and becomes king of the Scots of Dalriada-Scotland.
c. 501	Death of Fergus—Domangart Mac Fergus, Arthur's great-grandfather becomes king of the Scots.
c. 507	Death of Domangart—Comgall Mac Domangart, Arthur's great-granduncle, becomes king of the Scots.
c. 525	Gabhran Mac Domangart, Arthur's grandfather arrives in Manau.
c. 530	Birth of Aedan Mac Gabhran, Arthur's father.
c. 538	Comgall Mac Domangart, Arthur's great granduncle, abdicates—Gabhran Mac Domangart, Arthur's grandfather, becomes king of the Scots.
c. 540	Birth of Merlin-Lailoken and his twin-sister, Languoreth, at Cadzow-Hamilton.
c. 544	The Angles arrive under the warlord Ida.
547	Ida stages a coup and founds the Angle kingdom of Bernicia.
553	Emrys leads resistance to the Angles.
c. 557	Emrys takes the title *Pen Dragon*.

c. 558   Arthur's grandfather, Gabhran Mac Domangart, king of the Scots, defeated by Bridei Mac Maelchon, king of the Picts. Gabhran dies this year or perhaps the following year. Conall Mac Comgall, Arthur's second cousin once removed, becomes king of the Scots.

c. 559   Birth of Arthur Mac Aedan (Arthur).

c. 563   Gwenddolau becomes the second *Pen Dragon*, the "other" or *Uther Pendragon*.

563   Columba-Crimthann arrives in Scotland.

c. 568   The rebel lords rise against Conall, king of the Scots. Columba-Crimthann is given Iona.

c. 570   Aedan, Arthur's father, becomes king of Manau.

573   Battle of Arderydd. Merlin goes into exile in the Caledonian Wood.

574   Aedan, Arthur's father, becomes king of the Scots of Dalriada. Arthur takes the sword from the stone and becomes tanist and warlord of the Scots.

c. 574 to c. 575   Scots civil war—Battle of Delgon and Arthur's Battle of Glein.

575 to 576   The Council of Drumceatt.

c. 577 to c. 580   Arthur's four Battles of Douglas.

c. late-570s   Arthur kills Hueil the brother of Gildas.

c. 580   Merlin returns from exile. The Orkney campaign of Aedan, Arthur's father.

c. 584   The Battle of Bassas—Arthur defeats the Miathi-Pictish king, Bridei Mac Maelchon.

c. 586   Part one of the Great Angle War—Arthur is victorious in every battle:

Campaign of the Caledonian Wood

    The Battle of the Caledonian Wood

    The Battle of Guinnion

    The Battle of the City of the Legions

    The Battle of Tribruit.

c. 588 Part two of the Great Angle War—Arthur is victorious in both battles:
The Badon Campaign
    Battle of Agned-Breguoin
    Battle of Badon.

c. 592 Death of Muluag of Lismore.

593 Death of Éoganán Mac Gabhran, Arthur's uncle.

c. 596 Battle of Camlann and the death of Arthur.

597 Death of Columba-Crimthann.

c. 598 Gildas completes *De Excidio Britanniae*.
Battle of Catterick in which the Angles defeat the Gododdin.

c. 600 Merlin-Lailoken is forced from court by Saint Mungo Kentigern.

c. 603 Battle of Degaston at which the Angles defeat Aedan's army and the man now called Lancelot.

c. 603 to c. 608 Death of Aedan, Arthur's father.

612 Death of Rhydderch, king of Strathclyde, and of Saint Mungo Kentigern.

c. 615 The Angles cut Britain in two at Chester or Carlisle.

c. 618 Death of Merlin-Lailoken.

c. 830 Nennius completes *Historia Brittonum*.

c. 1136 Geoffrey of Monmouth publishes *Historia Regum Britanniae* (*History of the Kings of Britain*).

1152 Geoffrey of Monmouth becomes bishop of St. Asaph.

1485 Thomas Malory publishes *Le Morte d'Arthur*.

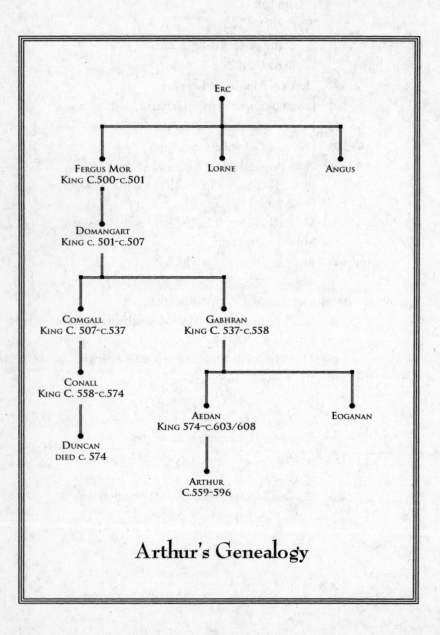

ERC

FERGUS MOR
KING C.500–C.501

LORNE

ANGUS

DOMANGART
KING C. 501–C.507

COMGALL
KING C. 507–C.537

GABHRAN
KING C. 537–C.558

CONALL
KING C. 558–C.574

AEDAN
KING 574–C.603/608

EOGANAN

DUNCAN
DIED C. 574

ARTHUR
C.559–596

Arthur's Genealogy

Glossary of Names

THE SCOTS

Fergus Mor Mac Erc, Fergus the Great, Arthur's great-great-grandfather, the
man who led a Scots army from Ireland to Scotland c. 500 (r. 500–501)

Domangart Mac Fergus, Arthur's great-grandfather (r. 501–507)

Comgall Mac Domangart, Arthur's granduncle, king of the Scots (r. 507–538)

Gabhran Mac Domangart, Arthur's grandfather, (r. 538–559)

Conall Mac Comgall, king of the Scots (r. 559–574), Arthur's second cousin
once removed

Aedan Mac Gabhran, Arthur's father, king of the Scots (r. 574–608)

Arthur Mac Aedan

Éoganán, Arthur's uncle

Duncan, Arthur's third cousin

STRATHCLYDE

Rhydderch, king of the Strathclyde Britons (r. 580–612)

Gwyneth, daughter of Morken of Cadzow, twin-sister of Merlin-Lailoken,
wife of Rhydderch, queen of Strathclyde, known as Languoreth (the
Golden One), The Swan-Necked Woman, The Lioness of Damnonia

Merlin-Lailoken, son of Morken of Cadzow, twin brother of Languoreth,
Rhydderch's chief counselor, a leading druid

Gawain, Arthur's nephew by the first marriage of his sister Anna

Cai (Kay), one of Arthur's warriors, perhaps his foster-brother

Gildas, *Gille Deas*, Servant of God, son of Caw of Cambuslang

Hueil, Gildas's brother
Domelch, a Pictish princess of Manau, possibly Arthur's mother
Ygerna/Igraine, a lady of Strathclyde, possibly Arthur's mother

THE PICTS
Bridei Mac Maelchon (Brude Mac Maelcon), king of the Miathi Picts
Guinevere, a princess of the Picts of Manau, Arthur's wife

THE ANGLES
Hussa, king of the Angles of Bernicia (r. 585–593)
Hering son of Hussa, an Angle prince
Aethelfrith, king of the Angles of Bernicia (r. 593–616)

THE GODODDIN
Mungo, son of Taneu (a princess of the Gododdin) and a lord of Strathclyde
Mordred, son of Arthur's sister, Anna, by her second marriage to Lot of the
    Lothians

"There is . . . no more difficult task than to substitute the correct '*sumpsimus*' for the long cherished and accepted '*mumpsimus*' of popular historians. All that the Author has attempted . . . is to show what the most reliable authorities do really tell us of the early annals of the country [Scotland], divested of the spurious matter of superstitious authors, the fictitious narratives of our early historians, and the rash assumptions of later writers which have been imported into it."

—W. F. SKENE, *Historiographer Royal to Queen Victoria*

Finding Arthur

Introduction

FOR MORE THAN A THOUSAND YEARS INNUMERABLE WRITERS HAVE invented stories about King Arthur. Even now, children all over the world grow up hearing tales of Arthur's legendary adventures with the Knights of the Round Table, his love for Guinevere, his friendship with the magician Merlin, and his mythical home in Camelot.

The writers telling these stories have been, by and large, Christian, English, and monarchist. Naturally, their Arthur has been portrayed, almost invariably, as a Christian English king—perhaps the greatest one of all.

But was he any of these things? Who was the historical Arthur, really? When did he live? Where did he live? What did he do? Why did he do it? Why is he so famous?

The question *Who was Arthur?* has confounded scholars for centuries. It has never been satisfactorily answered or, at least, it has never been answered in a way that allows all these other questions to be answered too.

Geoffrey of Monmouth's twelfth-century *History of the Kings of Britain* is one of the main pillars upon which the story of Arthur stands. According to Geoffrey, his *History* was based on "a certain very ancient book written in the British language," which was given to him by his mentor, Walter, Archdeacon of Oxford. Unfortunately Geoffrey did not identify this book, and it is now lost.

Some fifty years after Geoffrey wrote his *History*, a bishop of Glasgow commissioned a monk called Jocelyn of Furness to write a hagiography of a local saint, Mungo Kentigern (now patron saint of Glasgow). Jocelyn's *Life of Kentigern* contains much of what we currently know about the story of Merlin. According to Jocelyn, his book was based on a "codicil, composed in the *Scottic* style" that he found while going about the streets and quarters of Glasgow. Like Geoffrey of Monmouth, Jocelyn did not identify his source material, and it too is now lost.

Some 820 years after Jocelyn wrote his *Life of Kentigern*, I wrote in my previous book, *Finding Merlin*, of an "eighteenth-century book based on sixth- to ninth-century sources," in which I found evidence that enabled me to identify the historical Arthur. Like Geoffrey and Jocelyn, I chose not to name my source, as I thought it was more a part of Arthur's story than of Merlin's. Some readers were justifiably annoyed when I said I would identify this book but that this would "have to wait until later." Fortunately, unlike Geoffrey and Jocelyn, I am now able—and willing—to name my source: John O'Brien's *Focalóir Gaoidhilge-Sax-Bhéarla; An Irish-English Dictionary*, which clarified the connection between the earliest reference to Merlin, at the Battle of Arderydd in the year 573, and the presence of a historical Arthur at a place called Dunardry in 574.

Until I found that "eighteenth-century book based on sixth- to ninth-century sources," I had had no particular interest in Arthur or in Merlin. I liked television programs and films about the "Knights of the Round Table" when I was a boy, but I also liked Sword-and-Sandal epics and Westerns. The comics and the books I read as a child were as likely to be about Custer and his Seventh Cavalry, or Jason and his Argonauts, as Arthur and his Knights. I was an equal-opportunity hero-worshipper.

The Arthur who appeared in these children's stories was almost always the same character. The young Arthur was the pure and simple boy of the Disney cartoon *The Sword in the Stone*, a film inspired by T. H. White's book *The Once and Future King*. The adult Arthur could also be found in film—the musical *Camelot*; John Boorman's atmospheric *Excalibur*; the stolid *Knights of the Round Table* starring Robert Taylor—as well as in television shows such as *The Adventures of Sir Lancelot*. This Arthur was almost always an avuncular stay-at-home, who lost the woman he loved to his best friend, the dashing Lancelot. Worse still in the boyhood-hero-stakes, this Arthur lacked the warrior spirit and fighting prowess of his rival.

Like most people, I pictured King Arthur's Camelot as existing in some vague conception of the Middle Ages inspired by Thomas Malory's *Le Morte d'Arthur*: a place of turreted castles somewhere in England, inhabited by men in plate armor and women in pointed hats topped with chiffon. It was only later that I realized there was no historical Arthur in medieval English history, far less a "King" Arthur, and came to accept the general consensus that if there really was a historical Arthur he must have lived in the late fifth or early sixth centuries. Later still I found out that there was no historical Arthur in the late fifth or early sixth centuries either.

If I had known when I was a boy that Geoffrey's "ancient book" was in a "British language"—that is, in a Celtic language—and that Jocelyn's codicil was "Scottic," I might have guessed that Arthur was probably a Celt and possibly a Scot and looked to the north to find him. But along with almost everyone else I did not doubt the conventional wisdom that Arthur had lived in the south of Britain.

It was only in 1989, when I read Richard Barber's *The Figure of Arthur*, that I realized there was another possible Arthur, a Scottish one. However, after considering a goodly number of possible Arthurs, Richard Barber concluded that "Short of some fantastic invention, a time machine, say, or an equally fantastic discovery, an inscription naming him from a period which has barely left a word engraved on stone, Arthur himself will always elude us."[1]

I thought Barber was right and accepted that Arthur would always elude us, unless, of course, someone discovered something fantastic. I didn't imagine that I'd be the one to make or even to pursue such a discovery. Why would I? People who set out on such quests—and they do usually refer to them as quests—often end up as eccentrics, at best. Then, by sheer chance, I came across the source I've already mentioned, and the real story became clearer than I ever thought possible.

Several years ago, I was researching my family name in advance of a trip I'd planned with my young son to Argyll, Scotland, where our family had lived before they became part of the Protestant Plantation of Ireland in the seventeenth century. As I researched, two things helped me to look where no one else had looked and find what no one else had found: first, that our name, Ardrey, is rare in the extreme, and second, that very few people are interested in family trees other than their own. In a great many ways, I was lucky.

When I was at school in Scotland, "British" history—in effect English history—was promoted and Scottish history was played down. Despite or perhaps because of this cultural indoctrination, I came to number among my heroes Scots who had been all but airbrushed out of history: men like William Wallace (of the film *Braveheart*) and Robert the Bruce, the real braveheart of history. This one-sided schooling left me open to the possibility that the story of Arthur too could have been worked on and warped for political purposes.

Anyone who, like me, believes in democracy not monarchy and in people not the supernatural will find it easier to picture a pre-Christian Arthurian Britain than someone like Queen Victoria's Historiographer Royal for Scotland, W. F. Skene, would have. A man in thrall to organized religion, Skene had a Christian Monarchist blinker on one eye and a British Monarchist blinker on the other. Even so, there are places in his work where it seems he might have known the truth but been too cautious to say it, lest he lose his prospects of further preferment. Even the great Charles Darwin waited twenty years before publishing his ideas about evolution because he was wary of the Church's potential reaction.

If the search for Arthur in the south of Britain was ever in a period of upward momentum, it would now be possible to say that it has ground to a halt. Some southern-leaning historians claim there was no historical Arthur, others that there was no single historical Arthur but lots of proto-Arthurs. At best they are reduced to relying upon some soul's slight echo in history to found their claims.

The dearth of substantial evidence in the South has not led to a vigorous search for evidence in the North. In the North, fear of being labeled parochial shrivels "scholarly" inquiry. Fortunately, now that evidence is more widely available, popular culture has started to place Arthur in Scotland, in films like the otherwise risible *King Arthur* in 2004. But despite the fact that many of them are as clever as screenwriters, professional historians do not appear to be as open to new ideas or, indeed, evidence.

Living in Scotland I was well-placed to find evidence, literally, on the ground. Indeed I had so much evidence while writing *Finding Merlin* that I neglected to say that the purportedly magical spring of Barenton, where Merlin is supposed to have met a woman called Vivienne and which is said to be in the forest of Brocéliande in France, is really in Barnton, Edinburgh. The spring is still there, for all to see.

Medieval writers added romance and magic to their stories for the same reason that modern screenwriters add special effects to their films —these additions are popular with audiences. I have tended to ignore the magical references in the sources because magical things do not happen in real life. And while I believe in romance, I have also treated romantic events in the Arthurian canon with skepticism, because in real life such things do not happen nearly so often.

We in the twenty-first century have been saturated with film and television from an early age, so we're more aware of how storytelling works and how powerful the "front office" can be. Things were much the same in the Middle Ages, except that audiences were more gullible. To the same extent that producers of modern films dare not upset powerful commercial interests, men like Thomas Malory, who wrote perhaps the most influential Arthurian book of them all, *Le Morte d'Arthur*, dared not challenge the predominant powers of his day, the aristocracy and the Church. I have allowed for the fact that writers like Malory obscured and omitted truths they might have told openly because they were afraid such truths would have upset the powers-that-were.

According to Lewis Thorpe, in his introduction to Geoffrey of Monmouth's *History of the Kings of Britain*, "Geoffrey had several clear-cut political reasons for what he wrote . . . [including] his wish to ingratiate himself with his various dedicatees."[2] Geoffrey did not set Arthur's birth at Tintagel in Cornwall, England, because Tintagel had anything to do with Arthur. He did so because the castle belonged to a relative of his patron.

Nor did Malory say Merlin was acting under the orders of a Christian archbishop when he organized the sword and the stone event because the addition of an archbishop improved Malory's story. It did not, as evidenced by the fact that the archbishop is conspicuously missing from every modern depiction of this event. Malory inserted an archbishop to keep the Church from persecuting him. In my research, I have allowed for such biases.

I have also given less weight to evidence that seemed "too good to be true," unless there was other evidence weighing in its favor. Arthur and Mordred fighting in single combat to the death at the Battle of Camlann seemed too much like the kind of thing a modern screenwriter would add to a story for it to be believable.

If an account favored a writer's personal interests I have treated it as suspect, and I have given special weight to evidence that went against such interests. Fortunately for history, the Church only required that writers not alarm the largely uneducated majority, as distinct from the nobility, and so self-censoring writers only removed from their work the more obvious challenges to established opinion. As a result, while the only evidence we have available today has been percolated through Christianity, it includes information that these writers overlooked or were too lazy to delete. There is just enough left to re-root the story of Arthur in its proper place and time.

The life of Arthur and the legends that grew up around his name cannot be understood without reference to the various forms of Christianity that were making inroads among the people of Britain and Ireland in the sixth century. I have nothing to say about modern Christianity in any of its many manifestations or about anyone who professes to be a Christian today. My only interest is in those who promulgated the various forms of Christianity that vied for power in the sixth century.

The Celtic pre-Christian Arthur—the Arthur the novelist Bernard Cornwall called the "Enemy of God"—was a challenge to the churchmen who controlled Western society from the fall of the Roman Empire to the Renaissance. For this reason, Arthur's origins were disguised. It is difficult for us, steeped in Christianity as we are, to believe that the Church–State partnership that dominated Western Europe for so long under the brand-name Christendom expunged the historical Arthur from the record and created an alternative Arthur in its own image, but that's exactly what happened.

Other peoples may justly claim foundation myths of equal power to the Arthurian Cycle: the *Mahabharata* of the Indians; the *Iliad* of the Greeks; the sagas of the Icelanders; *The Five Books* of the Chinese; the *Nihongi* of the Japanese; and, less well known, the epic of the Mongol peoples that tells of the valiant Geser, who ruled the legendary Kingdom of Ling. However, only the Arthurian story-cycle has survived the molestations of a bitter rival with the power to reward and punish in this life and the ability to convince people that its baleful influence would follow them beyond the grave. That rival is of course Christianity. The Arthurian cycle survived Christianity. This makes the Arthurian cycle special.

I use the term *Scots* to designate members of a particular sixth-century group, and it should not be confused with today's Scots. Today, at least in my opinion, the term *Scot* includes all people who have made their home in Scotland and want to be part of the Scottish community, as well as those who live elsewhere but feel at home in Scotland and want to be called Scots. On the other hand, what we now know as Scotland and England did not exist in the sixth century, and so rather than continually say "what is now Scotland" and "what is now England," when I say Scotland and England I mean the areas covered by the modern countries.

Without William Wallace and Robert the Bruce, Scotland would have died. Without Arthur and Merlin, it would not have been born. Scotland is only a small country on the edge of Europe, but if it had ceased to exist as an independent nation or had never been at all, then there would have been no Camelot. Not the place called Camelot but the ideal that *is* Camelot.

I believe Richard Dawkins is right when he encourages us to always demand evidence. If the evidence I have found stands up and my reasoning is sound, then 10 percent of British history should be rewritten, the foundation myth of the English-speaking world flies away, and everything is different.

1

The Four Horsemen
of History

THE STORY OF "KING" ARTHUR IS THE FOUNDATION MYTH OF THE
English-speaking Western world. Almost everyone knows about
Arthur, Merlin, and Camelot; their story was told in one of the first
books printed in English, and for more than five hundred years it has
not fallen out of favor. It changed over the centuries as it was told and
retold, and it was written and rewritten in innumerable manuscripts for
the best part of a thousand years before ever it came to be fixed in print.
The result is that the Arthur best known today is a fictional figure: an
English, Christian, medieval king.

The historical Arthur—if there was a historical Arthur (the matter is much disputed)—should be looked for somewhere in the middle
of the first millennium, somewhere in Britain. Almost everyone agrees
about this, but there almost all agreement ends. Until recently most
of those who have looked for the historical Arthur have been Christian,
Anglophile monarchists, and so, perhaps unsurprisingly, they have
concluded that Arthur was a Christian English king (when they have
not concluded that he did not exist). However, just as it is often said
that the Holy Roman Empire was not holy, Roman, or an empire,
there is evidence that suggests Arthur was not a Christian, an Englishman or a king.

What is the truth about Arthur? Was he a historical figure? If he was, then who was he, when did he live, where did he live, what did he do, why did he do it, and who did he do it to?

THE EARLIEST DIRECT evidence of the man who became the legendary Arthur is the poem *Y Gododdin* written around 600 CE by the bard Aneirin in the land of the Gododdin, which included modern Edinburgh.

Of the thousands of male and female bards in the sixth century, the names of only five survive: Talhaearn Tad Awen; Bluchbard; Cian; Taliesin, and Aneirin. Of these five the works of Talhaearn Tad Awen; Bluchbard and Cian are entirely lost. Of the works of Taliesin and Aneirin only a small number of poems have survived and these only in much amended forms. It is a tragedy of epic proportions (literally) that lifetimes of work by countless bards have fallen prey to the vicissitudes of time and the depredations of Christians who calculatingly destroyed what they did not want people to see, lest people learn what the Christian Church did not want them to know: that there was another way, that things did not have to be the way they were.

Aneirin's most famous poem, *Y Gododdin*, describes a disastrous campaign waged by the Gododdin Britons against the Angles. Having praised warrior after warrior in verse after verse, Aneirin delivers near the end of his poem, with reference to a warrior called Gwawrddur, the most devastating one-line introduction in literature:

> He charged before three hundred of the foe,
> He cut down both center and wing,
> He excelled in the forefront of the noblest host.
> He gave from his herd steeds for winter.
> He fed black ravens on the rampart of a fort.
> But he was no Arthur.

Arthur, it seems, was the standard by which heroes were measured at the turn of the sixth century in eastern Scotland.

Y Gododdin also contains one of the earliest references to Myrddin, a man indelibly linked to the legendary Arthur and better known as Merlin. In the poem, Myrddin-Merlin makes a financial contribution to the campaign. "Myrddin of song, sharing the best / Part of his wealth, our strength and support."[1]

De Excidio Britanniae (*The Ruin of Britain*) by Gildas, a Christian fanatic, contains the earliest surviving indirect reference to Arthur. This reference is only "indirect" because Arthur is not named. Gildas refers only to the Battle of Badon, one of the legendary Arthur's most famous victories: "From then on victory went now to our countrymen, now to their enemies . . . This lasted up till the year of the siege of Badon Hill, pretty well the last defeat of the villains, and certainly not the least."[2]

De Excidio is more a concentrated rant against everything Gildas disapproved of than an attempt to write a sensible account of historical events, but it is the only contemporary history of the sixth century we have. The received wisdom places the writing of *De Excidio* in the first half of the century, around the year 540, although Michael Winterbottom of Oxford University says, of Gildas, "we cannot be certain of his date, of where he wrote, of his career, or even his name."[3]

Whatever its origins, *De Excidio* has been enormously influential. The *Ecclesiastical History of the English People*, written in 731 by Bede, a monk of Jarrow in the far north of England, clearly uses Gildas as a source when it says, "Thenceforward victory swung first to one side and then the other, until the Battle of Badon Hill."[4] Bede, the father of English history, does not name Arthur either and can hardly be considered an independent source of evidence.

Two hundred years after Bede, in the early ninth century, an appealing cleric called Nennius wrote his *Historia Brittonum* (*History of the Britons*) because, he said, "the scholars of the island of Britain had no skill, and set down no record in books."[5] Nennius collected Roman annals, Church chronicles, writings of the English, writings of the Irish (which included writings of the Scots), and no doubt all the oral history available to him, and provided a rather endearing account of his methods: "I made a heap of all that I have found." He used this heap to write his *Historia*, taking care to include everything that he could find that "the stupidity of the British had cast out." I picture Nennius in an untidy room delving into his heap, taking bits and pieces from here and there to use in his great work. The end result understandably reflects his apparently haphazard working methods and the arbitrary nature of his sources.

Nennius mentions Arthur three times in his *Historia*, the first instance being a list of twelve battles that he attributes to Arthur. This list is, perhaps, the single most important item of Arthurian evidence.

> Then Arthur fought against them in those days, together with the kings of the British; but he was their leader in battle. The first battle was at the mouth of the river called Glein. The second, the third, the fourth and the fifth were on another river, called the Douglas [*Dubglas*] which is in the country of Lindsey [*Linnuis*]. The sixth battle was on the river called Bassas. The seventh was in the Celyddon Forest [*Celidonis*] that is the Battle of Celyddon Coed. The eighth battle was in Guinnion fort, and in it Arthur carried the image of the holy Mary, the everlasting Virgin, on his (shoulder or shield?) and the heathen were put to flight on that day, and there was a great slaughter upon them, through the power of Our Lord Jesus Christ and the power of the holy Virgin Mary, his mother.[6] The ninth battle was fought in the city of the Legion. The tenth battle was fought on the bank of the river called Tryfrwyd [*Tribruit*]. The eleventh battle was on the hill called Agned. The twelfth battle was on Badon Hill and in it nine hundred and sixty men fell in one day, from a single charge of Arthur's, and no one laid them low save he alone; and he was victorious in all his campaigns.[7]

It is generally accepted that when Nennius said Arthur fought "together with the kings of the British; but he was their leader in battle," he meant Arthur was a leader of kings but that Arthur was not himself a king. A one-off manuscript discovered in the Vatican in the early nineteenth century makes this even clearer, in a version of the above passage that begins:

Then it was that the magnanimous Arthur, with all the kings and military force of Britain, fought against the Saxons. And though there were many more noble than himself, yet he was twelve times chosen their commander, and was as often conqueror.[8]

The two other references to Arthur in Nennius come under the heading "wonders." The first is a paw print on a stone, said to have been put there by Arthur's dog while hunting boar. Nennius says men may remove the stone and carry it away for the length of a day and a night but that the next day it will always be back in its former place. Wonder two is the grave of Arthur's son Amr, and Nennius describes its miraculous qualities thus: "Men come to measure the tomb, and it is sometime six feet long, sometimes nine, sometimes twelve, sometimes fifteen. At whatever measure you measure it on one occasion, you never find it again of the same measure. . ."[9] Needless to say, these wonders are not particularly helpful to someone looking for the historical Arthur.

The *Annales Cambriae*, the Annals of Wales, were compiled in the tenth century and claim to be an annual record of events starting in 447. There are only twelve entries for the first hundred years, however, and they mainly record the births and the deaths of saints. The entry for the year 516 reads, "The Battle of Badon, in which Arthur carried the Cross of our Lord Jesus Christ for three days and three nights on his shoulders and the Britons were the victors." The entry for the year 537 is as follows: "The Battle of Camlann, in which Arthur and Medraut [Mordred] fell: and there was plague in Britain and Ireland."[10] If these entries are accurate twenty-one years separated Arthur's last two battles.

The *Annales Cambriae* also contain one of the earliest references to the man called Merlin to survive. The entry for the year 573 reads, "The Battle of Arderydd between the sons of Eliffer and Gwenddolau son of Ceidio; in which battle Gwenddolau fell; Merlin went mad." The Battle of Arderydd was not fought in Wales however, but at the fort Caer Gwenddolau, which would now be in the hamlet of Carwinley on the Scotland–England border.

The Anglo-Saxon Chronicle, started in the ninth century and considered to be England's most important historical record of pre-Norman history, covers many events during the age of Arthur but has nothing to say about him. We are left then with only four sources of evidence of a historical Arthur: Aneirin's *Y Gododdin*; Gildas's *De Excidio*; Nennius's *Historia*; and the *Annales Cambriae*. After Nennius, Arthur becomes increasingly elusive as, in effect, he passes from history into legend.

In the early seventh century the written word in the south of Britain was controlled by the Christian Church, which consequently was able to promote its own stories—predominantly tales from the lives of saints—to the exclusion of almost all others. This meant that the stories of Arthur had to flourish as part of the oral tradition or not at all. Fortunately for Western literature and indeed for history, the written word was restricted to a few compliant clerics, but the oral tradition was like the Internet—accessible to the masses and almost impossible to control.

Christian clerics, almost by definition deskbound men, created heroes in their own self-image (and in their own self-interest). They liked their heroes to be saints, not warlike men like Arthur. They also omitted almost all references to sex, pagan religions, and the druids, so Merlin was absent too. This gave the stories of Arthur a certain advantage. While the *Lives* of saints were bolstered by magical miracles, they were still deadly dull compared to the thrilling tales of Arthur and his men, which made the latter increasingly popular in the oral tradition. Anyone who doubts this should compare the action-packed, epic, heroic poem *Y Gododdin* with any of the vast number of sloth-slow hagiographies that have survived. Given a choice, the people of the late first millennium CE favored stories of Arthur over the Christian propaganda that the Church shoveled at them *ad nauseam*, although, of course, they were not always given a choice. This struggle between the popularity of Arthur and the propaganda of the Church resulted in stories in which Arthur was the villain.

In Lifric of Llancarfan's late eleventh century *Life of Saint Cadoc*, Arthur and his friends Cai and Bedevere are playing dice when they see a young man and a young woman (who will become Cadoc's parents) being chased by armed men. Instead of going to their assistance immediately, as the Arthur of later legends would have done, Lifric's Arthur becomes "violently inflamed with desire" for the young woman and has to be talked out of raping her.

Later, when Cadoc is Abbot of Llancarfan he gives sanctuary to men who had killed three of Arthur's soldiers and refuses to hand them over. All Arthur is able to win as compensation is a herd of cattle, but even then he is beaten by Lifric's saintly hero, the clever Cadoc, because the cattle soon turn into bundles of ferns. People who were prepared to believe that cattle could turn into ferns would surely also have believed that Arthur was active in Wales if Lifric told them this was so.

The Life of St. Padarn tells of a tyrannical Arthur who ruthlessly demands Padarn's tunic. When Padarn refuses to hand it over, Arthur becomes enraged and curses and swears. This wicked Arthur then stomps away, only to creep back later and steal the tunic. Before he can make his getaway, however, Padarn causes the ground to open up and swallow him. Arthur has to apologize before Padarn will set him free. This is a rather sad little story. Arthur is portrayed as a tyrant, but what great crime is he said to have committed? Stealing a tunic. This shows the mindset of the clerics who wrote these accounts. They thought of Arthur as the enemy of their church, *the fount from which for them all blessings flowed*—why else would Arthur be portrayed as the villain?—and so they maligned him as a tyrant who . . . stole a tunic. Monks, who lived together in close proximity, may have thought the theft of a tunic a dreadful thing, but it is hardly a momentous offence outside cloisters. The world in which these monks lived may have been limited in the extreme, but when it came to punishments their imaginations knew no bounds—at the end of the story we have nothing less than the earth opening up and swallowing the wicked Arthur.

According to the *Life of Gildas* by Caradoc of Llancarfan, Arthur murdered Gildas's brother, the warrior Hueil. Of course, as saints could not be bested in Christian books; in the end Arthur surrendered to Gildas and "in grief and tears, accepted penance . . . and led an amended course, as far as he could, until the close of his life." (This was the same

Gildas who omitted the name of the historical Arthur from his history of Britain.)

These early attempts to portray Arthur as a villain were unsuccessful. No one really believed that Arthur was a villain, they pretended to believe it but they didn't, *not really*. A heroic Arthur continued to thrive in the oral tradition, although these stories increasingly lost touch with their historical roots as romance and magic were added to make them even more popular (just as today we add romance and special effects to films). Since Arthur wasn't going away, something needed to be done to bring him into the fold. Arthur needed to become a Christian, an Englishman, and, for good measure, a king.

Geoffrey of Monmouth, a twelfth century Welsh cleric who worked for much of his life in the schools of Oxford, made Arthur even more popular with his wonderful book *The History of the Kings of Britain*, written in 1136. While much of Geoffrey's *History* is obvious nonsense, "history keeps popping through the fiction," Lewis Thorpe writes. "What nobody who has examined the evidence carefully can dare to say is that Geoffrey . . . simply made-up his material."[11]

It is clear that while writing his history Geoffrey had popular opinion in mind. "I had not got thus far in my history," he writes, "when the subject of public discourse happening to be concerning Merlin, I was obliged to publish his prophecies."[12] Knowing and liking Merlin from the oral tradition Geoffrey's audience insisted that he write more about Merlin, despite the fact that his work was ostensibly a history of kings. In any event, in the middle of his *History*, Geoffrey rather awkwardly inserted a tedious catalog of what are said to be prophecies by Merlin.

Geoffrey was not a man to miss an opportunity, however, and so, in the late 1140s he followed up on the success of his *History* with his *Life of Merlin*. The Merlins portrayed in these two works are very different characters. The Merlin of the *History* is a more magical figure than the Merlin of the *Life*, who is more firmly rooted in history. This suggests that Geoffrey did not simply invent his Merlin; if he had, it is unlikely he would have so radically changed the nature of his invention between books. It also suggests that Geoffrey gained access to a more historical source material sometime between writing the *History* and the *Life*.

Geoffrey had three main sources: "a certain very ancient book written in the British language" (that is, in a Celtic language) given to him by his patron, Walter Archdeacon of Oxford; Walter himself was "a man most learned in all branches of history"[13]; and the oral tradition.

Geoffrey's *History* contains most of what is commonly known today as the story of "King Arthur." He writes of Arthur's conception, which he says took place when Arthur's father, Uther Pendragon, raped Arthur's mother, Ygerna (Igraine); of Arthur's sister Anna, mother of Gawain and Mordred; of Arthur's defeat of the "Saxons" at Mount Badon, which he places in Bath, in the south of England; of Ganhumara's—that is, Guinevere's—adultery with Modred [*sic*]; and of the Battle of Camblan [*sic*], where Geoffrey says Arthur killed Modred.

According to Geoffrey, Merlin magically changed the shape of Uther, Arthur's future father, to the shape of Gorlois, the husband of Arthur's future mother, and by this deception facilitated Arthur's conception. This is, of course, obvious nonsense. Geoffrey's Arthur becomes king without a sword or a stone and goes on to unite the kings of Britain. Then Guinevere, who is said to have been of noble Roman birth, makes an appearance, marries Arthur and commits adultery, not with Lancelot, as is popularly supposed, but with the treacherous Mordred. Geoffrey also makes one of the earliest references to Arthur's sword, Excalibur, which he calls Caliburn, and to the Isle of Avalon, where he says Arthur was taken after being mortally wounded by Mordred at the climactic Battle of Camblan [*sic*].

Geoffrey's Arthur is impossibly active all over mainland Britain: in Cornwall in the far southwest of England; at Loch Lomond in the southern highlands of Scotland; and in the Orkneys, in the far north of Scotland. He also has Arthur conquer Norway, France, the island of Gotland in the Baltic, and Iceland in the northern Atlantic. To top off all this, Geoffrey claims, more than somewhat anachronistically, that Arthur also defeated a Roman army! Why not? After all, Geoffrey was writing fiction, albeit fiction with a historical foundation, and penned some quite unashamed nonsense.

Wace, a Norman Frenchman writing in France in the twelfth century, followed Geoffrey in many respects in his *Roman de Brut* but changed the name of Arthur's sword from Caliburn to Excalibur. He also introduced the Knights of the Round Table. A generation later another Frenchman, Chrétien de Troyes, introduced Camelot, which he said was Camulodunum (today's Colchester) in the far south of Britain. Chrétien also introduced Lancelot and had Lancelot, not Mordred, commit adultery with Guinevere. Lancelot appears as a bit-part player in Chrétien's story *Erec and Enide*, but his breakthrough tale is Chrétien's *The Knight of the Cart*.

Lancelot was then taken up and made into a major hero by the Cistercian monks who compiled *The Vulgate Cycle* of stories, before becoming the Lancelot we know today from Malory's fifteenth-century *Le Morte d'Arthur*. The importance of an increasingly fictional Lancelot was continually played up at the expense of both Arthur and real Celtic heroes like Gawain and Kay. The courtly love phenomenon of Chrétien's day dictated that knights paid court to married women such as Chrétien's patron, Marie of Champagne, but it is remarkable that Chrétien downplayed Arthur in favor of Lancelot to the extent that he did: courtly love did not allow for outright adultery. To paraphrase Gore Vidal, it was not enough for the romancers of the Christian courts of Europe that Lancelot succeed, it was also important that Celtic warriors of the Old Way failed.

From the twelfth century onward the heroic Arthur of history is steadily reduced. He ends up a man who cannot even retain the affection of his own wife and who, compared to the dashing Lancelot, is a somewhat stolid figure. In time, as the emphasis in the stories shifted from Arthur to Lancelot, Celtic champions like Kay and Gawain came to be portrayed as somewhat dull characters, in comparison with "perfect," "pure" Christian knights such as Galahad and Perceval (a milquetoast twosome it is impossible to picture in a real fight). In effect, stories of Arthur ended up starring Christian knights who were amalgams of fictional saintly heroes and real warrior heroes.

Toward the end of the twelfth century, in Glasgow, the monk Jocelyn of Furness wrote an authorized version of a local saint, Mungo Kentigern. Jocelyn's *Life of Kentigern* is one of the main pillars upon which the story of Merlin stands. Jocelyn set about gathering source-material, and to his dismay he found that Mungo's Christianity was not the same thing as his bishop's Christianity. This was a problem for Jocelyn but not for long:

> For by your command, I went around the . . . city, through its streets and quarters, searching for a written life of . . . [Mungo] Kentigern . . . I have discovered . . . a codicil . . . which is filled with solecisms all the way through and yet it contains a more unbroken account of the life and acts of the holy bishop. Seeing therefore the life of so esteemed a bishop, who was glorious with signs and portents and most famous in virtue and doctrine, perversely recited and turned away from the pure faith. . . I confess I suffered greatly. On that account, I therefore accepted to mend this life . . . and by binding my method to your command, to season with Roman salt what had been ploughed by barbarians.[14]

Not only was Jocelyn prepared to "mend" history to suit his bishop's book, he was also proud of what he had done and anxious that his bishop should know about it (no doubt because he expected some reward). Men like Jocelyn and his bishop controlled the written and the printed word in the millennium after the death of Arthur, and used this power to faithfully "cleanse" the historical record on an industrial scale. They left little unchanged or undeleted that they thought was contrary to the interests of the Church, and they unscrupulously added whatever inventions they thought might promote their ends. It is only through the dark glass of "histories" created by men like these that we can consider the matter of Arthur today.

Innumerable authors contributed to the story that became the legend of Arthur before Thomas Malory wrote *Le Morte d'Arthur* in the fifteenth century. Malory, who described himself as a "knight prisoner," was accused of ambush, abduction, extortion, and rape, among other things (although there is reason to believe he was not guilty of rape, the woman being willing, the husband less so). Much of *Le Morte d'Arthur* was written while Malory was in prison. He was also a Member of Parliament.

The printing of books for general consumption was introduced about the time Malory was active and so it was that with the publication of *Le Morte d'Arthur* the legend of Arthur came to be fixed in the common consciousness. Certainly, before I came to read about Arthur, Merlin, and Camelot for the purposes of this book, the Arthurian story I knew was Malory-based, albeit with additions from a variety of other sources, including the poetry of Tennyson, the musical film *Camelot*, and the *Hotspur* comic for boys. The following account is what I remembered as the story of Arthur before I came to research this book.

Uther Pendragon, king of England, calls upon the wizard Merlin to help him seduce Igraine, the wife of the Duke of Cornwall. Merlin agrees to help on one condition: he is to be given charge of any child born of the union of Uther and Igraine. Uther agrees and so Merlin uses magic to change Uther's shape to that of the Duke of Cornwall and so deceives Igraine into having sexual intercourse with Uther. By this means is Arthur conceived. The scene of this conception was always Tintagel in my mind, because this is what both Malory and Geoffrey said and because Tintagel is simply a spectacular location.

That night, the Duke of Cornwall is killed, which is fortunate for everyone except the Duke. Igraine discovers what has happened but still agrees to marry Uther and even more mysteriously agrees to hand over her newborn baby, Arthur, to Merlin. Merlin puts Arthur into the care of a foster family headed by the kindly Sir Ector—a family that includes Ector's oafish son, Sir Kay—but still keeps in touch with Arthur over the years, as Arthur grows up bullied by Kay. (This part of my memory came primarily from Disney's *The Sword in the Stone*.)

No one except Merlin knows who Arthur's real father is, including Arthur, and so, when Uther dies, no one acclaims Arthur as king. Merlin suggests that a tournament be held in London, to which every knight in the realm will be invited, and where the matter will be decided. In London, Merlin reveals a large stone upon which stands an anvil with a sword stuck into it. Upon this Stone-Anvil combination is written, "Whoso pulleth out this sword of this stone and anvil, is rightwise king born of all England."[15]

Ector, Kay, and Arthur (by now Kay's squire), go to London for the tournament along with everyone else of importance. One day, as he is on his way to a joust, Kay notices that he has forgotten his sword and sends Arthur back to their lodgings to fetch it. On the way there Arthur sees a sword sticking out of an anvil in the middle of a churchyard. (Apparently Arthur was not one for keeping up to date with current affairs and had not heard of this sword, although it must have been the talk of the town.) Rather than go back to their lodgings to get Kay's sword, Arthur decides he will save some time and trouble and take the sword in the anvil instead. The fact that the sword is not his and that he will have to steal it does not seem to have occurred to Malory's Arthur. (Of course, Malory was not writing a history but an entertainment based on historical material, and his priority was a good story. The story he produced is one of the greatest stories ever told.)

Arthur takes the sword from the anvil and presents it to his foster-brother, Kay, who, unlike Arthur, has obviously been listening to the news. Kay recognizes the sword and uses it to pretend he is the rightful king. Everyone heads back to the churchyard, and Kay is told to put the sword back in place and show everyone how he took it out. Of course Kay cannot get the sword out of the anvil-stone, because of course Kay is not the rightful king (whatever a rightful king may be). Other knights try but none of them can take the sword from the stone.

Eventually Kay confesses that the sword was given to him by Arthur, and Arthur explains what happened. Then, before all, Arthur removes the sword from the anvil-stone. As I remembered the story, everyone then recognizes Arthur as the true king. Under the circumstances, who would be so churlish as not to recognize him?

Arthur sets up court at a place called Camelot and marries Guinevere who, just as one would expect, is very beautiful. (Her name means "most fair," "very lovely," "exceedingly beautiful," "awfully good-looking"—something like that.) He then creates an order of knights whose members ride out on quests, in the course of which they right wrongs. This usually involves slaying dragons and fighting villainous knights in single combat. These knights also protect the meek and the weak, although these tend to include a disproportionately high number of good-looking women.

At first, this questing consists of knights looking for good deeds to do, but with the arrival of knights like Galahad and Perceval, it mutates into knights seeking religious totems, such as the famous Holy Grail.

The Round Table is a common feature of every Arthurian story. It is usually said to have been made round to avoid any one knight having precedence. Even before I re-read Malory I thought this part was just more nonsense. While there may be no head to such a table, the most prestigious place would clearly have been near the king, especially the place at the king's right hand. Whatever the reason for the table being round, in the stories I knew knights travel from far and wide to join the Knights of the Round Table, including the best knight of all, Lancelot of the Lake, who comes from France to become Arthur's friend and right-hand man.

Before I started researching *Finding Merlin* I thought the sword Arthur takes from the stone was Excalibur. I had forgotten the equally famous story in which Arthur is given Excalibur by the Lady of the Lake. It was only when I re-read *Le Morte d'Arthur* that I realized that the sword Arthur takes from the stone is broken in battle and that Merlin later brings Arthur to a lake in the woods, where a woman's arm rises from the water, holding Excalibur. This lady of the lake then gives Excalibur to Arthur. My memory of this event has always included the startling slow-motion version from John Boorman's film *Excalibur*, with the words of Tennyson as my personal voice-over: ". . . an arm / Rose up from out the bosom of the lake, / Clothed in white samite, mystic, wonderful,/ Holding the sword . . ."[16]

Having taken part in this last great set piece in the early part of the Arthurian legend, Merlin becomes a hindrance to achieving the conflict required from a good story. Until this point everything he has done for Arthur has been successful; he has arranged Arthur's conception and his elevation to the throne, supervised the creation of the Round Table, provided Arthur with a magical sword, and seen him married to a nice girl. Now, for the story to remain interesting, everything has to go awry. This would be difficult to explain if a man as wise as Merlin were still around and so Merlin has to go. In the film versions Merlin is quite literally written out of the picture. He usually just slips away without any fuss, leaving Arthur to deal with things on his own.

On the few occasions when Merlin is the center of attention, usually in the written versions of the stories, he is given his own romantic interest: sometimes Viviane, sometimes Nimuë but always a beautiful young woman determined to learn all he knows about magic. Merlin falls in love with Nimuë, and, although he knows she will use his teachings against him, tells her all his secrets. Viviane-Nimuë uses the power Merlin has given to her to imprison him in a rock or a tree or a crystal cave, or some such thing.

With Merlin out of the way, Guinevere and Lancelot start their adulterous affair. There is a clear turning point in the stories around the time Merlin disappears. Until then Arthur has been the central hero and the plot has revolved around him, but now Arthur begins to take second place to Lancelot. It is also usually around the time Merlin disappears that Mordred, always the villain, appears on the scene.

Mordred is either Arthur's nephew or, in more explicit tales, Arthur's son-nephew, the result of an incestuous relationship between Arthur and his sister (what I think of as the *Chinatown* versions). I always found it curious that Arthur, who until this point has always been a heroic figure, should suddenly be portrayed as engaged in an incestuous relationship. This is not the kind of thing one expects of a hero.

Mordred hates Arthur and is jealous of Lancelot. Ambitious to be king, he plots to divide the Knights of the Round Table by telling Arthur of Lancelot's affair with Guinevere. Lancelot is forced to flee (people never just ran away in those days, they always fled). Arthur, bound to enforce the law, condemns Guinevere to death, but before she can be burned at the stake, Lancelot rides into town and snatches her away from the flames. Again, Arthur is made to look weak, especially in comparison to the heroic Lancelot.

The Knights of the Round Table are divided. Some remain loyal to Arthur. Others side with Mordred. Civil war breaks out. The two armies meet in battle at a place called Camlann. In the course of negotiations between the opposing armies, an adder appears near a knight's foot. The knight draws his sword to kill the adder. The soldiers on the other side, thinking they are about to be attacked, also draw their swords and the battle begins.

Arthur wins but it is a hollow victory:

> And thus they fought all the long day and never stinted till the noble knights were to the cold earth; and ever they fought still till it was near night, and by that time was there an hundred thousand laid dead upon the down. Then was Arthur wood wroth out of measure, when he saw his people so slain from him.[17]

Arthur engages Mordred in single combat and strikes him through the body with his spear. Mordred pushes the spear up to the limit to get close to Arthur and then strikes him hard on the head before falling "stark dead to the earth."[18]

That Arthur kills Mordred in single combat while at the same time receiving a mortal wound was always too Holmes-and-Moriarty-going-over-the-Reichenbach-Falls-together for my liking. This kind of thing just seemed too melodramatic to be true, as did the boy-meets-girl romantic elements and the Lady of the Lake—simply the medieval equivalent of special effects. The death of Arthur as described by Malory reads like pure fiction.

Arthur, severely wounded, is carried from the field by Bedevere, one of his few remaining knights. Believing himself close to death, Arthur orders Bedevere to take Excalibur and throw it into nearby water, usually described as a lake, although Malory simply says water. Twice Bedevere hides Excalibur under a bush and tells Arthur he had obeyed his orders. It is only when he is commanded for a third time to throw Excalibur into the water that he does what he has been told to do. A woman's arm rises from the surface of the lake, catches the sword and brandishes it before drawing it down, back into the water.

Then women arrive in a barge and take Arthur away with them to tend to his wounds in Avalon, an island somewhere in the western sea. There Arthur is to remain until his people need him again. He is Arthur, *Rex Quondam Rexque Futurus*, The Once and Future King.

This, broadly, is the story I grew up with. I got my visuals from comics and then from films in which the English countryside (it was always England) often looked a lot like California. John Boorman's film *Excalibur* eventually supplanted most of these images.

No one today seriously suggests that Malory was even trying to write history, any more than anyone today would claim that Mel Gibson was trying to produce a historical documentary when he made the film *Braveheart*. But this doesn't mean that Malory and Mel Gibson created their fictions from nothing or that Arthur and William Wallace were not real historical figures.

2

The Would-Be Arthurs

MANY BELIEVE THERE WAS NO HISTORICAL ARTHUR, WHILE OTHERS believe that several figures formed a foundation upon which the legend of Arthur was built. The conventional wisdom current among those who believe there was a historical Arthur has him living about the turn of the fifth century, give or take a generation; and a southern British, Christian king who became famous fighting the Anglo-Saxons. There is no consensus as to who this Arthur was, when he was active, where he was active, what he did, why he did it or who he did it to. No one who cleaves to the conventional wisdom can answer many, far less all of these questions while pointing to a historical Arthur.

Suggested historical Arthurs include Lucius Artorius Castus, a Roman military leader who lived circa 140 to 197 CE. This was the man played by Clive Owen in the 2004 film *King Arthur*, the first major film to place Arthur north of Hadrian's Wall. Despite living long before any possible historical Arthur, it is said Castus was remembered as a hero and injected into British history hundreds of years after his death, although no one has come up with a good reason why this might be. He did nothing of an importance that would justify such a development, certainly not in Britain. It is likely that the simple similarity of the name Artorius and the name Arthur led to the conclusion that he must have had something to do with the legend of Arthur.

Even slighter similarities of name have not stopped other claims, including Arthun, son of Magnus Maximus, a Western Roman Emperor who ruled from 383 to 388; Arthwys ap Mar of the Pennines, who lived between approximately 450 and 520; Arthwys of Elmet, West Yorkshire, born circa 479; Arthfael ap Einudd of Glamorgan, who lived circa 480 to 550; St. Arthmael, formerly King Athrwys of Glywyssing, who lived circa 482 to 552; Arthfoddw of Ceredigion, circa540 to 610; Artúir ap Pedr of Dyfed, circa 550 to 620; and Athrwys ap Meurig, a Welsh king, circa 610 to 680.

The net has been cast wide. These would-be Arthurs span five hundred years, from long before the early sixth century—the time when most historians place the historical Arthur—until long after this time. All these men are from the south of Britain, although some people have sought to buttress a favored candidate's claim by asserting that their man had northern connections. Lucius Artorius Castus is said to have been posted to Hadrian's Wall, and Arthun to have lived for a time at Caerleon (Carlisle)—both in the far north of England, near, but not quite in, Scotland.

Possible southern Arthurs include almost everyone known to have lived in Britain in the five hundred years before the mid-seventh century whose name begins with the letters *Ar*. There are almost as many interpretations of the name Arthur as there are "Arthurs." The most popular holds that the name Arthur is derived from the fifth-century P-Celtic Welsh words *art* or *arth*, which are said to mean "bear" with the addition of "ur," which is said to be P-Celtic Welsh for "a man." This produces Arthur, Bear-man. Alternatively, the P-Celtic Welsh word *arth*, meaning "bear," has been added to the Latin word *ursus*, which also means "bear," and so we end up with *Arthursus* (a name with double the bear-iness of other names).

In early Q-Celtic *art* also means "bear," although John O'Brien's eighteenth-century *Irish-English Dictionary* says that the name Arthur may also be derived from *art*, meaning "noble" or "generous." In either event, "bear" names work just as well in Scotland as they do in the south.

Scotland has only one Arthur-candidate, Arthur Mac Aedan, the son of the king of the Scots, a man of the late sixthcentury. His claim has been "debunked" on the grounds that little is known of his life.

"Artuir Mac Áedáin [*sic*] might be the historical Arthur but, even if he was, there is nothing else we can say about him,"[1] writes academic Guy Halsall in a recent book that sets out to undermine the very idea of finding a historical Arthur. Halsall notes that the reference to Arthur in *Y Gododdin* (circa 600) "might be the earliest mention of [the legendary] Arthur," but it goes on to say that,

> No fewer than three genuine historical Arthurs are mentioned around the end of the sixth century. One was a son of King Aedan of the Scots. . . This interesting cluster of three Arthurs appearing close together in the historical record might be proof of the reality of a great Arthur a generation or two before their birth, thus sometime in the early to mid-sixth century.[2]

One might think the existence of three late-sixth-century Arthurs is more likely to be proof of the reality of a late-sixth-century "great Arthur" (rather than an earlier "great Arthur"), but, then, this would be counterintuitive for those who hold to the conventional wisdom. (It was not clear to me who the two other Arthurs referred to were.)

A similarity of names is not always deemed essential for a historical candidate. Owain Ddantgwyn, White Tooth, of Powys in North Wales, has been put forward as a possible historical Arthur. The supposition is that the name Arthur was a nickname, and the "proof" is that his son was said to have driven a chariot called "the receptacle of the bear"—the word "bear" in P-Celtic is *arth*, as I mentioned earlier. The idea seems to be that the son was the father's charioteer.

The most famous potential historical Arthur is not actually called Arthur either: he is the shadowy Riothamus who went to the aid of a people called the Bituriges, in central France in about 468. Riothamus is said to have been king of the Britons, but it is more likely he was the king of the Bretons of northern France. It is unlikely a British Riothamus would have had the strength or the motivation to invade central France in the middle of the fifth century when there was more than enough to occupy him at home. If he did invade France from Britain, why did Gildas, who wrote of this time in the following century, not mention him? The little that is known of Riothamus does not suggest he was an especially successful warrior; on the contrary, all we know of his one campaign is that his army was routed and that he "fled with all his men" toward Burgundy, before vanishing from history. The weightiest evidence for Riothamus is that in Burgundy there is a place called Avallon, although it was not called Avallon in the fifth century, and there is nothing to suggest Riothamus was ever there.

Geoffrey Ashe, one of the most prominent advocates of Riothamus as the historical Arthur, also favors a connection between Arthur and Glastonbury, where, some say, Arthur was buried. According to Ashe, "The Arthur-Riothamus equation might be thought adverse to the [Glastonbury] grave, on the grounds that if [Riothamus] died overseas he would not have been buried in Glastonbury. Yet if his mortal career ended in Burgundian country, at the real Avallon for instance, his remains might have been brought back later for re-interment . . ." This would seem to preclude Avallon being, well, Avalon.

Riothamus has only a slender connection with Britain, if any, and none at all with any one of the twelve battles on Nennius's battle-list or with Camlann, or with any Round Table, or with Camelot, or with anything much that has anything to do with the legendary Arthur—not even a name. It is difficult to see that, as Geoffrey Ashe says, "In the High King called Riothamus we have . . . a documented person as the starting point of the legend," or that "[Riothamus] is the only such person on record who does anything Arthurian."[4]

There is almost nothing to connect anyone whose name sounds a little like "Arthur"—or indeed anyone whose name does *not* even sound a little like Arthur—to any one of the battles attributed to the legendary Arthur: at least no one who hails from the south of Britain.

Y Gododdin is looked upon as a southern British, specifically Welsh, poem, despite it having been written in the Edinburgh area circa 600. It is never easy to identify the origins of a first millennium source, far less to place an individual in a clear historical or geographical context. Any chance that Nennius might have made things clear was probably lost when he made a heap of his sources before writing his *Historia*. It has been said that the Nennius list of battles has provoked more commentary than any other passage of early British history, which, even if not exactly true, is not far from the mark. The

Nennius battle-list is to the matter of Arthur what the Rosetta Stone was to understanding Ancient Egyptian hieroglyphs before Champollion deciphered it.

The archaeologist Leslie Alcock once wrote, "The most serious danger for the historian is the scribe who knows, or thinks he knows, more than the original, and who cannot resist the temptation to insert his knowledge."[5] At least one such scribe appears to have worked on the *Annales Cambriae*. Writing long after the earliest years covered by the *Annales*, the scribes who compiled them had very limited sources to work with. They did, however, know about Arthur and Merlin, at least as stories: everyone did. They also had empty spaces in the historical record of the south of Britain. The solution was to put the stories of Arthur in those empty spaces.

It was a match made in heaven. Arthur's most famous battle, the Battle of Badon, was inserted as the entry for the year 516, and Camlann, Arthur's last battle, was said to have been fought in 537, thus creating an instant "Arthurian Age." If these entries were accurate, not only would it mean that twenty-one years separated Arthur's last two battles, but also that Arthur died thirty-six years before Merlin was active at the Battle of Arderydd in 573. Some scholars have solved this problem by saying there must have been two Merlins.

The Badon entry and the Camlann entry in the *Annales Cambriae* "are now discounted as historical evidence,"[6] and increasingly it is accepted that these entries were inserted long after the events they purport to record, to fill the gaping hole in southern British history that is the sixth century. They are just too good to be true—too like the kind of thing someone would insert if they wanted to place Arthur in the early sixth century. Furthermore, they come without any sensible context or corroborative evidence, and the entries for the fifty years before the Badon entry and the fifty years after the Camlann entry refer to people who have little or nothing to do with the south of Britain. No champion of any potential Arthur can rationally show that any, far less almost all, of the people mentioned in the *Annales Cambriae*, in any possible "Age of Arthur," are connected to a southern Arthur.

Lewis Thorpe, in his introduction to *The History of the Kings of Britain*, says, "Geoffrey had several clear-cut political reasons for what he wrote . . . [including] his wish to ingratiate himself with his various dedicatees."[7] It was Geoffrey who located Arthur's magical conception at Tintagel. The castle ruins at Tintagel today are from the early thirteenth century. They stand on the site of an earlier castle built by Richard, Earl of Cornwall, around the year 1141. Richard was the brother of Geoffrey of Monmouth's patron, Robert, Earl of Gloucester, and so it is possible, indeed probable, that Geoffrey set the scene of Arthur's conception in Tintagel to ingratiate himself with his patron. It was not until 1478 or so that Arthur was first said to have been born in Tintagel, no doubt because a birth site was more commercially appealing than the site of a rape. Today there is a thriving tourist industry founded on Geoffrey's identification of Tintagel as Arthur's birth place.

Geoffrey and Malory both say Arthur's father was Uther Pendragon; indeed, the first words in Malory's *Le Morte d'Arthur* are "It befell in the days of Uther Pendragon, when he was king of all England,"[8] but there is no Uther in the history of the south of Britain or a sensible explanation of the name. The second name is usually taken to mean Head Dragon—in effect, Chief Dragon—but the origin of this name is much disputed. The first name *Uther* is simply a mystery, at least in the south of Britain. According to Geoffrey Ashe, "Uther . . . is not real. Before Geoffrey he only figures as 'Uthr Pendragon', in uninformative Welsh verse."[9] Likewise, Guinevere, Lancelot, and Mordred have no part to play in southern British history. No one has placed them separately or together in a historical setting with anyone who might have been a historical Arthur.

Geoffrey, like Jocelyn of Furness, was happy to change evidence to suit his book, to please his patrons and his audience. Fortunately Geoffrey did not change all the evidence, and so there are a number of Scottish place-names in his work that hint at the true origins of his sources.

Choosing a "king" by means of a sword-from-a-stone test is unknown anywhere else in history, myth, or legend. Some say the legend of the sword and the stone is an echo of a Sarmatian practice that involved the veneration of swords stuck into the ground. There is nothing to suggest that this practice involved the selection of a king, nor would a sword stuck into the ground be difficult to remove. Scandinavian folklore contains a story of a sword stuck in a tree, but this was a test of strength and not part of any inauguration ceremony or coronation. Another alternative explanation claims that when people saw early blacksmiths extracting metal from iron ore and using it to make swords, they thought something magical was happening—something, we must suppose, involved with becoming a king.[10] Others have claimed there was a time when kingship disputes were settled by combat, with a sword going to the winner as a prize, and that these swords were left lying on a nearby stone until the fight was over. It has even been claimed that the Latin word *saxum*, said to mean a large stone, was confused with the word *Saxon*, and that when Arthur took the sword out of the stone he, in effect, took the fight out of the Saxons. Not one of these ideas comes with an Arthur attached.

In the late twelfth century, the French writer Chrétien de Troyes introduced *Camelot* as the name of Arthur's capital. He mentions it only once: "On a certain Ascension Day King Arthur was in the region of Caerleon and held his court at Camelot . . ."[11] Chrétien places his Camelot in the region of Caerleon, usually taken to be Carlisle in the far north of England, near the border with Scotland. By way of contrast, Malory's Camelot is in Winchester in the far south of Britain. Others say Camelot was Camulodunum (Colchester) because it begins with "Cam," although Colchester is an unlikely place for any Briton to have had his capital in any possible Age of Arthur because it was within Saxon lands at any time when any Arthur might have been active. Geoffrey did not mention Camelot, but this has not stopped Tintagel, Cornwall, where Geoffrey says Arthur was conceived, from being put forward as a possible Camelot.

Probably the most popular location for Camelot is Cadbury in Somerset, because Cadbury has a fort and there are several "Cam" names nearby. The idea that Cadbury was Camelot took off after the antiquary John Leland, writing in the sixteenth century during the reign of Henry VIII, said that local people referred to the area as *Camalat*. If they did, it was probably because there was a fort and some "Cam" names nearby, and because for some four hundred years the monks of nearby landlocked Glastonbury had been trying to pass off their monastery as the Isle of Avalon where Arthur was supposedly buried.

In Scotland, according to local tradition, Camelot was the village of Camelon in the Falkirk district, although local tradition also said that Camelon was the site of the Battle of Camlann, Arthur's last battle.

The twelfth-century French writer Wace introduced the Round Table. He said Arthur made the table round, "On account of his noble barons, each one felt he was superior, each considered himself the best, and none could say who was the worst, Arthur had the Round Table made, about which the British tell many a tale. There sat the vassals, all equal, all leaders; they were placed equally around the table, and equally served. None could boast he sat higher than his peer; all were seated near the place of honor, none far away."[12]

This is marvelous nonsense. Sitting in a circle might suggest equality to modern readers but not to someone in the sixth century. One thing the Celts of the sixth century felt strongly about was "pride of place." Everyone at a feast would have known who the most important person there was, and that the second most prestigious place was at that person's right hand. If the real Arthur truly did have a Round Table, equality was not the reason.

Robert de Boron, active a generation or so after Wace, tried to curry favor with those in power by Christianizing the Round Table, saying that Merlin made it in imitation of the table used at the Last Supper. This is but one of many attempts to give a Christian gloss to a non-Christian story. (Of course no one knows the seating arrangements at the Last Supper. In Leonardo da Vinci's *Last Supper* everyone is facing the same way, which seems unlikely, but . . . who knows.)

The *Annales Cambriae* say that "Merlin went mad" at the Battle of Arderydd in 573. Arderydd was fought at Caer Gwenddolau—today the Liddel Strength—a fort eleven miles north of Carlisle on the Liddel Water that forms the modern Scotland–England border. The battlefield lies just outside Longtown in the parish of Arthuret, centered on Arthuret Church. Close by lie the hills of Arthuret and seven miles away there is a hill called Arthur Seat.

The reference to Merlin at the Battle of Arderydd, coupled with the local Arthur-connected place-names, presents a problem for those who hold to the conventional view that Arthur was a man of the early sixth century who lived in the south of Britain and died in 537.

Arderydd was fought in the north in 573. Those who favor a southern Arthur have to decide whether their Arthur was a contemporary of Merlin, and, if they were contemporaries, whether they lived in the early or late sixth century. They also have to explain why a southern Arthur traveled north to fight at Arderydd. To solve this problem, it has been suggested there were two Merlins. The first Merlin is said to have been a contemporary of an early-sixth-century southern Arthur, a man who fought and won a memorable battle on the same battlefield where, in 573, a second Merlin fought in the Battle of Arderydd.

It is sometimes said that *Arthuret* originally meant "Arthur's Head" although Skene, Queen Victoria's Historiographer Royal for Scotland, said it is a modern form of *Arderydd*.[13] It seems Skene knew there was a connection between Arthuret and Arderydd but, at a loss to explain what it was, he simply conflated the two. One recent book in which scorn is cast on the very idea of finding a historical Arthur avoids the whole issue by calling the Battle of Arderydd, the Battle of Arthuret.[14]

The name Arthuret has inevitably led to this area being associated with the legendary Arthur. Some say he was buried there. It has also been said that Camelot was there and that Camlann, where Arthur fought his last battle, was fought in this area.

It has been supposed that Arthur was initially portrayed as a villain because he raided church property and stole the flocks and herds of priests and monks (and, we must suppose, tunics too), but there is reason to believe that the Church's early aversion to Arthur came from his association in the oral tradition with Merlin-Lailoken, an obviously non-Christian figure. This would have made Arthur anathema to Christian clerics.

The litmus test for the historical Arthur is the Battle of Badon, the only battle on the battle-list of Nennius to be mentioned in any of the other early sources: Gildas's *De Excidio* and the *Annales Cambriae*. Why is the test not to connect a southern Arthur with all twelve battles? Better still, why not all twelve battles in some sensible order? The reason this is not done is because, in the south of Britain, it is all but impossible to find a historical Arthur who is connected to a place called Badon, far less one connected to all twelve of the Nennius battles, far less all twelve of the Nennius battles in a sensible order. As Geoffrey Ashe says, "Four of the battle sites—'the river which is called Bassas', 'Fort Guinnion', 'the river which is called Tribruit' and 'the mountain which is called Agned'—have defied identification."[15] Other sites have proved all too easy to identify, albeit over and over again in many different places. The map in Alcock's *Arthur's Britain* shows a number of the battles including six Badons, all spread throughout Britain in no particular order, some as far apart as five hundred miles.[16]

All of the twelve Nennius battles have innumerable purported locations. The battle-list begins, "The first battle was at the mouth of the river called Glein." [17]

Alistair Moffat, measured and fair, plumps for the River Glen in Northumberland, England, as the location of Glein battlefield, although he admits he has only a reasonable reading of geography and good dictionaries to back this up.[18] There is even less evidence to associate, as some people do, the River Glen in Lincolnshire, England, with any possible Arthur or with any battle in which someone who might have been Arthur might have been involved.[19] Norma Lorre Goodrich ingeniously suggests that Glein was Gullane, east of Edinburgh, but the dissimilarity of the names and absence of corroboration says this is a desperate throw.[20]

Glein is said to be *glen* and to have been derived from the Gaelic for "pure," although my dictionaries say pure is *glan*. *Glé*, meaning "pure" or "bright," is the nearest word I could find to *glen*. The "pure" meanings of *glein* are unnecessarily complicated, especially when there is another rather obvious meaning available. *Glein*, according to all five of the Gaelic-English dictionaries I looked at, means "glen," the Scots word for valley. Applying Occam's razor—by which a simple answer to a question is always preferable to a complex answer—it would seem more likely that *glein* means "a glen" rather than something pure. But then, you might ask, who would call a river "the River Valley"? Well, there are innumerable rivers called Avon, and Avon is simply the Gaelic word *abhon*, meaning "river," and so we have a lot of River Rivers.[21] It is possible that whoever named Arthur's first battle did not know that a glen was a valley because he or she did not speak Gaelic. And so we have the River Glen when, in fact, the battle was fought in a river with a glen running through it or even in a place of rivers and glens in general.

The second entry on the battle-list reads, "The second, the third, the fourth and the fifth [battles] were on another river, called the Douglas which is in the country of Lindsey." The fact that Nennius lists four Douglas battles lends support to the idea that his battle-list had a real base in history. It is impossible to believe, if Nennius's list was a work of fiction, that the person who thought up the other eight names on the list was unable to invent another three names and so avoid repeating Douglas three times.

The Latin version of the battle-list reads, ". . . *Super aliud flumen quod dicitur Dubglas et est in regione Linnuis.*"[21] The place-name Linnuis has been blithely translated as Lindsey and identified as Lindsey near Lincoln in England. John Morris wrote in his *Age of Arthur*,

> One identifiable site is the river Dubglas in the district of Lin-nuis . . . Linnuis translates as Lindenses, the men of Lindsey about Lincoln; the only significant river of Lindsey is the Witham, whose ancient name is not known but which might have been Dubglas. A campaign may have entailed four nearby battles, but the more likely explanation is that this battle received four stanzas in the poem, the others one each. On any interpretation, it was evidently regarded as the most important of the battles, apart from Badon.[23]

Instead of using the name to find the place, this writer, it seems, has taken a place and adapted the name to fit it. He says the River Witham "might have been Dubglas." So might any river in Britain. There is no evidence that the Witham was once called Douglas. Lindenses is far from an obvious translation of Linnuis.[24] Lincoln is however in the south of Britain, and that seems to have been sufficient to outweigh the absence of the name Douglas in the vicinity, not to mention the absence of an Arthur and any time when something approaching the battles in question might have taken place in the vicinity of Lincoln. There is a River Douglas on the other side of England, in Lancashire, but this river has no Linnuis association. This has not stopped this Douglas also being put forward as a possible location for the second to fifth battles on Nennius's list.

Innumerable other places have been suggested as possible Douglas battle sites, but there is no substantial evidence to back up any one of them. Indeed some have neither a hint of a Douglas nor a Linnuis, which, given that places called Douglas (from *Dubh Glas*, meaning "Black Water") were common throughout Britain in the sixth century, suggests that someone was just not trying hard enough. Without some evidence to back up their claims, these places cannot be considered as possible locations of the battles of Douglas.

John Morris says four stanzas were given to the Battle of Douglas because, apart from Badon, it was the most important battle on the list. It is not easy to see why anyone would emphasize the importance of a battle by listing its name over and over and over again. On this basis it would be reasonable to expect Badon to be listed at least five times.[25] According to Morris there may have been a Douglas campaign that included four Douglas battles, but as there is no historical foundation for even one such battle in the area, it is pushing things a bit to jump to four battles. The proposition just does not make sense.

Those who are determined to have the battles of Douglas in the south of Britain have a choice. They can have a location on the east coast, which has a Lindsey but no Douglas, or a location on the west coast, which has a Douglas but no Lindsey. Leslie Alcock says,

> The best philological opinion is that Linnuis should derive from a British-Latin word like Lindenses, "the people of Lindum" or Lindensia, "land of Lindum." Neither of these British-Latin words is in fact recorded, but there seems to be no doubt that such words must have existed as derivatives of the word Lindum.

Yes, well, maybe, but that seems to be stretching the evidence just too far. Alcock says these supposed words subsequently developed and became Linnuis. He then asks where Lindum was. "The most obvious candidate" is Lincoln, he says, although, as he then goes on to say, "The only snag is that no Douglas . . . appears to be known in Lindsey [the area about Lincoln]."

There is however another Lindum, in Scotland. Why is this Scottish Lindum not "the most obvious" Lindum? Alcock does not say, but it may be because a Scottish location is too far north to weigh in favor of a southern Arthur. All Alcock is prepared to concede is that "This [Scottish site] could conceivably have been the scene of an Arthurian battle against the young Scottish kingdom of Dalriada, but it seems an unlikely place for four battles."[26]

What he means is that this Scottish site is an unlikely place for a southern Arthur to have fought four battles. It is not, of course, an unlikely place for someone from Dalriada to have fought four battles; on the contrary, this Douglas is on the border that separated Dalriada from the lands of the Picts, and so it is a likely place for someone from Dalriada or someone from the land of the Picts to have fought four battles.

The problem for those who would prefer a southern Arthur is that if this Scottish location is accepted it means their southern Arthur would have had to travel north to fight a full third of Nennius's twelve battles against the Scots of Dalriada. This would raise the question of why any southern Arthur would do such a thing. A southern Arthur would have had enough to do in the south, where his people were increasingly losing in battle to the Angles and the Saxons.

John Morris looked to the Witham, a place that "might have been Douglas." Leslie Alcock relied upon words which had not been recorded but which, he said, "must have existed." The matter would have been so much simpler if only they had been able to give serious consideration to the possibility that Arthur was a man of the north.

Britain has been fine-tooth combed for evidence of the location of the sixth battle, the Battle of Bassas. More than any other site on Nennius's battle-list, Bassas has caused scholars to despair. Some have said it just could not be identified, while others would not even speculate with regard to its whereabouts. The English nominees include, among others, Bassington near Cramlington and Bassington near Alnwick, both in Northumberland; Baschurch, Shropshire; Basford, Nottinghamshire; Baslow, Derbyshire; Bassingbourn, Cambridgeshire;

and Basingstoke, southwest of London. If it has "Bas" in its name, it is a contender.

In Scotland, the most favored location is the Bass Rock in the Firth of Forth off East Lothian. The fact that the Bass Rock is not much more than 500 feet across and is more than a mile from the mainland, never mind from the nearest river, has not prevented it from having its share of supporters. Bass, near Inverurie, Aberdeenshire, in the northeast, and Bass Hill, near Dryburgh, in the Scottish Borders, have also been considered but, like the Bass Rock, they have only their names to recommend them.

It is hard to believe, but Cambuslang a few miles southeast of Glasgow has also been put forward as a Bassas battle-site, although connecting "bas" with "bus" appears tentative in the extreme. Dunipace, where I say in *Finding Merlin* Merlin-Lailoken was assassinated, has also been thrown into the ring as a possibility due to an early alternative name, Dunibas, but perhaps this is also too tenuous a connection to be true.

It is commonly allowed that Nennius's seventh battle, the Battle of the Caledonian Wood, was fought in Scotland; but this is only because there is no real alternative, given that Caledonia, the Roman name for the north of Britain, is undeniably Scotland. Having said that, J. A. Giles, ever determined to place Arthur in the south, suggests that the Battle of the Caledonian Wood may have been fought in the forest of Englewood, between Penrith and Carlisle, making it just over the Scottish border into England. This is rather sad really.

There is no such consensus with regard to the eighth, ninth, and tenth battles—the battles of Guinnion, the City of the Legion, and Tribruit. Where were they fought? When were they fought? Who fought in them? And why? There are no answers to these questions in the south.

Suggested locations for Guinnion include Caer Guidn, Cornwall, in southwest England; Binchester, County Durham, in northeast England; and Winchester, Hampshire, in the far south of England. J. A. Giles favored the Roman station at Garionenum, near Yarmouth, Norfolk, in the far east of England. The City of the Legion has been identified as Chester or Carlisle, both northwest England; Exeter, southwest England; and Portsmouth, on the southern coast of England. For centuries Tribruit has been acknowledged by those who have looked for Arthur's battles as a nightmare. It has been said that the prefix "tri" refers to the city of Troy, for no reason other than the coincidence of the first two letters of the two names. An alternative opinion has the whole name mean "The Strand of the Pierced or Broken Place," although this suggestion does not come with any particular strand attached.

The "strand" element echoes in the Scottish-Gaelic word *tràigh*, which means "a shore." When *bruach*, a bank, is added to *tràigh* it produces the composite word, *tràigh-bruach*, which, at least, sounds something like *Tribruit* and fits Nennius's battle-list entry, which says the tenth battle was fought on the bank of a river. However, the Battle of the "Shore and/or Bank" is too tautological to make sense, and, even if it did make sense, which shore, which bank? *Ruathar* (which apparently means "violent onset") has also been added to *tràigh* to give a battle-name akin to "Skirmish on the Shore," which may be thought too bland to be a name for a battle.

J. A. Giles, ever anxious to set Arthur's battles in the south of Britain, said the battle-name *Tribruit* should really be "Ribroit," which he identified with the River Brue, Somerset, or the River Ribble, Lancashire. Don't ask me how. The rivers Severn in Gloucestershire in the far south of England and Eden in Cumbria in the far north of England have also been thrown into the pool of possible Tribruits.

Early in the twentieth century R. G. Collingwood interpreted the "tri" prefix as "three" before adding *bruit*, which apparently means "rushing" (as in the water of a rushing river). He concluded that Tribruit might have been the triple estuary of Chichester Harbour when the tide was coming in fast. How likely is that? In Scotland Tribruit has been identified as the place where the Rivers Forth, Teith, and the Goodie Water meet, west of Stirling, a claim which would have more force if these rivers actually met. The River Frew, once the River Bruit, another candidate, runs nearby.

According to the conventional wisdom there are two alternative eleventh battles in the list of Nennius. The eleventh battle most often referred to is in the Harleian manuscripts[27]: "the eleventh battle was on the hill called Agned." The alternative eleventh battle is in Vatican Recension–related manuscripts:[28] "The eleventh [battle] was on the mountain Breguoin, which we call Cat Bregion." The so-called Gildensian manuscript of the *Historia*[29]—effectively the Harleian manuscript with a few changes—confuses the matter further with a composite version of the Harleian- and Vatican-related manuscripts: "Mount Agned, that is Cat Bregomium [*sic*]." Somewhat surprisingly, given the general propensity among scholars to place Arthur in southern Britain, Edinburgh is the generally accepted location of the Battle of Agned. Even J. A. Giles, a man ever determined to place Arthur in the south of Britain and whose primary location for the Battle of Agned was Cadbury in Somerset, allowed that Edinburgh was a *possible* location.

It is ironic that Geoffrey of Monmouth, who did so much to make Arthur a southern hero, contributed so much to this Agned-Edinburgh identification, albeit indirectly. Geoffrey referred to Alclud, literally Clyde Rock, in modern-day Dumbarton and then, in the same sentence, to Mount Agned, which, he said, "is now called the Maidens' Castle."[30] Geoffrey did not say the Maidens' Castle was in Edinburgh. However, about the same time as Geoffrey was writing his *History* (circa 1136), David I, King of Scots, in circa 1142 referred to Edinburgh Castle as *Castellum Puellaram*, Castle of the Maidens. This conjunction led to the association of Agned and Edinburgh, even by those who favored a southern Arthur.

If Agned was the Castle of the Maidens and if the Castle of the Maidens was Edinburgh then, it followed, Edinburgh was Agned. That was the reasoning. However, many more places than Edinburgh were called "Castle of the Maidens" and so the Edinburgh identification does not necessarily stand. Maiden references are quite common in Scottish place-names, especially "Nine Maidens" references.

It may, however, still be argued that there is corroboration for the Agned-Edinburgh connection. Skene says, "The eleventh battle was fought in *Mynydd Agned*, or Edinburgh, and here too the name is preserved in *Sedes Arthuri* or Arthur's Seat." Arthur's Seat, the great volcanic rock that looms above the new Scottish Parliament, may well be connected with Arthur, but it does not necessarily follow that this has anything to do with the Battle of Agned. And of course the Arthur-was-a-man-of-the-south diehards do not accept that Agned was in Scotland, irrespective of evidence. One even claimed that "Agned" was a spelling mistake made by a copyist who had really intended to place the battle in Gaul in the fifth century.

The alternative names, Breguoin and Bregion, used in the identification of Nennius's eleventh battle in the Vatican-related manuscripts, and Bregomium, in the Gildensian manuscript, have inspired a range of variations that include Bravonium, Branonium, Bremenium, Brewyn and even Cathregonium, among many others. There are several suggested Breguoin-Bregion-Bregomium battle sites: Brent Knoll, Somerset; Ribchester, Lancashire; Cirencester, Gloucestershire; High Rochester, Northumberland. All are in England, and not one of these suggested sites comes with anything resembling a substantial evidential foundation.

Sometimes not even three common letters are needed—two will do—and so we have Roman place-names like Bravonium and Branonium put forward as possibilities. The *g* that appears in names like Breguoin is absent in these Roman names and in most of the others. This problem has been "solved" by the argument that *Breguoin* was a transcription error and what was really meant was "Bretagne" (Britain), which would make the eleventh battle the Battle of Britain. How Nennius in the ninth century could have used French is not clear, and, besides, if the eleventh battle was important enough to justify it being given the name of the whole island, would not this name be used in every manuscript, including the Vatican-related manuscripts? In any event, the "Battle of Britain" does not help identify an exact site.

Norma Lorre Goodrich puts forward a name that includes a *g* but she had to look to a very late source to find it. In *The Prose Lancelot*, written in Old French in the twelfth century, the name Breguoin is given as Bredigan. According to Goodrich the etymology of Bredigan is "astonishingly simple": *bre* means "promontory," *di* means "at," and *gan* (or *llan*) means "a meadow" or "church enclosure." This produces "the battle of the promontory at the meadow or church enclosure," which seems an unlikely name for a battle. Whether this is so or not, as with *Bretagne*, this construction takes us no closer to finding an actual battle site.

The site of the Badon battlefield has also been disputed for centuries; Bowden Hill, Lothian; Dumbarton Rock, Strathclyde; Mynydd Baedan, Glamorgan; and Little Solway Hill, Somerset have all been suggested as sites of Mons Badonis. Every Badbury in England—in Devon, Dorset, Wiltshire, Berkshire, Warwickshire, Northamptonshire, and Lincolnshire—has its champion. However, those who prefer an English location for everything Arthurian generally recognize Bath as the site of the Battle of Badon, despite the fact that there is nothing to connect the all but hill-free Bath with any historical context within which a historical Arthur might have existed. There is no evidence of any battle at Bath at any time which might have involved an Arthur, far less of a battle that was the last in a campaign of twelve.

The Romans name for Bath was Aquae Sulis, the place of the waters of a local deity called Sul. It was not given the name Bath until after any possible southern Arthurian period. (According to the *Anglo-Saxon Chronicle*, Bath (*Baðanceaster*) was captured by Saxons in 577, although it was probably not given its new name until sometime after that.) But even if the Britons had defeated a Saxon army at Aquae Sulis—and there is no evidence that this ever happened—why would these Britons name the battle *Badon*, the word for "a bath" in the language of their defeated enemy? This makes little sense.

Those who would like Arthur to have been a man of the south probably picked Bath as the site of the Battle of Mount Badon because *Badon* was reminiscent of *Badonici* and *Badonis*: this despite the absence of any corroborative evidence and the fact that there is plenty of evidence to the contrary. Bath does not have a hill for starters: there is nothing a Scot would call a hill in or near Bath. Little Solsbury Hill, three miles north of Bath is usually said to be the site of the battle. Howard Reid, considering the site of the Battle of Badon (which, he pleasingly describes as "of no . . . fixed abode"), refers to how low the "hills" around Bath are, before writing, "Just to make matters worse it would be hard to argue honestly for any site [for Badon] in south-west England."[31]

If those who favor a southern Arthur were to allow that the Battles of the Caledonian Wood and of Agned-Breguoin, and the four Douglas battles were fought in Scotland, this would mean half of Nennius's twelve battles were fought in Scotland, which would stretch the idea of a southern Arthur to breaking point.

There is no consensus regarding the location of Arthur's last battle, the Battle of Camlann. In the absence of any real evidence for a southern Camlann, southerners have relied overmuch on the battle-name itself until almost anywhere with "cam" in its name has its supporters. The Roman Fort of Camboglanna, now Birdoswald on Hadrian's Wall; the River Cam, near Salisbury, Somerset; and Slaughterbridge, Camelford, Cornwall, have all been put forward as potential Camlanns, all in England. Only one, Slaughterbridge, is able to boast a possible battle (although recent archaeology has shown that this battle was fought in the ninth century, too late to have had anything to do with any possible historical Arthur).

Identifiers of Welsh Camlanns are less picky about "cam" connections. Their Camlanns include the "Cam"-free Rhinog Mountains in northern Wales and Dolgellau in northwestern Wales.[32] Wales, like England, lacks a historical Arthur who might have fought in these battles, whenever and wherever they may have been fought. Not one of these places stands within a sensible historical framework that might include someone who might have been Arthur; just like every one of the twelve Nennius-battles attributed to the legendary Arthur there is no convincing, far less conclusive evidence, as to where Camlann was fought and far, far less evidence that it was fought by an actual historical Arthur.

The date of the battle is an even bigger problem for those who believe in the traditional southern-British Arthur. Dr. John Morris says there is evidence to suggest Camlann was fought, "a year or two either side of 515," beyond this, he says, "nothing . . .is known of the battle or its cause, or even of its whereabouts."[33] The *Annales Cambriae* disagree with Morris, putting the date at 537, but neither of these dates has a historical hinterland: no Arthur, no campaign; no *casus belli*, nothing to enable anyone to decide whether to favor circa 515 or circa 537 or to dismiss them both.

Almost everyone agrees that women took the dead or dying Arthur to the Isle of Avalon after the climactic Battle of Camlann, although the precise name of this island varies: *Insula Avallonis*,

Insula Avallonia, *Ynys Avalon*, *Ynys Afallach*, *Avilion*, *Avilon*, and *Avallon*. This last alternative is the name of a town in Burgundy, France. This may seem preposterous but there is another, equally daft suggestion that is frequently trotted out as if it makes sense, because some people really want to believe it is true, because it is in southern Britain—Glastonbury.

The fact that Glastonbury is landlocked has not prevented it from being identified as Avalon. Glastonbury proponents, from Gerald of Wales in the twelfth century onwards, have claimed that in the middle of the first millennium the land about Glastonbury was not well-drained and that consequently the land about Glastonbury was often flooded, making the Tor, the hill near the town, stand up out of the water, island-like. This means that not only the high Tor but also the low-lying Abbey must have stuck up out of the water and been confused with an island, because it was in the low-lying Abbey that the monks said they found the grave of Arthur. Gerald should just have done what Malory did: delete the word *island* and inserted the word *vale*—it would have been simpler.

The real reason Arthur is said to be buried in Glastonbury is money. In 1184 a fire damaged Glastonbury Abbey and the monks needed funds to carry out repairs. Being enterprising monks they realized there was money to be made if they could attract pilgrims. They also knew that Geoffrey had associated Glastonbury with Arthur and that stories of Arthur were popular among the people of England at this time. Theirs was an age of relics, usually corpses or parts of corpses, and the monks concluded that if they were to bring in visitors, they needed a popular relic, ideally a corpse.

So it was that in 1191 the monks of Glastonbury said they had discovered Arthur's grave in the Abbey grounds[34] and, just in case there was any dispute, they also "discovered" a lead cross, upon which were written the words, *"Hic iacet sepultus inclytus rex Arthurius in insula Avalonia cum uxore sua secunda Gwenneveria*—Here lies the renowned King Arthur in the isle of Avalon with his second wife Guinevere." (This cross had everything necessary to promote pilgrim-tourism but directions to and the opening hours of the medieval equivalent of a gift shop.)

In recent centuries it has been pointed out that the lettering on this cross, supposedly found in a sixth-century grave, was twelfth-century, the century in which it was "found." This cross subsequently disappeared, although copies of it had been made. Later it was claimed it said only, *"Hic iacet sepultus inclytus rex Arthurius in insula Avalonia."* Guinevere had been left lying on the cutting room floor.

It is now generally accepted that the Glastonbury grave was a hoax created to suck in gullible religious-tourists and make money from them, and it worked: from the twelfth century onward many credulous people flocked to Glastonbury and spent money there, thinking the place had something to do with the historical Arthur—some still do. Realizing they were on to a good thing the monks went on to "discover" and display the bodies of several Christian saints, including Gildas and, amazingly, St. Patrick (these monks had chutzpah). For good measure they also claimed that Joseph of Arimathea, said to be the great-uncle of Jesus of Nazareth, had visited Glastonbury. This too boosted the pilgrim-trade and the monks' profits. Before the twelfth century, however, nothing linked Arthur with Glastonbury; indeed, several writers referred to Glastonbury in detail without reference to an Arthurian, far less an Avalonian, link.

Another favorite site for Avalon is in Wales—Bardsey Island, off the Llŷn Peninsula. Historians Steve Blake and Scott Lloyd, however, with reference to early Welsh manuscripts, have said Avalon was sited at a Bronze Age fortification in the Clwydian Mountains in Flintshire in Wales.[35] They overcome the absence of an island in the Clwydian Mountains by reading *ynys*, which is usually read as "island," as "realm," and by taking *afallach* to be, not "apples" but a personal name. The result is *Ynys Afallach*, Realm of Afallach. Apples, however, have a recurring connection to Avalon, as further examples will show.

So why would anyone plump for locations like Glastonbury and the Clwydian Mountains when the island of Anglesey, off the coast of northwest Wales, is at least an island in the western sea, just as Avalon is said to be an island in the western sea? The answer is because Anglesey was the headquarters of the people of the Old Way of the druids. This made it a non-starter. Why did they not then go for the Isles of Scilly in the Atlantic? They too are at least islands and in the western sea. The answer here is because the Scillies were inaccessible to pilgrim-tourists, and because no one would have thanked anyone for such an identification.

Looking for Avalon in the south of Britain is like looking for a black cat in a dark room that isn't even there—the coasts of southern Britain have very few islands at all. On the other hand, there's no shortage of islands off the west coast of Scotland; it's near impossible to set out to sea from the Scottish mainland and avoid an island. Laurence Gardner suggested the Isle of Arran as a possible Avalon. He said the Fir Bolg, an early Irish people, installed their kings on an island, an "eternal paradise," an "enchanted isle" called *Arúnmore* and that this enchanted isle lay where Arran lies, between Antrim in the northeast of Ireland, and Lethet, which, Laurence Gardner said, is the stretch of land between the Clyde and Forth. It has been said Arran was once called *Emain Ablach*, the place of apples, although the *Oxford Dictionary of Celtic Mythology* says this connection cannot be correct.

Another Isle of Avalon was the "Island" of Invalone, an island it is said once lay between the Rivers Forth, Teith, and Allan, near Stirling.[36] Besides Wales, England, and Scotland, Avalon has also been placed in Australasia, Sicily, India, and in the Mediterranean by writers from the twelfth to fifteenth centuries. It is always possible that Avalon was an island in a lake or a loch, although by tradition the Avalon was ". . . an Island in the Western Sea."[37] This matter of the western sea is perhaps unsurprising given that almost all the offshore islands of Britain and Ireland lie off their western coasts. This also is in accord with the beliefs of many pre-Christian peoples, who pictured the souls of the dead being borne westward to ". . . an Island in the Western Sea . . ."[38] This too is perhaps unsurprising, because the sun sets—that is, dies—in the west. The dead of the First World War were said to have "gone west." Christians explained this by claiming "west" meant west from the battlefields of France, home to England, when in fact this saying is but one of many surviving folk-memories of the Old Way.

In the "Stanzas of the Graves" in the *Black Book of Carmarthen* is the line, "*Anoeth bid bet y Arthur.*" This has been translated in several ways: "a wonder of the world is the grave of Arthur"; "a difficult thing is the grave of Arthur"; "a mystery to the world is the grave of Arthur";

"impossible to find in this world is the grave of Arthur". All of these things are true except, perhaps, the last one.

William of Malmesbury, writing in the early twelfth century attributes the name Avalon to "a certain Avalloc, who is said to have lived there with his daughters because of the secrecy of the place." This was probably inspired by a Welsh tradition at least as old as the twelfth century, which says that the name Avalon was derived from the name of a man called Avallach, the father of a woman called Morgan (from whom the legend of Arthur is said to have acquired Morgan le Fay, Morgan the Fairy). Place-names were often personalized and attributed to eponymous fictional figures; there probably never was an Avalloc.

In his *Vita Merlini*, Geoffrey describes Avalon as "*Insula pomorum quae fortunata uocatur*—The island of apples, which men call the fortunate isle."

> There [in Avalon] nine sisters rule by a pleasing set of laws those who come to them from our country. She who is first of them is more skilled in the healing art, and excels her sisters in the beauty of her person. Morgen [*sic*] is her name . . . Thither after the Battle of Camlann we took the wounded Arthur . . .

The Welsh poem *The Spoils of Annwn* says that after the Battle of Camlann the druid-bard Taliesin brought the wounded Arthur to the *Insula Pomorum*, Isle of Apples, and left him there under the care of Morgan, who was skilled in the arts of healing and who was the chief maiden of the nine maidens who lived on Avalon.

The Welsh for "apple" is *aval* or *afal*; in old Welsh it is *abal* or in the plural *aballon*.[39] In Scottish Gaelic "apple" would be *abhall*,[40] pronounced "aval." The Avallon in Burgundy also has an apple meaning—one that springs from the ancient Celtic-Gaulish languages that once prevailed in France. The apple connections that work in the south of Britain work equally well in the north. Apples were said to be a magical fruit in the Celtic world; they evoked ideas of immortality spent in some heaven or paradise, "like those of the Hesperides, or of Celtic otherworld regions."[41]

In the first few centuries after Arthur's death the Church ignored his memory, hoping it would just fade away. When this did not happen clerics tried to include Arthur in their Christian writings as a villain, in the hope that this would erode his heroic status. When this did not work they abandoned their negative tack, bit the bullet, and made Arthur a Christian, an Englishman, and, for good measure, a king.

By the time this change of tack was taken Arthur was already somewhat damaged goods. In contrast, the stock of the man who came to be called Lancelot was on the rise. Lancelot was said to be a better fighter, younger, better looking and an all-around more glamorous figure than Arthur, and, just in case this was not enough, Lancelot, the new up-and-coming Christian hero, was said to have cuckolded Arthur. The matter of sex suggests that if the legend of Lancelot had a foundation in history it lay in a time before Christianity controlled the written word. Lancelot also stands in stark contrast to that relatively late addition to the Arthurian cycle, Galahad, a true Christian hero and an all but sexless knight.

Despite the best efforts of the purported southern Arthur, whoever he was, the Anglo-Saxons conquered the south of Britain, created Angle-land or England, and pushed the native Celtic-British into what is now Wales.

The Anglo-Saxons had little interest in Arthur, because in the original stories they, or at least the Angles, were the enemy. In later centuries, after Arthur was presented as an English king, new enemies had to be found for him and so he ended up fighting in France (although this was probably to please Geoffrey's French audience), before going on to fight a Roman Emperor (long after Roman Emperors had ceased to be).

The Norman French who conquered the Anglo-Saxons in the eleventh century saw Arthur as a useful propaganda tool and were pleased to associate themselves with him. This was not because they were pro-British but because they were anti-Anglo-Saxon. This led to the story of Arthur—originally a Celtic story before it was subjected to Germanic, Anglo-Saxon influences—becoming popular on the mainland of Europe and falling under the pens of the Norman-French.

In Norman-French England and on the mainland of Europe the story of Arthur cross-fertilized with French and German influences and grew exponentially. The Celtic-British origins of the stories were played down even more, and the Celtic material was absorbed and adapted to appeal to English, French, and German audiences. By the twelfth century the story of Arthur had become a staple of the romantic canon of the Troubadours.

In England, when Edward III needed the support of his Welsh subjects to fight the French he "revived" the order of the Round Table to win Welsh favor, although he dropped this idea after his victory at Crécy in 1346. The remains of the 200-foot-diameter hall that Edward started to build in Windsor, but which he did not complete, have only recently been discovered.[42]

In the fifteenth century, Henry VII Tudor, a Welshman, coveted the English crown and tried to curry favor with the English by naming his firstborn son Arthur. This Arthur died before he became king, leaving his brother Henry, the abominable Henry VIII, to be king in his place. Henry VIII also jumped on the Arthurian bandwagon. He renovated a round table in Winchester, which he said was *the* Round Table, although it was really a fourteenth-century fake.

Arthur's story became entangled in the histories of England and Wales, and so we have Edward III, an English king, associating himself with Arthur to ingratiate himself with the Welsh and Henry VII, a Welsh would-be king, associating himself with Arthur to ingratiate himself with the English. In the twentieth century U.S. President John F. Kennedy and his staff preened themselves by promoting their Whitehouse as Camelot, and Charles Windsor, Prince of Wales and heir to the British throne, has Arthur among his many names to enhance his Welsh connections. The legend of Arthur is evidently a useful and much used legend.

In the film *The Man Who Shot Liberty Valance* a newspaper man says "When the legend becomes fact, print the legend." The legend of Arthur contains perhaps the most famous legend of them all: the Holy Grail. The idea of the Grail as a vessel was perhaps inspired by the magic cauldron stories of Celtic mythology, although Wolfram von Eschenbach of Germany in his poem *Parzival*, written in the early thirteenth century, said the Grail was a magic stone. Robert de Boron, about the turn of the twelfth century, inserted the Holy Grail into the legend of Arthur and provided them both with a communal Christian spin. Robert's Arthur was a Christian and his Holy Grail was the bowl Jesus used at his last supper, a bowl later used by Joseph of Arimathea to catch the blood of Jesus while he hung on his cross. This Holy Grail was said to have been brought to Glastonbury Abbey by Joseph of Arimathea, although William of Malmesbury, who wrote about the abbey in the twelfth century, appears to have known nothing of this. Joseph of Arimathea only appears in the second edition of his book, after William was dead. From the twelfth century on, the search for the Holy Grail is a common staple of Arthurian tales. These Grail expeditions tend to be called quests.

In the early fourth century, Christianity became the state religion of the Roman Empire. In the early fifth century the western empire collapsed and the Christian Church moved in to fill the vacuum. Until then, the people of the Old Way, all over the empire but especially in Gaul (France) and Britain, had been free to believe whatever they wanted, provided their beliefs did not impact the welfare of the community as a whole. This was the Roman way. Early Christianity was not like that. Early Church leaders told people what they should believe and so started a "Dark Age" that lasted until the fifteenth century, at which point the Renaissance allowed in a little light. The middle of this Dark Age saw the highpoint in the worship of relics, of which the Holy Grail was the epitome.

The idea of the Grail was first conceived at a time when fake relics provided a major source of income for the Church. Think of the vast number of people even today who expend energy and cash getting themselves to places like Santiago de Compostela in northwest Spain, hoping to see pieces of the corpse of St. James and pay for the privilege, on the understanding that they will be rewarded while they are alive or in some afterlife. The advantage the Grail had over other relics (usually human body parts) was that it did not exist, and so people could continue looking for it forever. The Grail became the acceptable face of relic worship, the quintessential user-friendly relic, the myth that kept on giving.

According to the conventional wisdom, as everyone knows from innumerable stories, Arthur's "knights" were "noble" men who spent much of their time righting wrongs. It is extremely unlikely that this happened in reality. The historical Arthur was not a social reformer. It is more likely that the stories that came to be attached to Arthur were echoes of the spirit of the Old Way of the druids that remained alive in the oral tradition, despite all the efforts of churchmen to eradicate every trace of the Old Way and its works.

.   The Old Way allowed for alternative ways of living to be discussed. The very fact that new ideas, such as Christianity were allowed space to grow is proof of this. There was almost no persecution of Christians by people of the Old Way. Columba-Crimthann of Iona was allowed to visit Inverness, an Old Way stronghold, and to challenge the druids he met there. It is almost impossible to imagine this scene reversed at almost any time in the next thousand years, when Christianity was in power: a druid seeking to challenge Christians on Christian ground would have been lucky to escape with his life (and many did not).

One of the few records in which the druids *are* mentioned is Pliny the Elder's *Naturalis Historia*, in which they are described not just as magicians but as natural scientists and doctors of medicine.[43] They were, in effect, a professional class.

Given their various specialties, there was no one person in authority and so no one authorized right way to do things. By the tenets of the Old Way, knowledge was valued, acceptance of the beliefs of others was the norm, and women and gay men had a proper, respected, natural place in the community. No Galileo of the Old Way would ever have been sacrificed to preserve some dogma. On the contrary the Old Way engendered individuality, and so disputation, both of which are good for humanity and bad for those in charge.

It was difficult to control people who wondered how to sort out their own problems because, being individuals, they tended to come up with individual answers. It was much better in the view of those in authority to have *one* answer and a people who were bound to accept that answer. The freedom of the Old Way contrasted strongly with the authoritarianism of the Church. The Old Way was the antithesis of Christendom.

After Christianity came to power people, through the oral tradition, remembered the time when the Old Way held sway. Even if they did not, being human they would have been inclined to reason, question, and argue anyway, because that is the human "default" position. It was only natural that people would associate their vague memories of the Old Way with the time of their greatest hero, Arthur, a man of the Old Way. He was, after all, the last hero standing when the twilight of the druids gave way to an age of darkness.

In time the philosophy of the Old Way and the legend that came to be attached to the historical Arthur became confused, until stories arose of Arthur's Camelot as a place where righteous "knights" vied with each other to see who could do the noblest deed. In effect, the ideas of the Old Way became conflated with and personalized by the celebrity status of the by-then-legendary Arthur and his men.

Inherent in the concept of "doing good deeds" is the question, What is good? As everyone knows, once you start asking that kind of question you are on the slippery slope to philosophy, and philosophy always leads to disagreement. Such a thing was unacceptable to a prescriptive and authoritarian Christianity. The Church told people what was good and what was bad and that was that. Unwilling to allow freedom of thought even in story form, the Church decided to keep the quests but have the "knights" search not for opportunities to stand up for the weak against the powerful but for a physical object. The idea of simply doing good protecting women, the weak, and the poor soon took second place to the idea of "knights" looking for the Grail.

It did not matter what the Grail was because the search was the whole point of the exercise. The fact that no one knew what the Grail was did not stop some deluded people from actually looking for it—some are still looking. And so it was that just as Lancelot replaced Arthur as the main hero in the stories, the MacGuffin in the stories changed too: from righting wrongs to questing for the Holy Grail. Questing for this Holy Grail, as opposed to doing good, enabled the Church to avoid the tricky question, What is good?

As the power of the Church grew, the fighting-the-strong-in-defense-of-the-weak elements in the stories were diluted and the searching-for-religious-relics elements became predominant. The fact that it was unclear what the Grail was had the advantage of preventing anyone from "finding" it and spoiling everything.

Given that there is no evidence that the Grail, whatever it was, ever existed, it is likely that the Grail is a fiction invented, like the anvil in the story of the sword and the stone, to distract attention from the real story of Arthur—a story that was steeped in the Old Way of the druids.

There is an answer to Chrétien's Grail question, "What is the Grail for?" The Grail was invented to stop people asking the "wrong" questions: that is, just about any questions but especially what is right and what is wrong. The Grail was and is a distraction: that is what the Grail was and is for.

3

Why Arthur Is Lost to History

WHEN THE CHURCH CONTROLLED THE WRITTEN WORD PEOPLE GOT the *Lives of Saints* whether they wanted them or not. When they were free to choose for themselves people went for stories of Arthur, just as they would today. Modern action movies are the equivalent of late-first-millennium tales of Arthur. The *Lives of Saints* have no such contemporary resonance: once the Church lost its media monopoly, the boring lives of saints proved to be too boring to survive, even when liberally larded with special effects (miracles).

The Christian Church was determined to promote its own interests no matter what, and, as not every historical fact suited its book, the Church destroyed a lot of historical material. Gerald of Wales, who was present when the monks of Glastonbury pretended to find Arthur's grave, said that Gildas destroyed several "outstanding books" that spoke well of Arthur. Jocelyn ignored the evidence he had found about Merlin-Lailoken, and Mungo Kentigern and produced the book his Bishop wanted him to produce. Non-churchmen too—men like Malory with his authorized books and unauthorized books—followed the party line to keep themselves safe.

Many inactive men today (it is usually men) like fantasy heroes.

It was the same in the past: Christian clerics liked fantasy heroes too. Today we have mild-mannered Clark Kent who becomes Superman, and the unremarkable Peter Parker who is Spiderman. In the past they had mild-mannered, unremarkable men like Cadoc and Padarn, who could turn cattle into ferns and open up the earth.

Unfortunately for the early clerics, people still preferred stories of warriors (especially when they involved attractive women) to hagiographies of saints, which were bereft of sex and action. No matter what the clerics did Arthur remained popular among the people, and, as a hero of the Old Way, he distracted people from the propaganda of their church. The Church could not compete with romantic tales, because they had only saintly heroes and so no scope for romance. Lifric of Llancarfan did his best with his story about Cadoc's parents, but no one—not then, not now—wants to hear a story about the love life of the main character's mum and dad. The Church had to find other tactics and it did. Stories in which the hero was a composite of a cleric and an action hero were written, and so we have vapid heroes like Galahad and Perceval.

In the early 590s, Pope Gregory I the Great told his churchmen not to destroy places that were held to be special by people of the Old Way but to commandeer them and use them for their own ends. This policy was applied not just to places of worship but also to stories of Arthur and Merlin.

In Evelyn Waugh's *Brideshead Revisited*, Lord Marchmain was contemptuous of the Christian Church but was said to have accepted Christianity just before he died, despite being too far gone by then to have had a meaningful say in the matter. When Arthur was dead and the oral tradition too weak to allow meaningful opposition, Arthur too was claimed as a Christian. He was, in effect, *marchmained*.

When it was recognized that the stories of Arthur and Merlin-Lailoken were not going to go away, a different tack was taken. Arthur and Merlin-Lailoken were absorbed into the body of acceptable Christian writings. Arthur was a man of war and not primarily associated with a particular way of thinking and so it was relatively easy to pretend that he was a Christian. Merlin-Lailoken was a man of ideas and so more of a problem. Too closely associated with the Old Way for anyone to believe in a Christian Merlin (despite some rather half-hearted efforts to portray him as just that), the best that could be done was to make him a tame, sexless, avuncular figure—a sort of in-house wizard. This did not work either. Merlin-Lailoken was just not a believable Christian. The best that could be done was to ensure that he was always portrayed as operating under the aegis of the Church.

The most famous story of Arthur and Merlin is the one in which Arthur is said to have taken a magic sword from a magic stone and so proved that he was the rightful king of "England." Malory took a historical event and changed it to create the wonderful supernatural story everyone knows today (the stone from which Arthur really took a sword is still there to be seen—see chapter 6).

Malory did not dare allow the magic of the sword and the stone episode to be at the instigation of Merlin, and so he has his Merlin ask the Archbishop of Canterbury to lend his authority to the occasion. Choosing a king was an important matter and so it had to be seen to be controlled by the Church or, at least, by a Christian. Merlin was just too obviously not believable as a Christian to be in charge of this event.

Christianizing the stories was only part of the process. Arthur and Merlin also had to be made men of the south of Britain. The scene became London and the whole sword-in-stone episode was said to have taken place under the auspices of Merlin who was, of course, acting under the authority of a Christian Archbishop. The supernatural elements in these stories are obviously fictional. London, in Geoffrey's day the capital of England, is an obvious anachronism. Merlin-Lailoken was a champion of the Old Way and an inveterate enemy of Christianity. He would never have acted under the authority of a Christian Archbishop. Besides, London was Saxon, and there were no Christian Archbishops about at any possible time when any of this might have happened in history.

The matter of romance leads us inevitably to the matter of sex, something the Christian authorities deplored almost above all things. Consequently, just as with films until the 1950s, if characters had to "do it," particularly outside marriage and, worse still "enjoy it," then they had to end up unhappy. So it was with Guinevere, who, according to Geoffrey, because of her adultery, "took her vows among the nuns, promising to lead a chaste life." That is, in effect, a warning against the dangers of promiscuity. *Let that be a lesson to you all.*

This adding of a Christian gloss to almost everything of importance for a thousand years served only to promote the Church and obscure what really happened, although not entirely. Over centuries the emphasis in the stories was to shift from the more Celtic Arthur to the more Anglicized, and later more Frenchified, Lancelot. It is, however, still possible to discover what really happened when Arthur took a sword from a stone; what Excalibur really was and where it came from; and where Guinevere really spent her last years.

The written word was restricted to a few compliant clerics who essentially did what they were told to do. For a millenium clerical apparatchiks—men like the monk Jocelyn in Glasgow, Saint Mungo Kentigern's hagiographer—censored stories of Arthur and Merlin-Lailoken to create the affront to history that is the legend of Arthur best known today. Remember Jocelyn in the twelfth century going out into the "streets and quarters" of Glasgow looking for source material to help him write a biography of Mungo Kentigern? Jocelyn was fortunate. He found a source that contained a truthful account of Mungo's life. Most biographers would have been delighted by such a find but not Jocelyn, because the source he had found showed that Mungo's Christianity was even further removed from the Christianity of his bishop than the original *Life of Kentigern* that had presented a problem in the first place.

Of course, Jocelyn, like almost all of his fellow clerics, ignored the evidence and wrote what suited the Church of his day. The original *Life of Mungo* and the even earlier source material Jocelyn found were allowed to disappear or (and this is more likely) were deliberately destroyed shortly after Jocelyn finished his new and authorized version. If even sources that related to Christian heroes like Mungo were deliberately warped or destroyed, it is even more likely that material that showed the people of the Old Way in a good light or that even showed them at all would not survive untouched, if it survived at all.

Men like Jocelyn and his bishop had both the means (almost complete control of the media) and the motive (maintaining that control) to create a version of past events that suited their ends. For over a thousand years men like Jocelyn and his bishop made the changes they wanted to writings that contradicted their worldview. From the time of Columba-Crimthann and the Council of Drumceatt (the Wannsee Conference of the early Christian Church) people of the Old Way were marginalized, castigated, and on occasion exterminated. At first many went underground and many became the less threatening "bards." Later most of the people who in another time would have been druids assimilated to a degree, thinking for themselves while going through the motions of the required rituals. They had to do this to survive. (It was more difficult for women. There was no place for educated women in the new Christian world.)

Is it any wonder that even a glimpse of the true story of Arthur has been lost to us for so long?

More recently, in 1599, the Indian Church of St. Thomas, said to have been founded in the mid-first century by Jesus' disciple Thomas, held records that contradicted the professions of the more powerful Church of St. Peter in Rome. That year the Archbishop of the Roman Church, Menezes of Goa, following a synod at Diamper (Indian equivalent of Drumceatt) burned the books of the people of the Church of Thomas. Only four manuscripts from before 1599 are known to exist in India today. It is possible, indeed likely, indeed almost certain, that almost all of the work of Taliesin and Aneirin were similarly deliberately destroyed.

More than the works themselves were destroyed; the fact that they were destroyed and, more, the very fact that they had existed at all was nearly erased from the common consciousness.

THE EUREKA MOMENT

As a child I had never dreamed that Arthur wasn't the southern English king I knew from books and films. It was only in July 1989, when I read Richard Barber's *The Figure of Arthur*, that I realized there was a Scottish Arthur-candidate: Arthur Mac Aedan of Dalriada. I was fifteen years old when I read in *The Steps to the Empty Throne*, the first part of Nigel Tranter's Robert Bruce trilogy of novels, that the Scottish Gaelic for high king was *Ard Righ* (*righ* has the same root as *rex*, *roi*, *rui*, regal, etc.).

I was sure this had to be more than a mere coincidence and that there had to be a some connection between the hero king, Robert Bruce, and me. This was partly because *Ard Righ* and my surname, Ardrey, sounded somewhat similar, but this was mainly because I was fifteen years old. Until then all I had known about my second name was that it was uncommon in the extreme. I always had to repeat it and spell it out to people I met for the first time, and every Ardrey I knew or had heard of was related to me and there were very few of them.

My imagined royal connections quickly disappeared when reality clicked in. I had started out in life in a "room and kitchen" in Coatbridge, the "Iron Burgh," in the dark heart of industrial Lanarkshire in central Scotland. I was also "good at school," but neither of these things was consistent with royal connections. Besides, common sense told me that even if my name did mean high king in Gaelic this did not make me special in any way, because in real life I was only a wee bit Ardrey. I was just as much a Palmer, Watson, Thompson, Milligan, Hostler, Wood, Dunlop, McEwan, Justice, Neilson, Dempster, Mitchell, Judge, Brown, Walker, Comrie, Cross, Campbell, Brankin, Smith, and all the other countless other names borne by my ascendants. Even at age fifteen, I knew there were no such things as objectively special families.

When I became a lawyer and notary public I needed something akin to a motto to put on my official seal, and so I used my second name translated into Latin. When I asked a Gaelic scholar at Glasgow University to confirm that Ardrey was derived from *Ard Righ* and that it meant "high king," I was told that Ardrey was actually derived from *Ard Airigh* and that *Ard Airigh* meant not high king but high pasture. I was going through a left-wing phase at the time and so this was fine by me.

My old Roman Law teacher translated high pasture into Latin for me and so *Ager Altus*—literally, high field—became my "motto." I suspected Ardrey, *Ard Airigh*, high pasture, was a combination of an occupational name and a place name and that it had probably become attached to my ascendants because in the summer months they had tended the stock that grazed on the shielings, the high summer pastures.

I assumed that they had been Campbells or MacDonalds or some other relatively common name, and that to distinguish themselves from others of the same name, they had added "of the high pasture" to their clan name and that addition had ended up as my second name.

Soon after my marriage I took my new wife, Dorothy-Anne, to visit a place called Ardery outside Strontian in Sunart in the north of Argyll. There we found a working steading and met a man called Jimmy "Ardery," who told us that Ardery was not his real second name but, as he had always lived at Ardery, that is the name people called him by. This seemed to confirm what I had been thinking: that my people, living for much of the year on the high pastures, had lost their original second name and come to be called simply Ardrey. I was quite happy that my second name meant high pasture. If my family's most distinguishing feature was that they spent a lot of time in the hills with sheep . . . well, it could have been much worse.

One thing gave me pause, however—something I came to think of as the *Rìgh-Airigh* conundrum. I could not understand how *rìgh* meant "king" and *airigh* meant "pasture" when the words *rìgh* and *airigh* had so much in common and "king" and "pasture" did not.

In the late 1990s Lucy Marshall of New Zealand, an Ardrey on her mother's side, provided me with evidence that our common ascendants had lived in the Townland of Mullnahunch, County Tyrone, Ireland. I couldn't find Mullnahunch on any map and mentioned this to an Irish friend, Eugene Creally, just before he went home to Ireland one Christmas. Eugene told his father this and his father, who happened to "know the Ardreys," kindly sent me a map on which Mullnahunch was clearly marked. Unfortunately, when I visited Ireland in 2004 with my son Eliot I forgot to take Eugene's father's map with me, and so we drove by memory as near to Mullnahunch as we could before stopping at a petrol station to ask directions, just as a delivery van drove up. Delivery van drivers usually know where places are and so I asked the driver if he knew where Mullnahunch was and told him why we were looking for it. He knew exactly where it was because, as it turned out, he was an Ardrey on his mother's side. All there is at Mullnahunch today is a few fields, a few houses, and an Orange Hall (rebuilt after it was blown up in the religious troubles of the late twentieth century). My Ardreys had lived and run a little shop there in the nineteenth century and been buried in the churchyard of the Protestant Church of Upper Clonaneese nearby.

In 1603, following the death of Elizabeth I, James VI, King of Scots and son of Mary Queen of Scots, became King of England too. He immediately set about quelling any notions of freedom and independence the majority of the people of Ireland might have harbored, by planting among them Protestants who were loyal to the Crown or, at least, antagonistic towards Roman Catholicism.

Over the next century most of those who settled in Ulster, the most northerly of Ireland's four provinces, came from Scotland. A disproportionately high number of these were Scots from Argyll, although Scots had been going back and forth across the North Channel since time immemorial, and Antrim and Down were densely Scottish in population even before the plantation.

The fact that anyone living in the north of Ireland is Protestant strongly suggests Scottish roots, and as far as I knew my people had always been Protestants. This meant my people were almost certainly not native Irish; that is, they were not among those Scots who were living in Ireland before the influx of Protestant settlers in the early seventeenth century. All the evidence I found suggested that my people were part of the Protestant Plantation: Scots who had emigrated from Scotland to Ireland, probably in the late 1600s.

In 1665, a William Ardrey sailed to Virginia in the Americas. There is no record of his port of embarkation and so I cannot be sure that he was one of my people, but our second name was uncommon, even in the seventeenth century, and so it is probable that we are related, even though it is impossible to say in what degree. The political, religious, and economic pressures that drove this William from his home would have applied in equal measure to his extended family, and so it is possible that others, perhaps his siblings, left Scotland for Ireland at the same time. All that is certain is that by the late 1600s /early 1700s there were Ardreys of Scottish descent in Ireland.

The records for the year 1714 refer to George Ardree of Aghervilly;

Thomas Ardree of Lislea; and Mark and Matthew Ardry of Munburge, all County Armagh. In 1725 there was a John Ardrey at Glasger and in 1731 a John Ardree at Glaskerberg, both County Down. A Mary Ardrey was married in a Quaker ceremony at Charlemont on the Armagh-Tyrone border in 1733, and Robert Ardrey leased land in Banbridge, County Down, in 1755. On November 14, 1791, William and Sarah Arderley had their daughter Margaret Arderley baptized and registered in Donaghmore, the town that for administrative purposes covered the Townland of Mullnahunch. This William and Sarah were probably also the parents of John Ardrey, who was born in 1798 and who is the first person in my direct line I can put a name to with certainty.

John of 1798, my great-great-grandfather, was a farm laborer who lived and died in 1866, in Mullnahunch. He married Ann McCewan and they had five children: George, born in 1834; an anonymous daughter, who probably died young; Sarah Anne (date of birth unknown); John, born in 1843; and my great-grandfather David, born in 1846.

The 1860 *Roll of Valuation of Tenements for the Parish of Killeeshil, Co. Tyrone*, names twenty-two property holders in Mullnahunch, including, as the last name on the list, John of 1798. He held three roods (3,630 square yards of land), on which were erected a house and an outhouse. The largest landholding in Mullnahunch was sixty acres or 290,000 square yards. Even John's next door neighbor, John Beadmead, had four acres three roods or 22,990 square yards.

My John was obviously of modest means; indeed, if the value of his tenement is anything to go by, he seems to have headed one of the poorest families in the area. When John of 1798 died, his youngest son, David, my great-grandfather, signed his father's death certificate with his mark, a cross, which means, almost certainly, that my grandfather Adam was the first in my direct line of Ardreys who could read and write.

Illiteracy was common in Ireland in the nineteenth century, and consequently family names, especially unusual family names, were often variously spelled. Men such as my great-grandfather had to rely on clerks to listen carefully and make an accurate record. There was the added complication that, for political and economic reasons, Scottish names were often Anglicized by people whose first language was not

Gaelic, hence the innumerable spellings of my second name in the records: these include Ardray, Ardary, Ardery, Ardry, Ardree, Ardrie, Airdrie, Airdrey, Ardrea, Arderly, Artrey, Arderey, Arderry, Artery, Adderley, Aredrey, Ardarie, Ardare, Ardarike, and even Dare. (This sometimes had unfortunate consequences. My great-grandfather David's brother, George, married Eliza, John Bedmead's daughter, the girl-next-door in the village of Mullnahunch. Eliza's name was written into the records as, variously, Bedmaid and Bedmate by clerks who no doubt thought this was funny. And it is . . . a bit.)

John Bedmead (father of Eliza of the user-friendly name) brought shoemaking into my family and by the middle of the nineteenth century my Ardreys were running a small shop in Mullnahunch where they manufactured and sold boots and shoes and pots and pans, and sold candles, salt, clothes, and eggs and other farm produce.

Following his father's death, my great-grandfather David immigrated to Scotland and found work as a car conductor. It was in the early 1990s while I was looking for David's first home in Glasgow— 60 McLean Street, Plantation—that I came across an Ardery Street, a mile and a half away, over the river on the north bank of the Clyde. I wondered if this Ardery Street had anything to do with my David, though the spelling differed from my own name. I did not think that this may have been where the man called Merlin lived in the last two decades of his long life, after he was driven out of town by Mungo Kentigern's Christians. I was not to discover the evidence for this for more than a decade.

In the 1870s a young Martha Milligan was sent from her home in Kilmarnock to work as a domestic servant in Glasgow. I picture her meeting my great-grandfather David when she was a passenger on his bus going to her work. They were married in 1877. Martha's family found David work as a railway pointsman in Riccarton, Kilmarnock, and by the time their first son, John, was born they were living in Railway Buildings, Barleith, Kilmarnock. Seven other children followed; the last of them was my grandfather Adam. He was born in 1893, after David and Martha had moved to Coatbridge and opened a shop where they made and sold boots and shoes. The only surviving photograph of David shows a man with a large moustache wearing an apron and standing at the door of his shop near the fountain that marks the center of Coatbridge. My grandfather Adam, an Assistant Registrar of Births, Deaths, and Marriages in Baillieston, Glasgow, had two sons; my father, another David, was the older of the two.

I served my legal apprenticeship in a solicitor's office that, I have always suspected, was a portal to the world of Charles Dickens. One of my jobs was to catalog deeds that had been left untouched in black tin boxes in the basement since before I was born. It was on one of these frolics, while working on documents concerning property in Argyll, that I crackled open a title deed that was dry in every sense and saw my second name on a map, on the banks of Loch Awe, Argyll. The spelling was slightly different, *Ardray*, but I knew old spellings were variable things. I had not known that my name had any connection with Argyll until then, but I had always known of my Protestant Irish connection and so an Argyll connection made sense.

I contacted the Forestry Commission and the people there sent me older and more detailed maps. In the early 1980s, with these to guide me, I drove north along the east side of Loch Awe, past the remains of the ancient church of Kilneuair and the ruins of Fincharn Castle, looking for the lands of Ardray. There is now a picnic site at Ardray, but when I was looking for it that first time there was nothing to suggest where it was, and so I had to use dead-reckoning. I estimated how far it lay from the crossroads at Ford at the southern end of the loch and used my car odometer to count the miles. I also counted burns as I passed, having worked out that Ardray lay between the fifth and sixth burns that ran into the loch, but identifying what was and was not a burn wasn't easy, far less telling one burn from another. I might as well have followed the second star to the right for all the good any of this did me. I searched all day but found nothing.

On my last night in Argyll, in the bar of the Ford Hotel where I was staying, I told the Forestry Commission workmen who were drinking there my problem. They said they knew where Ardray was and that there were ruins there. They then took a broken dart from the hotel dartboard and a red paper napkin from a table and promised me that on their way home that night they would mark the site of Ardray by pinning the napkin to a tree with the dart. The next day I saw the napkin, walked uphill into the woods, and found the Ardray ruins, a stone shell of a building standing on the bank of a burn.

A few years later, on the same weekend in which we visited Ardery in Sunart, I again tried to find Ardray on Loch Awe, to show it to Dorothy-Anne, but I couldn't find it. It was only later that I wondered what she must have thought as she stood there in the rain watching me, her new husband, slipping and sliding as I ran in and out of the trees looking for what, at that time, I was calling my "ancient family home." It was not a scene that compared well with Mr. Darcy showing Pemberley to Elizabeth Bennet.

Ardray was not always such an obscure place. It is clear from Timothy Pont's sixteenth-century maps that there was something significant there in his day.[2] Pont marks Ardray (or, as he spells it, Ardery) with a symbol that looks like two tubes above a small circle, but as no one knows what Pont meant by many of the symbols he used and because he was not always consistent, it is impossible to be sure from his map what was originally there or when it was built. The Ardray-Ardery symbol, two parallel tubes, is very uncommon, if not unique. I can find no other symbol like it on Pont's maps.[3]

The nearest things to the symbol Pont used to mark Ardray-Ardery on Loch Awe are the symbols he used to mark relatively important buildings: churches and fortified places. Almost all of Pont's churches and fortified places have a circle symbolizing a settlement nearby, as does Ardray-Ardery.

I was a new lawyer, with lots to learn, and so I did not pursue the matter of my name and family further at that time. Almost ten years later, in 1993, I was driving south of the Kilmartin Glen, along the side of the Crinan Canal to the Mull of Kintyre, to view land that was the subject of a legal dispute in Dunoon Sheriff Court, when I saw a hand-painted sign nailed to a tree with the word *Dunardry* written on it.

I understood this *Dunardry* to be *Dun Ard Airigh*, "Hillfort of the High Pasture," a rather insipid name and one that did not seem right to me. There are high pastures all over Argyll. Why would anyone call such a vital fortified place, one that commanded the most important route in Argyll and which was situated only a short distance from

Dunadd, the ceremonial capital of Dalriada, by such a bland name? Hillfort of the High Pasture just did not make sense.

Dunardry is a large flat-topped hill that looms over the portage route that ran along the narrow neck of land that separated Knapdale and Kintyre for thousands of years, until the Crinan Canal was built in the early nineteenth century to connect Loch Fyne and the interior of Scotland to the Sound of Jura and the Atlantic Ocean. Dunardry was of vital strategic importance, even more so than the more famous hillfort at Dunadd, the first seat of the Scots kings of Dalriada, which lies less than two miles to the north.

Dunadd, a rocky plug some 175 feet high, stands proud in the Moine Mhor, the Great Moss that stretches west to the Sound of Jura. (The Great Moss is now a bird sanctuary.) In its prime Dunadd had four walls on different levels, with terraces accessed by massive gates. On the summit, carved in a flat expanse of rock, is the figure of a boar, a symbol of Argyll; a cup shape, for which there is no generally accepted explanation; and a footprint, which played a part in inaugurations of the kings of the Scots. Nearby is inscribed a single line of as yet untranslated ogham text.

Dunadd is generally accepted as the capital fort of Dalriada, although there is reason to believe there was another, now lost, capital. As the toponymist William Watson writes, "Where was the capital of Scottish Dalriada? Since the middle of the last century [the nineteenth] it has been supposed that Dunadd . . . was the capital—a theory championed by Skene . . . though some of the literary evidence used by him refers to another site, unidentified *Dun Monaidh*."[4]

I thought again of my *Righ-Airigh* conundrum. The men who gave the fort its name were warriors. Why would they have named a vital stronghold "the hillfort of the High Pasture," when the name "hillfort of the High King" was obviously more appropriate? Although I accepted what I had been told, I still felt that I was missing something. Perhaps, I thought, my name meant "High King" after all; perhaps *Dunardry* did mean "Hillfort of the High King"; perhaps it was and always would be impossible to be sure.

My surname was of interest to me because it was mine and so, naturally, of little or no interest to anyone else. The whole point of

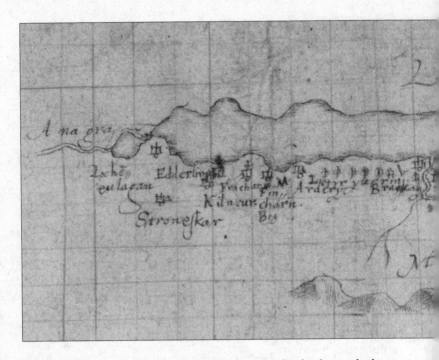

family history is that it is personal. Being personal, it leads people down un-trodden paths and allows them to find things no one else has found (primarily because no one else cares enough to discover them). That is how it was for me.

In the year 2000 I was planning a weekend break with my then nine-year-old son, Eliot, in Kilmartin, Argyll, because of its Ardrey associations. The Kilmartin Glen is one of the most important archaeological sites in Europe. There are at least 350 ancient monuments — stone circles, standing stones, cup-and-ring marks, and cist graves —within a six-mile radius of Kilmartin village. (I was proceeding in the belief that nine-year-old boys enjoy visiting ancient monuments. I did when I was nine.)

Kilmartin became famous in the 1980s following the publication of the book *The Holy Blood and the Holy Grail* and follow-up books that claimed that survivors of the Knights Templar came to Kilmartin as refugees after their order was destroyed by the French king Philip the Fair and his henchman Pope Clement V, on Friday, October 13, 1307.

Timothy Pont's sixteenth century map of Loch Awe showing one of the many Ard Airigh (Ardery/Ardrey) place-names in Argyll. This place-name on Loch Awe prompted my search for Arthur.

This idea added mystery to the history of the Glen and provided me with more stories to tell my son. (I was also proceeding in the belief that my son liked to hear me talk a lot. I did when I was nine.)

The scenery, the history, the mystery, the football (on the car radio), the good food, and watching *The Guns of Navarone* on the TV in our B&B made that weekend one of the best times of my life.

The day before we left for Argyll I went through the "secret" passage that led from the Advocates' Library where I work to the National Library of Scotland. I had often used this passage before to visit the National Library to research something or other, or just to read books at random. This time, looking for more Ardrey-family connections with Argyll, I found nothing that was new to me in the gazetteers, and the dictionaries only confirmed what I had been told years before: that my name, Ardrey, was originally *Ard Airigh* in Gaelic and that it meant "high pasture."

Then I found a dictionary that was new to me and everything changed.

John O'Brien, Roman Catholic Bishop of Cork and Cloyne in Ireland, wrote *Focalóir Gaoidhilge-Sax-Bhéarla: An Irish-English Dictionary* and had it privately printed in Paris in 1768. O'Brien said he compiled his dictionary,

> Not only from various Irish vocabularies . . . but also from a great variety of the best Irish manuscripts now extant; especially those that have been composed from the 9th & 10th centuries down to the 16th, besides those of the lives of St. Patrick & St. Bridget, written in the 6th & 7th centuries.[5]

It followed that O'Brien's definitions were more likely to reflect the way words were used in the sixth century, than were modern dictionaries, written to be used by people today.

According to O'Brien, *Airigh* did not mean a "summer pasture" or "shieling," as I had been told (in the first millennium summer pasture or shieling was *Airghe*). The first millennium meaning of *Airigh* was, "Certain, particular, especiall [*sic*] . . ." And, in a separate entry, "A Prince, a nobleman &c. [*sic*]."

This was my Statue-of-Liberty-at-the-end-of-*Planet-of-the-Apes* moment. I had been a happy high-pasture Ardrey ever since I had stopped being a happy high-king Ardrey. Now everything changed again. My second name was still *Ard Airigh*, but it no longer meant "high pasture"—now it meant "high prince" or "high nobleman." I was no longer fifteen years old and so I was not deluded into thinking I had become more prince-like or noble. But I knew I had become something much more important—I had become more knowledgeable.

Until then I had not been particularly interested in either the legendary or the historical Arthur, but after reading O'Brien I knew, even before I raised my head from the page, that I had evidence that the legendary Arthur was the historical Arthur Mac Aedan.

I already knew of many *Ard Airigh*/Ardrey place-names in Argyll, through my interest in my family's history, and that Arthur Mac Aedan had been active in Argyll after his father became king of the Scots there in 574. I also knew that an entry in the *Annales Cambriae* for the previous year, 573, contained the earliest surviving reference to the man called Merlin and that this entry placed Merlin at, "The Battle of Arderydd," a battle after which, it was said, "Merlin went mad."

Until I found the *Airigh* entry in O'Brien, all I had was an Arthur, Arthur Mac Aedan, in a place where there were innumerable *Ard Airigh* place-names and a Merlin involved in a battle at a place called Arderydd.

Arthur and Merlin were obviously connected, but what was the connection between, say, Arthur Mac Aedan's Dunardry hillfort, in Argyll, and Merlin's battlefield of Arderydd, one hundred miles away on the Scotland–England border?

"Hillfort of the high pasture" and the "battle of the high pasture," while possible, had always struck me as just too much of a coincidence to believe. Two important places—one a battle and one a fort, one associated with a Merlin and one associated with an Arthur, one in 573 and one in 574—and both named after pastures? This struck me as unlikely.

Why would the main hillfort in Argyll, the hillfort that dominated the most important land route in Argyll, be named the "hillfort of the high pasture"? Why were there so many *Ard Airigh*/high pasture names in Arthur Mac Aedan's Argyll? Why was a battle fought far from Argyll, on the Scotland–England border in P-Celtic speaking lands, given a Q-Celtic Gaelic, *Ard Airigh* name? How could these things be just coincidences?

There was no reason why pastures, high or otherwise, should have been connected to Arthur Mac Aedan. There were no especially high pastures in Argyll or on or near the battlefield of Arderydd—there were just, well, pastures.

Even if all the *Ard Airigh* place-names in Argyll meant "high pasture," despite the fact that they were not attached to places that were particularly high or pasture-like, there was no reason to believe that such a bland Q-Celtic place-name would have been given to a fort as important as Dunardry or to a battle as important as Arderydd. The "high pasture" meaning of *Ard Airigh* had always puzzled me and it had always been a dead-end. Until I found the *Airigh* entry in O'Brien, I had been unable to understand why so many places in Argyll had "high pasture" names.

O'Brien's definition of *Airigh* enabled me to make a sensible, albeit initially tentative, connection between the *Ard Airigh* place-names in Arthur Mac Aedan's Argyll and Merlin-Lailoken's Battle of Arderydd. (Merlin was the name used by his enemies. His friends called him Lailoken, Chief of Song. I will on occasion use Merlin-Lailoken from now on.)

"A prince, a nobleman," said O'Brien. It is now generally accepted that the legendary Arthur was not a king but a prince. I also knew that the historical Arthur Mac Aedan was a prince, the descendent of Scots warlords who had arrived in Argyll some sixty years before he was born; he died years before his father Aedan, king of the Scots. This was only a beginning but at least O'Brien's *Airigh* definition, "prince or noble-man," was relevant to both the legendary Arthur and Arthur Mac Aedan, while the "pasture" definition was not.

The Britons of southern Scotland spoke P-Celtic. Their neigh-bors, the Scots of Dalriada-Ireland and Dalriada-Scotland, spoke Q-Celtic. The words *ard* and *airigh*, from which *Arderydd* is derived, are Q-Celtic Irish-Scots-Gaelic words. *Airigh* is especially relevant to Ulster, the part of Ireland from which Arthur Mac Aedan's family came to Scotland at the turn of the fifth century. If *Ard Airigh* meant high prince or high nobleman it would not be surprising if the warriors who came to Scot-land from Ireland at the turn of the fifth century gave the places they found there *Ard Airigh* names.

Of course, Arthur Mac Aedan was only one among many sixth-century warlords of Dalriada, and so it did not necessarily follow that he was *the* high lord or even one of the high lords who inspired the *Ard Airigh* place-names of Argyll. But Arthur Mac Aedan did live in Argyll and so directly or indirectly there was some connection. Arthur Mac Aedan was also a contemporary of Merlin-Lailoken and Merlin-Lailoken fought at the Battle of Arderydd and so there was another connection. This was, of course, provided that the legendary Arthur (who was con-nected with a man called Merlin) and Arthur Mac Aedan were one and the same man. If they were not, then this was a most amazing coinci-dence. Two Arthurs both connected with a Merlin at different times and in different places—an amazing coincidence indeed.

How many other Arthurs lived at the same time as a man called

Merlin and shared *Ard Airigh* associations? None. In legend there was a Merlin and an Arthur. In history there was a Merlin-Lailoken in 573 (at the Battle of Arderydd) and an Arthur, Arthur Mac Aedan, in 574 (at Dunardry). The simplest solution seemed to me to be that these Merlins and Arthurs were one and the same.

Arderydd: the battle of the high pasture. Dunardry: the hillfort of the high pasture. It is not clear why anyone would give a battle and a fort such names. These translations did not make sense. Arderydd: the battle of the high lord or high lords. Dunardry: the hillfort of the high lord or high lords. These translations made sense. (I will from now on use the more user-friendly high lord or high lords in place of the clumsy combination high prince or high nobleman.)

It had never rung true to me that Dunardry, the most vital political, economic, and strategic hillfort in Argyll, was called *Dun Ard Airigh*, the hillfort of the high pasture. The men who named this fortress were warriors. The chances of these warriors calling their stronghold the "hillfort of the high pasture" when names such as the "hillfort of the high prince or princes" or the "hillfort of the high nobleman or noblemen" were available and more obviously attractive and appropriate options were slight in the extreme.[6]

It is reasonable to suppose that a place like Dunardry might well be called by a name that sounded of a high prince or nobleman and that a battle too might be named in memory of a high prince or nobleman (maybe not in its immediate aftermath, but certainly after that high prince or nobleman became the most famous hero in British history). Arthur Mac Aedan, certainly, especially, and particularly fitted the profile of the prince or nobleman after whom the fort and the battle were named. He lived in and was a prince in Argyll. He was a contemporary of Merlin of Arderydd, and, although I did not know this to begin with, Arthur Mac Aedan fought at the Battle of Arderydd.

If I was right and the battle-name *Arderydd* was a Q-Celtic name in a P-Celtic place and meant the "battle of the high prince or nobleman," this suggested the possibility that the battle-name *Arderydd* commemorated the Q-Celtic speaking Arthur Mac Aedan.

If Arthur Mac Aedan was not the high prince or nobleman commemorated in the battle-name *Arderydd*, then we would be looking for some other prince or nobleman with a Q-Celtic and an Argyll connection, who was active in 573 and who was or who became so famous that he inspired the name of this major battle.

Alternatively, the battle-name *Arderydd* and the *Ard Airigh* place-names in Argyll could be simple, albeit highly unlikely, coincidences. I did not think a simple coincidence was a reasonable possibility.

O'Brien's definition of *Airigh* provided me with a solution to what I had called the *Righ-Airigh* conundrum. I had been unable to understand how, if *righ* meant "king" and *airigh* meant "pasture," the words *righ* and *airigh* could be so similar when "king" and "pasture" are so different. If however *righ* meant "king," which it does, and *airigh* meant "prince or nobleman," which, according to O'Brien, it does, then there was an obvious relationship. *Righ* and *airigh* were similar in the same way *bishop* and *archbishop* are similar. The dichotomy that was the *Righ-Airigh* conundrum ceased to exist.

Welsh scholars cannot say what Arderydd means with any certainty or authority or with reference to any convincing sources because they have been looking for answers in the wrong place among the wrong people and at the wrong time. One Welsh academic with whom I corresponded, wrote to me,

> A battle was fought at Arderydd (or Arthuret) in c. 573 CE between various British factions, which became the epitome of heroic battle. As such it is frequently mentioned in Welsh literature . . . I have never seen an explanation of the name, and it could contain several elements: possibly *arf* ("weapon"), and some form of *dâr* ("oak"), although *deri* (not **derydd*) is the usual plural form.

Battle of the Weapon Oak seemed to me to be as unlikely a name for a battle as Battle of the High Pasture. "High prince" or "nobleman" place-names in Argyll and a battle involving high lords made more sense to me. If my *Ard Airigh* interpretation is accepted, no tortuous interpretation of *Arderydd*, involving weapons and oaks, is needed.

I looked for corroboration of O'Brien's *Airigh* entry and found it in MacBain's *Etymological Dictionary*, where *Airigh* is defined as follows:

"*Airigh*: worthy, Irish *airigh* (Ulster), *airigh*, nobleman . . . Old Irish *aire(ch)*, primas, lord; Sanskrit *árya*, good, a lord; *ârya*, Aryan, *âryaka*, honourable man." There are two categories of meaning in MacBain's dictionary. The first includes "worthy," "good" and "honourable." The second includes "nobleman" and "lord." O'Brien's definition "prince" falls into MacBain's second category.

MacBain says *Airigh*, in the sense of "worthy," is derived from Irish sources and in particular from the Irish of Ulster, the most northerly of Ireland's four provinces. It was from Ulster that the Scots came to Argyll in the early centuries of the first millennium and from which Arthur Mac Aedan's immediate and direct ascendants came in circa 500 to found Dalriada, the first kingdom of the Scots in what is now Scotland. If Ulster-Scots brought the word *Airigh* with them from Ireland and used it to name places in Argyll, this goes some way toward explaining the high frequency of *Ard Airigh* place-names in Argyll.

Until I found O'Brien's "high lord" definition of *Ard Airigh*, I had given no more thought to Arthur, Merlin, and Camelot than I had to innumerable other subjects, and none at all to writing books about any one of them. I had not been looking for anything to do with the Arthurian canon that day in the National Library. I had been looking for something to do with my second name and that is all. However I found evidence that threw light on the matter of Arthur, and so I decided to see if I could find more evidence.

I knew I had a solution to the *Righ*-king, *Airigh*-pasture conundrum when I read O'Brien's definition of the word *Airigh* because, unlike *king* and *pasture*, *Righ*-king and *Airigh*-lord were obviously connected. I had never accepted that it was merely coincidental that Arthur Mac Aedan lived in Argyll among innumerable *Ard Airigh* place-names, such as Dunardry, and Ardery on Loch Awe, and that completely separately and one hundred miles from Argyll, Merlin had fought in an *Ard Airigh* battle, the Battle of Arderydd.

I had always suspected that there had to be some connection between the *Ard Airigh* names in Argyll and the battle name, Arderydd, but when I thought *Ard Airigh* meant "pasture" I could not see what this connection might be. Why should so many places in Argyll and a battle fought on the Scotland–England border have high pasture names?

However if *Ard Airigh* meant "high lord" things made sense. It made sense that a warrior people, like Arthur Mac Aedan's Scots, would name their most important fortress *Dun Ard Airigh*, Dunardry, hillfort of the high lord or lords, and that a battle would be called the Battle of *Ard Airigh*, Arderydd, the battle of the high lord or lords; after all, Arthur Mac Aedan was a high lord and his men were high lords (at least high lords of war).

I knew I was onto something when I saw O'Brien's definition of *Airigh*, and so I tried to remember all I could about Arthur and Merlin and Argyll, to see if there was anything that worked for or against my provisional conclusion that Arthur Mac Aedan was the legendary Arthur. All the time I was doing this I knew I was missing something. I stopped to think what it might be, and when that didn't work, I tried not thinking about it at all, in the hope that the answer would just come to me. But that didn't work either until it did . . . well, almost.

I suddenly knew that what I was looking for was on a map, but which map? I had not been looking for evidence of Arthur until that day (indeed, I could not remember the last time I had even thought of Arthur—probably the last time I had seen him played in a film or read a book in which he featured, and that had not been for a long time). It followed, therefore, that if the map I was looking for was not primarily Arthur-connected it, probably had something to do with my name and was perhaps one of my maps of Argyll. If it was a map in a book I had looked at in passing and then put aside, then I had a problem.

When I got home that day I looked at my maps of Argyll—the maps the Forestry Commission had given me, Ordnance Survey maps, and maps in books—until I found what I was looking for in a standard Collins roadmap. It was a place-name.

I had overlooked its Arthurian significance when I used this map to get about Argyll when I was researching my family-name. Its significance would have been obvious to anyone thinking about Arthur, but at that time I had not been thinking about Arthur.

The earliest surviving indirect reference to Arthur is in Gildas's *De Excidio*. It is "indirect" because Gildas hated Arthur and deliberately omitted Arthur's name. *De Excidio* was written in the early sixth century according to the conventional wisdom, but, by reckoning, it was compiled circa 598, although the exact date does not matter overmuch for these present purposes; what matters is that toward the end of his history Gildas writes, "From then on victory went now to our countrymen now to their enemies . . . This lasted up till the year of the siege of Badon Hill, pretty well the last defeat of the villains, and certainly not the least."[7]

Just over two hundred years after Gildas wrote *De Excidio*, Nennius listed twelve battles in which Arthur was in command in his *Historia Brittonum*. The last item on Nennius's battle-list reads, "The twelfth battle was on Badon hill and in it nine hundred and sixty men fell in one day, from a single charge of Arthur's, and no one laid them low save he alone."[8]

The *Annales Cambriae*, the earliest versions of which date to the early ninth century, contain records of four battles between circa 447, when the entries begin, and 600, when, everyone agrees, Arthur (whoever he was) was dead. These four battles include the Battle of Badon: "The Battle of Badon, in which Arthur carried the Cross of our Lord Jesus Christ for three days and three nights on his shoulders and the Britons were the victors."[9] This makes the Battle of Badon the only battle mentioned in all three of the generally accepted, most important early sources. Indeed, the Battle of Badon is the only one of Arthur's battles mentioned more than once in any of the early sources. The Battle of Badon has become the litmus test by which potential "Arthurs" are measured.

Arthur Mac Aedan lived at Dunardry-Dunadd. The place-name I had found on my Collins road map showed that the land between Dunardry and Dunadd is called Badden. This Badden extends north from the shadow of Dunardry to Dunadd, and east with the Badden Burn to Lochgilphead and Loch Fyne.

This Badden had the right name (allowing for the usual variations in spellings) and was the very place where Arthur Mac Aedan lived for much of his life and where his father was king. No case for any southern Arthur has evidence that can outweigh this one item of evidence that Arthur Mac Aedan was the man who became the legendary Arthur.

Once I knew what I was looking for and where to find it, I found Badden on other maps with ease, but these were all modern maps and so I had to find out if the name Badden was modern too. For all I knew some "New Scots"—say the Badden family from the south of England—had moved to Argyll and named the land between Dunardry and Dunadd after themselves or, worse still, used a corrupt variation of their hometown, Bath! The maps created when the railways were introduced to Argyll showed a place called Badden in the late nineteenth century, and so if my hypothetical family from the south of England had called their new home Badden, they must have done this before 1873.

It is arguable that a period of more than 130 years is long enough to establish Badden as a traditional name and to allow it to be fairly inferred that it had been called Badden for far longer. However, the further back I could trace the name, the more likely it would be that it had some connection with Arthur Mac Aedan's sixth century. I set out to see if I could fill the thirteen-century gap that lay between the sixth and the nineteenth centuries.

Fitzroy MacLean, writing of the sixth century in his book *Highlanders*, refers to the *Cinelbadon*, the family or "kin" of Baodan. This Baodan was a grandson of Lorne, one of the brothers of Arthur Mac Aedan's great-great-grandfather Fergus Mor, and so Arthur's second cousin twice removed. Unfortunately, Fitzroy MacLean did not identify his authority for this reference. MacLean did however parachute behind enemy lines during the Second World War, with instructions from Churchill to take the partisans in hand and beat the Nazis in Yugoslavia and he did just that. He was one of those men, who, if he said something, you could rely upon it: a man like that did not go about making things up. The very fact that it was he who was writing was good enough for me, but even Fitzroy MacLean was not around in the sixth century, and so it followed he must have had some authority for what he wrote.

I looked for MacLean's source material and found other Baodans in the *Senchus Fer nAlban*, the history of the men of Scotland. The *Senchus* is a genealogical record—in effect, a *Who's Who* of the sixth century. It shows several Baodans including a Baodan Mac Eochaid Mac Aedan Mac Gabhran Mac Domangart Mac Fergus (Arthur's nephew); and a Baodan Mac Ninnud Mac Duath Mac Conall Mac Niall of the Nine Hostages, who died in 586. This first Baodan was closely related to Arthur Mac Aedan. The second Baodan, although a contemporary of Arthur, was only distantly related to him (and to Columba-Crimthann who played a large part in events during Arthur's lifetime).

Whether a particular Baodan lived a generation before or after Arthur Mac Aedan or was related to him is immaterial, however. What really mattered was the very existence of men called Baodan in Arthur's day. Nor does it matter whether Lorne and Comgall were the sons, brothers, or grandchildren of Fergus Mor, Arthur's great-great-grand-father (the sources vary). What matters is that they gave their names to the lands of Lorne in the north and to the Cowal Peninsula in the south of Argyll, names that are still used today.

In the sixth century, when Scots of Ireland led by members of Arthur Mac Aedan's family invaded Argyll, they, quite naturally, replaced some of the place-names they found there with Scottish names. The aforementioned Baodans were in the right place at the right time to make these changes. It is likely therefore that the lands of Badden outside Lochgilphead were named after one of the many Baodans who were about at the time, which means, almost inevitably, a Baodan who was closely related to Arthur Mac Aedan. The existence of numerous Baodans in the time of Arthur Mac Aedan all but closes the gap between the sixth century and 1873. In any event, the legendary name Badon clearly echoes in the modern place-name Badden, a name that can be connected to the life and times of Arthur Mac Aedan.

Again, this evidence alone is more than anyone else can muster for any other possible location of the Battle of Badon. Furthermore, unlike so many southern sites, there is no shortage of hills around the lands of Badden, the most prominent being Dunardry. Dunadd was the ceremonial capital of Argyll, but Dunardry commanded the most important land route in Argyll and was its administrative capital. There is no more likely place for a sixth-century battle than the land about Dunardry; the land of Baodan-Badon-Badden.

There was reason to believe that the Battle of Badon had been fought on the approaches to and on the land about Dunardry and that, consequently, Dunardry is the legendary Mount Badon. In the American Civil War the North named battles with reference to geographical features, while the South named battles with reference the nearest town, and so we have Bull Run and Manassas, Antietam and Sharpsburg. If the South had named Nennius's twelfth battle it would have been the Battle of *Dun Ard Airigh*; if the North had named the twelfth battle it would have been the Battle of the Hill of *Boadan* (before it became in Latin the Battle of *Badonici montis* or *monte Badonis*, Mount Badon).

The Badon entry on Nennius's list contained three clues. The first clue was the battle-name "Badon." The second clue was that the battle had been fought on or in the vicinity of a hill. Both pointed to the Battle of Badon having been fought at Dunardry-Badden in Argyll. The third clue, the place of this battle on Nennius's battle-list, twelfth of twelve, remained to be solved.

The *Annales Cambriae* say the Battle of Badon was fought in 516 and the Battle of Camlann, Arthur's last battle, in 537. The entries in the *Annales Cambriae* for the fifty years before the Battle of Badon and for the fifty years after the Battle of Camlann mention twenty-two people. These include Columba-Crimthann, who lived in Dalriada where Arthur Mac Aedan's father was king; Mordred of the Gododdin, who lived on the border of Manau, Arthur Mac Aedan's father's kingdom; Gabhran, Arthur Mac Aedan's grandfather; Gildas of Cambuslang in central Scotland, Arthur Mac Aedan's neighbor; the sons of Eliffer, who included Rhydderch Hael, King of Strathclyde, Merlin-Lailoken's brother-in-law and a neighbor of Arthur Mac Aedan; Gwenddolau, defeated at the Battle of Arderydd fighting against Arthur Mac Aedan and the man known as Uther Pen Dragon; Merlin-Lailoken, Chancellor of Strathclyde, Arthur Mac Aedan's friend and partner in the Great Angle War; Brendan of Birr, an advisor to Columba-Crimthann and so connected to Dalriada, where Arthur Mac Aedan's father was king; Gwrgi and Peredur, probably lords of York and southwest Scotland respectively and contemporaries of Arthur Mac Aedan; Constantine, probably the son of Rhydderch of Strathclyde and Gwyneth-Languoreth, Merlin-Lailoken's sister; and lastly Dunod, probably a man of Dunadd, the ceremonial capital of Dalriada, where Arthur Mac Aedan's father was king.

It boils down to this—these early entries in the *Annales Cambriae* are not concerned with people and events in Wales, despite the title *Annales Cambriae* (the Annals of Wales), but with people and events in

Arthur Mac Aedan's late-sixth-century Scotland, and almost all of them are closely connected with Arthur Mac Aedan.

Gildas's *De Excidio* contains the earliest reference to the Battle of Badon. It is generally accepted that *De Excidio* was written in the early sixth century. "Gildas wrote his main work, the *Ruin of Britain*, about A.D.540 or just before," says one authoritative editor.[10] However, Michael Winterbottom of Oxford University said, "we cannot be certain of [Gildas's] date, of where he wrote, of his career, or even his name."[11] This uncertainty ceases to exist when Gildas, a name that means Servant of God in Gaelic, is looked for north of the Scotland–England border. There Gildas can be found and recognized as a man of southern Scotland who flourished as a Christian polemicist in the late sixth century. It is more likely that *De Excidio* was compiled by Gildas from earlier writings and completed in circa 598, some ten years after the Battle of Badon.

In the *Preface* to *De Excidio* Gildas says,

> I have kept silence, I confess, with much mental anguish, compunction of feeling and contrition of heart, whilst I revolved all these things within myself; . . . for the space of even ten years or more, my inexperience . . . and my unworthiness preventing me from taking upon myself the character of a censor.[12]

Gildas waited "ten years or more" before he completed his masterwork, but ten years or more from when? It makes sense to suppose ten years after the last major event in the "History" part of *De Excidio*. The "History" part of *De Excidio* ends with an account of a victory won by Ambrosius Aurelianus (who, in *Finding Merlin*, I identified as Emrys, the first Pen Dragon). This account segues smoothly into the Battle of Badon passage:

> From then on victory went now to our countrymen, now to their enemies: so that in this people the Lord could make trial (as he tends to do) of his latter-day Israel to see whether it loves him or not. This lasted right up to the year of the siege of Badon Hill, pretty well the last defeat of the villains, and certainly not the least.[13]

It seems to be common sense to suppose that the ten years during which Gildas "kept silence" followed the date on which he ended his *History*—that is, followed the date of the Battle of Badon. It would also be common sense to suppose that Gildas brought his *History* up to date, more or less. In other words, his history ended with the Battle of Badon, the last historical event he mentions. He then either waited ten years before writing about it, or, and this is more likely, he waited ten years before making his work public.

Gildas's Latin is obscure in the extreme and apparently notoriously difficult to translate. The translator I have quoted above says Badon was, "pretty well the last defeat of [the Angles], and certainly not the least." J. A. Giles interprets this vague passage differently: ". . . until the year of the siege of Bath-hill, when took place also the last almost, though not the least slaughter of our cruel foes."[14]

When someone feels the need to say something is "not the least" it usually means this something is pretty close to being "the least." When Gildas tries to give the Battle of Badon some added status, he doth protest too much, methinks. There is therefore reason to believe that although Badon was the most famous of Arthur's battles—because it is the only one mentioned more than one of the earliest sources, the four horsemen of history—it was far from his greatest battle.

It could be argued that if Gildas was writing some ten years after Badon and if Arthur Mac Aedan was the victor in the Battle of Badon, that Gildas would have mentioned this fact. Why does Gildas's Badon passage not mention Arthur? Gildas's *De Excidio* was not primarily a history but a piece of religious propaganda and so he mentioned very few individuals. In the whole fifth century he names only one person and one place and provides only one date (and he gets that wrong).

I have argued in *Finding Merlin* that when Gildas was a boy Emrys, the first Pen Dragon, saved the Britons from the Angles and consequently Emrys became Gildas's boyhood hero. This is why Emrys appears in Gildas's *History* (albeit burnished with spurious Roman antecedents and a grand name, Ambrosius Aurelianus). Gildas's relationship with Arthur did not include hero-worship; on the contrary, Gildas hated Arthur Mac Aedan, because Arthur killed Gildas's brother Hueil. In these circumstances it would be surprising if Gildas mentioned Arthur in his history. If Arthur was Arthur Mac Aedan he would have been a Scot in Gildas's eyes, and Gildas hated Scots (he said we were "like worms which in the heat of mid-day came forth from their holes"). If Arthur was Arthur Mac Aedan he was a man of the Old Way, and Gildas hated anyone who was not a Christian, in addition to a goodly number of people who *were* Christians: Gildas was big on hate. Even if Gildas had been bothered to name people in his *History*, and he was not, he would never have named Arthur Mac Aedan.

The main pillar upon which the dating of Gildas's *De Excidio* stands is a passage dealing with the legendary Arthur's famous Battle of Badon: "There is, perhaps, no passage in Gildas that has been more frequently discussed than that in which he appears to assign a date for the siege of the Badonic Mountain," explained the *English Historical Review* in 1926.[15] All attempts to date *De Excidio* center on this one corrupt passage in which Gildas refers to Badon and to his own age.

> From then on victory went now to our countrymen, now to their enemies . . . This lasted up till the year of the siege of Badon Hill, pretty well the last defeat of the villains, and certainly not the least. That was the year of my birth: as I know, one month of the forty-four years since then has already passed.[16]

This is usually taken to mean Gildas was born in the same year as the Battle of Badon. It is however a very corrupt passage. The English historian Bede, writing in the eighth century, lifted large passages from Gildas, including the above passage, but his version is somewhat different. Bede says, "Thenceforward victory swung first to one side and then to the other, until the Battle of Badon Hill, when the Britons made a considerable slaughter of the invaders. This took place about forty-four years after their arrival in Britain."[17]

This passage is more likely to reflect accurately what Gildas wrote because it makes some sense. One rule used when interpreting a law is to assume the law maker intended to make sense. Gildas either dated Badon with reference to his age or with reference to the arrival of invaders in Britain. He does not tell us when he was born nor does he tell us when the invaders arrived. If we assume Gildas intended his read-ers to make sense of *De Excidio*, then the Bede version of the Badon passage is more likely to be correct, given that it would be reasonable to expect that more people would know about an invasion than would know about Gildas's birth.

This passage in Bede may have escaped the depredations of those determined to place Arthur in the south because it was a little out of the Gildas mainstream and because, no matter what, Bede's history was considered sacrosanct by the Church. As late as the nineteenth century J. A. Giles, ever determined to place Arthur in the south, translates the passage in Bede as, "Bath-hill . . . was (as I am sure) forty-four years and one month after the landing of the Saxons, and also the time of my own nativity."[18]

Giles's translation is an overt attempt to place Arthur in the south. The Latin *Badonici montis* is blithely translated as "Bath-hill" because Giles wanted Badon to be Bath and so he wrote what he wanted. The Latin says *novissimaeque ferme de furciferis non minimae stragis*, that is, "pretty well the last defeat of the villains, and certainly not the least." There is no mention of Angles or of Saxons. Where did Giles get his Saxons from? Not from Bede. Bede does not mention Angles or Saxons in the passage in question. It is however clear from the immediate context that the villains to whom Bede refers are Angles. Why, if Giles wanted to mention a particular people, did he not refer to Bede's Angles? Perhaps this was because the Angles tended to be in the north and the Saxons tended to be in the south, and Giles wanted Arthur in the south.

If the received wisdom is correct and Gildas was born in the year of Badon, it follows that he ended the "History" part of *De Excidio* at about the time he was born. This is counter-intuitive. Gildas was per-manently worked up to frothing point about people and events of which he disapproved. A man like Gildas would have been certain to touch upon events that happened during his lifetime. He would not have been able to stop himself.

Why would Gildas not bring his history up to his time of writing and so cover the one period of which he had first-hand knowledge? There is no good answer to this question.

It makes no sense to suppose that Gildas was born in the same year as Badon. This would leave what is a very precise period of time, forty-four years and one month, hanging in mid-air. What is the point of saying, in effect, *I am forty-four years and one month old and the Battle of Badon was fought the year I was born*? Unless Gildas tells his readers the date when he is writing, his readers cannot know either the date of the Battle of Badon or when he was born—what is the point of that?

If the received wisdom is correct and the time period, forty-four years and one month, relates to the date of publication of *De Excidio*, which it must if Gildas was born in the year of Badon, this presupposes a known and exact date of publication (to the very month), a concept that would have been meaningless in the sixth century.

It is probable that the received wisdom is wrong and that Gildas was not born in the same year as Badon but forty-four years before Badon. If this is correct the above problems disappear. It seems more likely that Gildas dated the Battle of Badon forty-four years after the Angles landed in Britain: that is, forty-four years and one month after he, Gildas, was born, just as Bede said.

Of course, without a date for the arrival of the Angles this does not help date *De Excidio*. The Angles had been arriving on the east coast of Britain from at least the middle of the fifth century, and so if the "arrival" of the Angles is to have any meaning, Gildas must have meant some particular arrival. There is only one particular arrival this might be: the arrival of the Angle chief war-chief, Ida. Ida and his men came to fight as mercenaries on behalf of Vortigern, the Gododdin British King. When? We do not know exactly—Gildas is imprecise.[19]

All we know is that before long, Ida discovered that Vortigern was weak and so sent for more men: what Gildas calls "a second and larger troop of satellite dogs."[20] At earliest this would have been the following year. Ida and his Angles then inveigled themselves into positions of power, "sprouted in our [Gododdin] soil with savage shoots and tendrils." This would have taken some little time, say, another year. The Angles asked for supplies, which had been given to them, but then they demanded more. When more supplies were not forthcoming they rose up against Vortigern and overthrew him. For a short while Vortigern was kept on as a figurehead but before long he had taken to the hills to hide and Ida became king. The *Anglo-Saxon Chronicle* says Ida became king in 547.

Given that the Angles had been coming to Britain for a long time, there must have been something special about this particular arrival, and there was: Ida overthrew the British king and started a sequence of events that culminated in the Great Angle War of the 580s. I say this is the arrival of the Angles to which Gildas refers, because the arrival of Ida changed everything, especially for Gildas, who, by my reckoning, was born the year Ida's Angles arrived and who grew up a few days march from what was from then on hostile territory. By my calculation, and I accept this cannot be precise; Ida arrived some three years before he staged his coup in 547—say, in 544.

Following Ida's coup Gildas spent his childhood, like everyone else in southern Scotland, in fear of Angle invasion. He would have had reason to remember the arrival of Ida circa 544, especially if he had been born that very year. It is easy to picture Gildas when he was a boy being told that he was born the year the Angles under Ida arrived in Britain. Every one of his contemporaries would have known that date.

The above, if correct, throws the received wisdom into confusion because, according to the received wisdom, based upon the *Annales Cambriae*, Gildas traveled to Ireland in 565 and died there five years later. This would mean, according to the received wisdom, that Gildas went to Ireland at the age of about seventy-five. If, however, I am correct, then Gildas went to Ireland at the age of twenty-one and left Ireland five years later. Gildas departed Ireland, not this life, in 570.

In summary, in my view, Gildas was born circa 544, the year Ida's Angles arrived in Britain, and the Battle of Badon was fought forty-four years and one month later, circa 588. Gildas brought his history up to date, more or less. This means the "History" part of *De Excidio* tells of events in the late sixth century, which means the book was compiled or completed circa 598, when Gildas was an old man.

Gildas's *De Excidio* is the nearest thing we have to a contemporary history of the sixth century. This is why so much effort has been put into claiming it for the south. In the centuries that followed *De Excidio*, the historical record was kept alive in the poems recited and songs sung by the bards. Many of these poems and songs were of Arthur; indeed, it is likely he was one of the most popular subjects in the whole body of this work, because he was greatest hero of the Britons and, if he was Arthur Mac Aedan, of the Scots. "There is ample evidence," historian John Morris writes, "that in the 6th and 7th centuries many epics of Arthur were sung in Britain . . . but only two survive, the *Elegy of Geraint*, preserved in modernised Middle Welsh form, perhaps of the 8th or 9th century, and the Nennius epitome."[21] (Aneirin's *Y Gododdin*, which contains the earliest reference to Arthur and which originated in Scotland, seems to have been overlooked.)

The *Elegy of Geraint* is said to be based on sixth-century material. It mentions Arthur only in passing, "In Llongborth I saw Arthur's / Heroes who cut with steel." Geraint's father is said to have been king of Dumnonia (Devon), England; a place that is frequently confused, deliberately or in ignorance, with Damnonia, Strathclyde, Scotland. Even today *Damnonia* is sometimes simply translated as *Dumnonia*, irrespective of the spelling in the original. One translation of *De Excidio* reads in Latin, "est inmundae leaenae Damnoniae," and in the English translation, "whelp of the filthy lioness of"—not Damnonia (Scotland) as one might expect—but "Dumnonia" (England).[22]

A Geraint also appears in *Y Gododdin* as a man of the south active in the north. It may be that this Geraint was one of the many Britons who came north to join the fight against the invading Angles, first successfully, under Arthur Mac Aedan, and then, after the death of Arthur Mac Aedan, unsuccessfully under the Gododdin king who led the disastrous campaign commemorated in *Y Gododdin*.

As for the Nennius "epitome," with its battle-list of twelve battles, we will come to it—to all twelve battles.

4

A Fragmented Kingdom

ARTHUR MAC AEDAN MAC GABHRAN MAC DOMANGART MAC FERGUS Mac Erc Mac Eochaid was born to a Scottish father and probably to a British mother, probably in the kingdom of Manau in central Scotland, probably about 559.

In the early sixth century, Ireland and Britain were hodgepodges of kingdoms, sub-kingdoms, chiefdoms, confederations, and what in later centuries were called debatable lands, lands where no one's rule was certain or for long. Both islands were inhabited by Celts: the Gaels in Ireland; the Picts in Scotland (north of the Rivers Clyde and Forth); and the Britons everywhere else. The Scots, whose homeland was Antrim in Ulster in northeast Ireland, were a subdivision of the Gaels, who, in their turn, were a subdivision of the Celts.

As Gaels, the Scots spoke Q-Celtic Gaelic, a language that sprang from the Goidelic branch of the Indo-European family tree of languages. The people of Britain, Picts and Britons both, spoke P Celtic, from the Brythonic branch of the same linguistic tree. It is from this division that we get the saying "Mind your Ps and Qs"—watch how you speak.

When the Roman Empire collapsed and the last legions left Britain in the early fifth century, the Scots of Ireland, who, like the Picts of Scotland, had never been conquered by the Romans, increasingly raided the west coast of Britain. As always, they were looking for loot, but as the years passed, more and more they came looking for places to settle.

The people of the south of Britain, who had for centuries lived under the protection of Rome, were less martial than the Scots, but they were brave and sufficiently numerous to push the Scots back to their ships. Only in Argyll were the Scots able to establish substantial permanent settlements.

According to the second-century geographer Ptolemy of Alexandria, the native Pictish people of Argyll were the *Epidii*, the people of the horse. They were no less doughty than their British Celtic cousins in the south, but over hundreds of years close commercial ties had grown up between them and the Scots of Ireland and so they were less inclined to reject Scots incursions. Commercial ties naturally led to social interaction and from there to marriages and settlement until, by the start of the sixth century, a sizeable number of Scots were living in peace with the Picts in Argyll.

Left alone to get on with their lives the differences between the Scots settlers and the native Picts of Argyll would have blurred with time and the two peoples would have come together as one. But this was not to be; there were powerful people who saw an opportunity to advance their interests at the expense of others.

At the end of the fifth century, Arthur Mac Aedan's great-great-grandfather Fergus Mor Mac Erc, Fergus the Great son of Erc, a chief of the Scots of Dalriada-Ireland, pressed by dynastic competition at home, took advantage of the beachhead his fellow Scots had created across the water, marshaled an army, invaded Argyll, and founded a new Dalriada in what is now Scotland.

The simple picture commonly presented is of a native population usurped and replaced by an invading army of Scots. The real picture is more complicated. Put broadly, before Fergus arrived there was a mixture of Picts and Scots in Argyll, with the Picts in charge. After Fergus's invasion, there was a mixture of Picts and Scots in Argyll, with the Scots in charge and with Fergus in charge of the Scots. While Fergus had made himself king of the Scots of Dalriada, his kingdom was really a subkingdom of Dalriada-Ireland, a status it was to retain for seventy-five years until Arthur's father, the wily Aedan, backed by force of arms, negotiated the independence of Dalriada-Scotland.

Circa the year 500, Fergus was inaugurated king on the summit of the hillfort of Dunadd, Argyll's ceremonial capital. Dunadd still stands stark in the Moine Mhor, the Great Moss, through which the River Add twists on its way to the western sea. In Fergus's time the shoreline was closer to the fort than it is today and the marsh, now largely drained, was wider and deeper. The modern approach road that leads from the main road to a small car park would have been a raised causeway or a bridge-walk standing on stakes. This would have been the route Fergus took as he approached Dunadd, before walking through the entrance gate in the great stone wall that bounded the fort, and crossing the large enclosure that lay beyond. He would have then gone through another, smaller, gate that opened to allow him to climb the last few feet to the high-point of the rock.

As part of the inauguration ceremony favored by the local people, the Picts and the Scots of Argyll, Fergus placed his foot in a footprint carved into the bedrock of the summit. By this act he symbolized his rightful connection with the land and so with the people who lived upon it. This was standard practice when a king was inaugurated at Dunadd—indeed, standard practice among many of the people of the Old Way throughout Scotland.

We do not know the details of the doubtless colorful and complicated ceremonies involved in the inauguration of Fergus as king—these have been lost to history—but we may assume, given the evidence of subsequent inaugurations, that a list of his ancestors was recited by a *Seannachie*, a bard specializing in genealogy. In the early sixth century this *Seannachie* would have been a druid.

Fergus's inauguration included one novelty: the introduction of the *Stone of Destiny*. According to legend, thousands of years ago the Scots brought the Stone of Destiny from Egypt, across North Africa to the Iberian Peninsula, and then to Ireland. The surviving descriptions of the Stone suggest it was made of black marble or meteoric rock cut to the shape of a low seat, about eighteen inches high with volutes to make it easier to carry, and carved all over with symbols. If it had been in the hands of the Egyptians and the Celts, great stone-carvers both, for more than a thousand years, it could hardly have been otherwise.

When Fergus sat on the Stone of Destiny and placed his foot in the footprint cut into the summit of Dunadd, he was recognized as king of the Scots, at least by those who were present that day. Not everyone in Argyll recognized Fergus. He still had to fight to fully establish his authority.

Domangart, Fergus's successor and Arthur Mac Aedan's great-grandfather; Comgall, Arthur Mac Aedan's great-uncle; Conall, Arthur Mac Aedan's uncle; and Aedan, Arthur's father were all inaugurated kings of the Scots on Dunadd's summit, sitting on the Stone of Destiny, as were innumerable kings of the Scots in years to come.

The *Senchus Fer nAlban* is a genealogical record of the Scots of Dalriada, although the versions available today are a composite of several seventh-century sources that were only reduced to writing in the early tenth century. The end result is that the *Senchus* is not only inherently contradictory but also contradicts other separate sources.

One reading of the *Senchus* suggests that Fergus's new kingdom of Dalriada-Scotland was divided between Fergus's kin, with his brother Lorne taking the north of Argyll (still, to this day, the district of Lorne) and with his brother Angus, or at least the house of Angus, taking Islay and Knapdale. Other lands fell to other kin, but the *Senchus* is vague and confused, and it is impossible to know exactly who got what.

We do know that Cowal in southeast Argyll, near to the heart-lands of Strathclyde, was named after someone called Comgall. Fergus's grandson, Arthur's great-uncle, was a Comgall, and so it may have been him. If Fergus initially directed his efforts against the islands and the west coast, this would explain why these were named after Fergus's closest relatives, his brothers, Lorne and Angus. It would then make sense to suppose that it was left to the next generation to advance inland to the east, which would explain why Fergus's grandson Comgall gave his name to Cowal.

According to the *Senchus*, the *Cenél Gabhran*, Kin of Gabhran (Gabhran was Arthur Mac Aedan's grandfather) consisted of 560 households and could put 800 men in the field. The *Cenél Lorne* and the *Cenél Angus*, with 420 and 430 households respectively, could each field 600 men. Based on these figures, Dalriada-Scotland in its heyday was probably able to muster an army of between 1,000 and 2,000 warriors. The figures in the *Senchus* do not seem to be obvious exaggerations but seem reasonable enough to be relied on. They were probably based on records kept for fiscal purposes, or perhaps they were muster rolls.

Following his inauguration, Fergus marched north from Dunardry-Dunadd, against the Picts, taking the Stone of Destiny with him and fighting all the way. Within a year of landing he had taken the islands of Lismore and Iona and was in control as far north as Loch Linnhe. In the *Chronicles of the Picts and Scots and Other Early Memorials*, W. F. Skene says that Fergus built a town near Dunstaffnage Castle and installed the Stone of Destiny there. According to Hector Boece, the fifteenth-century Scottish historian, "Fergus . . . brought the chair [the Stone of Destiny] from Ireland to Argyll, and was crowned upon it. He built a town in Argyll called Beregonium, in which he placed it."

Beregonium, modern Benderloch, is only three miles from Dunstaffnage Castle, across the Bay of Selma, now Ardmucknish Bay. Ardmucknish Bay today is largely unspoiled and can be seen much as it was fifteen hundred years ago, when its strategic position commanding the approaches to the Sound of Mull, Firth of Lorn, and the great sea lochs, Linnhe, Creran, and Etive made it vital to anyone determined to hold the north of Argyll.

The Stone of Destiny was to remain at Beregonium during the reigns of twelve kings before it was moved south to "Evonium," Dunstaffnage. In the ninth century, when the depredations of the Vikings made it unsafe to keep the Stone of Destiny in the west, it was taken to Scone, near Perth, and kept there until 1296. In that year Edward I, king of England, "Hammer of the Scots," attempted to steal it as part of a campaign to denude the Scottish nation of its identity.

Fortunately for Scotland, the Stone of Destiny was hidden, and Edward was fobbed of with a lump of Perthshire sandstone. The fake stone was taken south to Westminster Abbey, where it was used in

English coronations until the Union of the Crowns of Scotland and England in 1603, after which the fake stone was used to crown *British* monarchs. It was "loaned" to Scotland in 1296 and is now kept in Edinburgh Castle.[1]

Following his successes against the Picts in the north of Argyll and having divided the land he had conquered among his supporters, Fergus set off back to Ireland to help quell a rebellion. He died when his ship was driven onto the rocks at what is now Carrickfergus. Fergus had been in Scotland for about two years.

Domangart Mac Fergus succeeded his father. Domangart was Arthur Mac Aedan's great-grandfather. He was known as Domangart of Kintyre, which suggests that while Fergus was fighting in the north of Argyll, Domangart was charged with subduing the south. It is perhaps indicative of the ferocity of the opposition mounted by the native people of Argyll that six years after becoming king Domangart too was dead (circa 507).

Domangart was survived by his two young sons, Comgall, who was to succeed him as king of the Scots, and Gabhran, Arthur Mac Aedan's grandfather. Fergus and Domangart had established a foothold only. It would be generations before their kin could say with reason that their hold on Argyll was secure. Then all Argyll would resound to the name of Arthur, at least for a time. Today Arthur's name echoes only faintly about the glens and hills where he fought most of his most famous battles, but echo it does

The visitor's information map at Cadzow Hill, Hamilton, where Merlin-Lailoken was born, shows the names of hills to the north and west. The name most worn by countless pointing fingers is Ben Arthur, the Hill of Arthur.

Ben Arthur is generally accepted as having been named in honor of the legendary Arthur, despite the fact that the legendary Arthur is usually said to have been a man of the south. Skene thought a southern Arthur came north, fought a few battles on the banks of Loch Lomond, and then went home, leaving behind the memory of his heroics to be commemorated in the hill-name, Ben Arthur. Why would a southern Arthur do that? It just does not make sense.

The alternative explanation is that the fame of some southern

Arthur was so great that, for some unknown reason, his name came to be attached to this a northern hill. This begs the question: Why this particular hill?

Ben Arthur, half way up the west bank of Loch Lomond, commands the great pass that leads up and over the aptly named *Rest-and-be-thankful* road to the heartlands of Argyll, and so it is perfectly placed to serve as the headquarters of someone charged with protecting the borders of Dalriada from the depredations of the Picts. In the sixth century Loch Lomond formed Dalriada's border with Pictland in the north and east, Manau in the south and east, and Strathclyde in the south. It is unlikely that that the name Ben Arthur and this strategic location are just a coincidence. It is more likely that Ben Arthur was given its name because it was associated with a historical Arthur, and there is only historical Arthur in the right place at the right time. If Ben Arthur was named in memory of Arthur Mac Aedan this would explain both the name and the location. This would also suggest that Arthur Mac Aedan was the man who became the legend that is Arthur and that the general consensus that Ben Arthur was named in honor of the legendary Arthur is well founded.

Head west, away from Loch Lomond, across the *Rest-and-be-thankful* road, you will find that the road falls steeply down towards Inveraray, the capital of Argyll. Beyond Inveraray a string of *Ard Airigh* place-names runs north–south down the spine of Arthur's Dalriada; these include, among others, Ardery near Strontian in Sunart, where I met Jimmy Ardery; Dun Creagach, the fort south of Connel named Ardery on Timothy Pont's sixteenth-century maps; Ardary and Aredrey on the banks of Loch Awe; and Dunardry at the southern end of the Kilmartin Glen.

In the sixth century the most important route in Argyll was the portage road that ran east–west along the line of the modern Crinan Canal, in the shadow of Dunardry. This made Dunardry the obvious administrative capital of Argyll. It is unlikely to be mere coincidence that at the very foot of Dunardry, exactly where one would expect business to be transacted, goods inspected, tolls levied, and travelers identified and given permission to pass, there is a place called *Tighean Leacainn*, the "smooth slope of the master or sovereign." Tighean Leacainn was probably, in effect, Argyll's commercial district. This lends weight to the view that Dunardry and other *Airigh*-places do not have pasture but lordly connotations.

Contiguous with Tighean Leacainn is *Dhaill*, a place-name that can and usually does mean a portion or a share, as in the place-name Dalkeith, the portion or share of the Keiths. The *Dhaill* at the foot of Dunardry stands alone and does not have a name attached to it, and so, if it was ever meant to signify some particular party's portion or share, that information has been lost. It is more likely however that this *Dhaill* at the foot of Dunardry, next to the smooth slope of the lords, where business was transacted and meetings were held, denotes a meeting place, a place of business and parley—literally a parliament, a place where people would meet to talk. (The name of the House of Representatives of the Parliament of the Republic of Ireland, *Dáil Éireann*, is from the same root.) Again, this suggests there was more to Dunardry than has hitherto been thought.

Airigh is an element in many modern Gaelic place-names. Sometimes it means a summer pasture or shieling; sometimes it has O'Brien's older meaning, lord. However, it would require someone more patient than me, with significant linguistic skills and some statistical ability, to work out which *Airigh* was which on each individual occasion. I suspect that even such a person would find it impossible to reach a definitive conclusion in every instance.

Not only do Q-Celtic *Ard Airigh* place-names speckle the heartland of Arthur Mac Aedan's Q-Celtic speaking Dalriada, they can also be found in the P-Celtic speaking lands of the Britons: Arderydd where Arthur Mac Aedan fought against Merlin-Lailoken in 573; Ard Airigh, now Ardery Street, Partick, Glasgow, where, I have submitted in *Finding Merlin*, Merlin-Lailoken lived toward the end of his long life; the town of Airdrie (*Ardrytoun* or *Ardry*)[2] in central Scotland; and, two miles north of Airdrie, Arderyth. If Arthur was Arthur Mac Aedan it would not be surprising that the *Ard Airigh* names found in Arthur Mac Aedan's Argyll also echo in the southlands of Manau, in Airdrie and Arderyth, where Arthur's father Aedan ruled and Arthur Mac Aedan patrolled the border.

East of Dunardry-Dunadd, upriver along the Add and past the

Dunardry hill, Dun Monaidh, Mount Badon, looking west along the Crinan Canal, Cairnbaan, Argyll

village of Kilmichael Glassary is Glen Airigh, traditionally the Glen of the Pasture, but which, if O'Brien's definition of *Airigh* is correct is really the Glen of the Lord or Lords. There is nothing particularly pasture-like about Glen Airigh. It is very much like many other Scottish glens. On the other hand it is where the kings of the Scots were based, from the time of Fergus (circa 500) until the middle of the ninth century when Viking pressure led the Scots to move their capital east to Scone, Perth. Is it not more likely that Glen Airigh, rather than being called by a "pasture" name, would have been given a name that something to do with a lord or with lords?

Located between Kilmichael Glassary and Glen Airigh is Lecknary, an obvious corruption of a Gaelic name. *Lecknary* is usually taken as a version of *Leac-nathrach* meaning "Flat Stone of the Serpent," *nathair* being "serpent" in Gaelic. But what serpent? Why should this stone, in this place, have anything to do with a serpent? Lecknary stands sentinel at the entrance to Glen Airigh, and so there is a more sensible interpretation of the name *Lecknary*. *Leac* means a "great stone" or a "flat stone": that is, a stone upon which something might be carved. It may be that a Pictish sculptor carved a snake on a stone in this place and so inspired the name *Flat Stone of the Serpent*, but is it not more likely, given that Lecknary stands at the entry to Glen Airigh, where the sixth-century equivalent of a road sign might have stood, that it was originally *Leac na Airigh*—the great or flat stone of the Lord or Lords?

The River Add runs through Glen Airigh, past the 482 meters of the hill Airigh Ard, which, according to the conventional wisdom, means "hill of the high pasture" although, again, this is for no obvious geographical reason. By my account, it is the hill of the high lord or lords. North of Airigh Ard and south of Ben Dearg is the source of the river. Beyond Ben Dearg the hills slope away, down to the town of Inveraray, the ancient seat of the Dukes of Argyll.

The town signposts say that the name Inveraray is derived from the Gaelic, *Inbhir Aora*. *Inbhir*, pronounced *inver*, means "an inlet," and *aora* means "rough water" (being derived from *aò-reidh*—literally, "not-smooth"). This interpretation says the reference to "rough water" is to two burns that run nearby, one of rough water and the other of smooth water, although it seemed to me when I read this explanation that even the writer did not find it convincing.

The Duke of Argyll's onetime factor, Mr. P. M. Fairweather, kindly told me in an exchange of letters that, "One of the earliest written references to Inveraray is . . . found on Timothy Pont's map circa 1590 on which there is a reference to the *Castel of Inreyra*." I knew this. This *Inreyra* reference is an obvious misspelling, probably based on a mishearing. Whatever the last part of the name may be, the first part is undoubtedly *inver*, "inlet," a word commonly used in place-names in the Gaelic speaking parts of Scotland, and one which describes the geography of Inveraray exactly. Mr. Fairweather went on to say, "[In] the Registrar of the Great Seal of Scotland there is an entry for 8th May 1474 referring to *Villam de Innowreyra*. In 1648 when King Charles I granted a Charter giving Royal Burgh status, the spelling appears to be

Inverarey. (This was supported by a Valuation Roll entry of 1648 when the spelling is *Inverairey*.)"

Innowreyra and *Inverairey* were new to me. I added them to a list that also included *Invedraray*, a name taken from a charter signed by a Duke of Argyll in 1669. The first of Mr. Fairweather's versions, *Innowreyra*, was probably recorded by a clerk who was unfamiliar with his informant's accent or perhaps even with his language, leading the clerk to write what he thought he had heard without checking that the end result was anywhere near right. The second version, *Inverairey*, was closer to what I had come to believe was the true source of the town-name, *Inbhir Airigh*, Inlet of the Lords. Inlet of the Lords makes sense. Inlet of the Rough Water does not make sense, well, not much sense: two burns, one smooth and one rough and they named the town after the rough one. How likely is that?

Given all the other *Airigh* place-names just over the hill to the south and the fact that in recent centuries Inveraray has been the main base of the lords of Argyll—indeed, even today the Duke of Argyll has his seat there—it is more likely that Inveraray is *Inbhir Airigh* and that it means the inlet of the lords. If this is so, the signposts that translate Inveraray as *Inbhir Aora* stand to be changed to *Inbhir Airigh*.

The name Arthur has been commemorated in the name of the Argyll clan of MacArthur, a name, it is said, that was "Ancient even in remote Celtic times." It is also said, albeit mainly by MacArthurs, that "There is nothing older, except the hills, MacArthur, and the devil." The MacArthurs fought for the hero king, Robert Bruce, in the Scottish War of Independence in the early fourteenth century and were rewarded with royal recognition of their titles to their lands. They were also awarded, as the spoils of war, lands taken from the Bruce's defeated enemies the MacDougalls. The most powerful MacArthur house, the MacArthurs of Loch Awe, was given lands that included Dunstaffnage Castle outside Oban (once the resting place of the Stone of Destiny) and Ardery and Aredrey on Loch Awe. This was the high point in MacArthur fortunes. In the early fifteenth century James I, King of Scots, favored the Campbells at the expense of the MacArthurs. When James executed Iain MacArthur, the Clan Chief, MacArthur fortunes waned and never recovered.

The Campbells went on to become the most influential family in Argyll.

That the MacArthurs hail from Argyll suggests there was an Arthur whose name and fame lived on after his death, whoever he was. If the MacArthurs were named for Arthur Mac Aedan and if Arthur Mac Aedan was the man who inspired the legend of Arthur, it would be easy to see where both the name and the fame originated.

MacArthur is not the only clan to imagine a connection with the legendary Arthur. In a Gaelic manuscript dated 1467, Dubhghall Albanach mac mhic Cathail (Scottish Dugald, son of the son of Cathal), staked a Campbell claim to descent from the legendary Arthur.[3] The first part of the 1467 manuscript is a Campbell genealogy that puts the legendary Arthur firmly in Argyll: "Young Colin son of Archibald son of Colin son of Allan son of Neil son of big Allan son of Archibald son of Dugald son of Duncan son of Archibald son of Gille Coliam son of Duibhne son of Eirenan son of Smeirbhe son of Arthur son of Uther, that is, the unopposed king of the world."

This was written a very long time after Arthur, and medieval records are notoriously unreliable, but one thing is clear—Scottish Dugald, or whoever provided him with his source material, thought to claim the legendary Arthur as an ascendant of one line of Clan Campbell of Argyll. While the reference to Uther makes the evidence of Scottish Dugald somewhat suspect, the fact remains that only clans in Argyll can make such claims.

Notwithstanding his Argyll connections, Arthur was not always a man of Argyll. He came there from the east, from Manau; indeed, there is reason to believe that to the people of Argyll Arthur was always an easterner really. The sixth century kingdom of Manau was centered on Stirling, which has been called "the brooch that holds Scotland together." Manau lay north of Strathclyde, south of the lands of the Miathi Picts, east of Dalriada, and west of the lands of the Gododdin, and so was of vital strategic importance. Echoes of the name Manau can still be heard in the names of the modern towns Clackmannan, nine miles east of Stirling, and Slamannan, twenty miles south of Stirling. According to Skene, Manau's western boundary was Slamannan, from which it extended east to the river Esk, although there is reason to believe Skene set Manau's western boundary too far to the east. This might be a moot point because in the 150 years between the departure of the Romans and the birth of Arthur, Manau's borders fluctuated wildly.

Wherever the border was at any given time, the site of what is now the town of Airdrie was the most important strategic location between the kingdoms of Strathclyde and Manau. From Airdriehill it is possible to look across the Clyde Valley to the Firth of Clyde and beyond to western Argyll. Ben Arthur and Ben Lomond are visible to the north, as is Tinto Hill to the south: hills that were not only observation points but signal-fire hills that enabled whoever held them to communicate over long distances. To control the contested lands that lay between Strathclyde and Manau it was necessary to control Airdriehill.

So who controlled Airdriehill in the time of Arthur Mac Aedan? The answer to this question may lie in the very name, Airdrie. Blaeu's 1654 maps[4] show Airdrie as Ardry. Peter Drummond in his *Place-names of the Monklands* calls it Ardrytoun. There is clearly some connection between Airdrie-Ardry-Ardrytoun and Dunardry, where Arthur Mac Aedan was active in 574. Airdrie is also on land that was ruled by Arthur Mac Aedan's father in 574. It is therefore reasonable to suppose some connection between Arthur Mac Aedan and Airdrie. The alternative would be to suppose that Arthur Mac Aedan's Dunardry association and Arthur Mac Aedan's Airdrie association were purely coincidental. It is more likely that for some similar reason Dunardry was called the hillfort of the High Lords and that the signal-hill Airdriehill was called the place of the High Lords: that is, because they were both associated with Arthur Mac Aedan's war-band, a war-band that was called something akin to the *Ard Airighaich* or the *Ard Airighean*, the High Lords. In effect, the High Lords of war.

Of course, it may be that the name Airdrie was inspired by some warrior or a war-band unconnected with Arthur Mac Aedan. If this is so then it would be necessary to explain why Merlin-Lailoken too was associated with Arderydd in 573, a battle fought far to the south on the border of Scotland and England.

Two miles north of Airdrie is Arderyth (now little more than a name on the map and a few houses). Arderyth and Arderydd are exactly the same name (*dd* is pronounced "th." I will use Arderyth for the Airdrie location and Arderydd for the battle location simply to avoid confusion).

The legendary Arthur fought and killed the warrior Hueil, the brother of the Christian polemicist Gildas. If Arthur was Arthur Mac Aedan this probably occurred in the twelve miles of contested land that separate Airdrie and Cambuslang. Hueil and Gildas were the sons of Caw, a chief of Strathclyde whose lands were centered on Cambuslang on the River Clyde, half way between Glasgow and Merlin-Lailoken's lands at Cadzow, and just across the River Clyde from Arthur Mac Aedan's Manau. There were several reasons why Arthur Mac Aedan and Hueil might have crossed paths and swords. Hueil was from Strathclyde and Arthur was from neighboring Manau, and so there would have been a local rivalry engendered by inevitable raiding. It is also reasonable to suppose that the family of the ultra-Christian "Saint" Gildas was also Christian. This would mean that Hueil and Arthur would have had religious differences because Arthur was a man of the Old Way.

While Arthur's humiliation in Caradoc's *Life of Gildas* is primarily propaganda, there is still reason to believe that some of what Caradoc wrote reflects what really happened, because much of it is contrary to Caradoc's interest. Southern writers did not invent Scottish locations; they had no reason to do this. On the contrary, given that their audiences were southern, it made more commercial sense for them to use southern locations. When Caradoc said that Gildas was the son of "the king of Scotia," that is, Scotland, it follows that either a southern Arthur went to Scotland to kill Hueil or that Hueil came south to be killed by Arthur. If, however, Arthur was Arthur Mac Aedan, there would be no need for Arthur to travel north to kill Hueil or for Hueil to "swoop down from Scotland," as one southern writer put it, to raid the lands of a southern Arthur and get himself killed in the process. All Hueil would have had to do was cross the Clyde and raid land that fell under Arthur's protection, once too often. I am not aware that anyone has ever thought that they both lived in the same area. Indeed, by one account Arthur is said to have chased Hueil to the Isle of Man, when it is much more likely that Arthur chased Hueil into Manau. Of course, to have identified Manau as the scene of the fight would have been to place Arthur and Hueil firmly in Scotland.

Manau sometimes stretched as far north as the Firth of Tay and east into Fife. As for the eastern marches of Manau, south of the Forth, geography almost dictates that these skirted the drum of hills that stands between Glasgow and Edinburgh.

Arthur Mac Aedan's Manau lay among the lands of the Picts, the Britons of both Strathclyde and the Gododdin, and the Scots of Dalriada. The people who lived there reflected this border-country status; they were predominantly Pictish with a large admixture of Britons, the descendants of the various peoples who had manned the Antonine Wall in Roman times, and, of course, Arthur Mac Aedan's Scots.

Arthur Mac Aedan's great-grandfather Domangart, king of the Scots, son of Fergus Mor, died around 507, probably fighting to secure his Scottish kingdom of Dalriada in Argyll. He left two sons to compete for the throne, Comgall and Gabhran, the latter of whom would be Arthur Mac Aedan's grandfather. The Scots of Dalriada did not practice primogeniture and so the elder son, Comgall, was not automatically bound to succeed. The Scots knew that simply allowing the firstborn male child of the last king to succeed to the throne would almost inevitably mean they would end up with a king who was not up to the job. These were dangerous times and they dared not take this risk. To ensure they had a leader who was at least adequate, they chose their king from a pool of candidates that included the late king's close male relatives: sons, brothers, nephews, and cousins.

A sitting king could try to sway the decision by choosing a tanist, a position akin to an American vice president in that while it did not provide the tanist with an automatic right to succeed, it certainly put him in the running. The final decision lay with the people or, at least, the chiefs among them. That said, Comgall and Gabhran were both very young when their father, Domangart, died, and there was probably very little of substance to distinguish them. So Comgall, the older brother, was chosen to be the next king, probably simply because he was the older brother.

While Comgall ruled from Dunardry-Dunadd, Gabhran was stationed in the east to man the frontier beyond which lay the threat of the great Miathi-Pict confederation. This took Gabhran far from the center of power but also allowed him an independent command, and so this arrangement probably suited both brothers. This posting to the eastern marches of Dalriada may be inferred from what happened next.

Gabhran proved to be an able general while fighting the Miathi Picts and this attracted the attention of the people of Manau, themselves a predominantly Pictish people. Around 525 they invited Gabhran to join them in some capacity, either as an ally or as a warlord in their army. Perhaps Gabhran was tired of playing second fiddle in Dalriada or maybe he saw an opportunity to advance his interests, but, in either event, he decided to try "pastures new." From then on, Gabhran and his descendants, including his grandson-to-be Arthur, were closely connected with Manau (indeed, the Men of Manau formed the core of the war-band that Arthur was to lead to everlasting fame).

Power descended through the female line among the Picts, and so when Gabhran married the Pictish Princess Lleian, the daughter or granddaughter of Brychan, king of Manau, and possibly the niece of Clinoch, king of Strathclyde, Gabhran gained high standing in the Pictish hierarchy. From this time on, Gabhran is described as a man who lived near the River Forth—that is, in Manau.

The ferocious Scots warriors who came with Gabhran to Manau, fresh from fighting the Picts, would have been invaluable to the people of Manau as they struggled to survive, locked as they were between four great powers. In these circumstances it is most likely that Manau sold its swords to various bidders, bobbing and weaving in and out of alliances, trying to ensure no one of its neighbors became predominant. I picture something akin to British foreign policy in the second half of the second millennium CE, when Britain worked to prevent any one nation on the European mainland from becoming powerful enough to pose a real threat to Britain's security.

Based upon what happened a few decades later (in the actual age of Arthur, when Manau became the dominant military power), it is likely that Manau unconsciously aped Athens in the age of Pericles. Athens grew strong by taking money rather than ships from members of the Delian League. This money enabled Athens to build even more Athenian ships and so to attain naval supremacy. Under Gabhran,

Manau stopped being the "pig in the middle" and started out on a road that would lead to the creation of a standing army of full-time professional soldiers, while Manau's neighbors continued with armies of predominantly citizen-soldiers (mainly farmers called up to support their kings' relatively small professional bodyguards).

All Gabhran had to do was require payment from his neighbors in exchange for Manau's acting as a well-armed buffer state, the implicit understanding being that whoever broke the peace would find themselves up against their target and Manau too. In this event it would have been in everyone's interest to maintain Manau. It would not have been in anyone's interest that Manau become too strong but, just as with Athens, this is exactly what happened.

Manau soon became the only body that could afford to maintain a strong permanent fighting force, because it was the only body that had permanent work for them. This force would not only have been engaged in the perennial raiding that was the leitmotif of the sixth-century warrior but also in border skirmishes with neighbors who wanted to test Manau's strength or to attack one of the other great powers and so had to cross Manau first.

The endemic fighting that was rife in Manau inevitably attracted free-lances, second-sons, the disinherited, and outlaws prepared to sell their swords for a place in a community that offered them the plunder that followed victory. In a time when only a king's bodyguard could be considered professional soldiers and when standing armies were too expensive to maintain, Manau ended up with an efficient fighting force that was out of all proportion to its size and population.

Under Gabhran, Manau bolstered its army with outsiders: first Gabhran's Scots and later, inevitably, men who were not much better than mercenaries. Manau became practiced in warfare beyond the experience of its neighbors. It became a Celtic Sparta, a Celtic Macedonia.

In fiction, the best and noblest knights came from afar to Arthur's Camelot to join the Knights of the Round Table. These fictional (and anachronistic) "knights" are said to have joined Arthur because they wanted to do good deeds. Such nonsense is just too milk-soppy to be true. In real life, the men who came to be called the Knights of the

Round Table were Arthur Mac Aedan's chosen men, the *ArdAirighaich*:
Men of Manau, Scots of Dalriada, free-lances, and others who gravitated to Arthur because . . . well, because Arthur was a winner. These
most warlike of men gravitated to Arthur, as they had to his grandfather
Gabhran, for purely mercenary motives. These men did not go about
doing good deeds. They went about killing people.

We can see in what Gabhran started the beginnings of the fighting-force that would win eternal fame under Arthur. It was only much
later, after much of the history had been rubbed away and the rest
blurred, that Arthur's war band, the *ArdAirighaich*, the high lords
(of war), came to be known as "The Knights of the Round Table."
Although it is not possible to say exactly how successful Gabhran was
in war, the deep inroads he made into the lands of the Miathi Picts,
fighting in Gowrie, near Perth, and in Forfar, suggest that Gabhran
was very successful indeed.

Comgall ruled Dalriada for more than thirty years. Gabhran
carved out a place for himself in the neighboring kingdom of Manau
before succeeding his brother as king of the Scots of Dalriada. Comgall
is said to have abdicated his Dalriada throne because of ill health in
about 537, although there is reason to believe that he was deposed.
In any event he died in retirement or exile, four years later.

Although Comgall left a son, Conall, it was Gabhran who in 538
was chosen as the new king of the Scots, probably because he had a
track record of success against the Picts and because his activities in
Manau had provided him with powerful allies. Gabhran had five sons
including Arthur's father, Aedan, who was born near the river Forth in
527, 530, 533, or 534 CE (the sources vary).

Aedan is unlikely to have visited Dalriada often, if at all, before
his father's inauguration in 538. Aedan's roots were in Manau, in the
east. Indeed, in later years he would be called, among other less com-
plimentary things, king of the Forth. As the son of a Pictish mother,
born and brought up in the east, Aedan must have been treated with
some suspicion if not outright hostility by the native Scots of Dalriada.
This would not have daunted Aedan. He grew up to be an able politician and to be known as Aedan the cunning or Aedan the wily (although
these appellations were attached to him by Christian writers and so they

must be read with some suspicion). Cunning and wily or not, Aedan was clever and ambitious. One may picture him, even as a young man, seeking out strengths and weaknesses in potential friends and enemies and forming alliances with chiefs of Dalriada.

Gabhran was married at least twice: first, to Aedan's mother, a Pictish princess and, second—to consolidate his position after he became king of the Scots—to a Scots woman of the House of Comgall, by whom he had a son, Éoganán.

In 558 Gabhran invaded the lands of the Miathi Picts only to be heavily defeated by the Pictish king, Bridei son of Maelchon. He died within the year, probably from wounds suffered in the battle. This defeat was a disaster for the Scots. The Picts recovered much of the land they had lost to Dalriada and Manau in the preceding decades. (It would be left to Arthur to avenge this defeat.)

There were two main contenders for the vacant throne: Aedan, son of Gabhran, and his cousin Conall, son of Comgall (the last king but one). Conall was older than Aedan and was Scots on both sides of his family, having been born and raised in Dalriada. Aedan was the son of a princess of the Picts and had spent his formative years in Manau. Not only did Aedan have Pictish blood, but his side of the family, the House of Gabhran, was tainted by recent defeat. Aedan had one other disadvantage. Even if all other things had been equal, and they were not, there was a tendency in tanistry to alternate the kingship between rival branches of the family. This meant that those whose favored candidate lost on one occasion would know there was a good chance that their man or someone from his branch of the family would be chosen next time. This took some of the steam out of the whole process.

Comgall had been succeeded not by his son Conall, but by his brother Gabhran. Gabhran was succeeded not by his son Aedan, but by his nephew Conall, Comgall's son. A king from the house of Comgall had been succeeded by a king from the house of Gabhran, and so a king from the house of Gabhran was succeeded by a king from the house of Comgall.

Aedan had been unsuccessful but he had not given up. He was now only one step away from being king in Dalriada. At this same time Bridei's Miathi Picts followed up on Gabhran's defeat by putting pressure on the defenses of Manau. Aedan saw an opportunity. It was probably about 560 that Aedan returned to Manau and made it once again his main base. In this he acted as his father had before him and for similar reasons—to avoid internecine strife in Dalriada.

From then on, throughout the 560s, Aedan made himself useful in Manau, preparing the army, organizing the defense of the borders, gathering taxes, and administering justice—in other words, placing himself in positions where he could curry favor and gain supporters. Aedan was primarily a politician, not a warrior.

Aedan's dates are muddled. He is said to have led the army of Manau against the Miathi Picts for thirteen years before he became king of Manau circa the year 569. Aedan is also said to have died in the thirty-eighth year of his reign. If 608 is the generally accepted date of his death, this means that Aedan became a king around 570, but where this happened is not clear. It is undisputed that he became king of the Scots in 574, and so if the record that says he died in the thirty-eighth year of his reign is correct, he must have been king of somewhere else for some four years before he became king of the Scots. This somewhere else was almost certainly Manau. (It is, of course, possible that Aedan did not die in the thirty-eighth year of his reign and that these timings are simply wrong—sixth- and seventh-century dates, like sixth- and seventh-century names are uncertain things.)

It seems likely, however, that Aedan spent the 560s strengthening his position in Manau, until in 570 he was strong enough to make himself king there. He had certain claims through his mother and his first wife, but his elevation was probably mainly because he was an adept and ruthless politician, backed up by military might. His son Arthur, a child in the 560s, must have grown up surrounded by ruthless ambition and terrifying uncertainty.

Aedan's success in Manau is corroborated by *The Tripartite Life of Patrick*, which says Patrick prophesized that Aedan would take the throne of *Fortrenn*, the Pictish province of *Fortriu*, the land between Stirling and Perth. This may be accepted as true, not because Patrick prophesized it (he did not—Patrick could no more prophesy than anyone else) but because Patrick's hagiographer, with the gift of hindsight, *said* Patrick prophesized it. It was common practice among clerics determined to boost the status of whatever saint they happened to be promoting to take something that had happened after the saint was dead and say the saint had predicted it would happen. The writer of the *Tripartite Life* says that this prophecy—that Aedan would be king of the land between Stirling and Perth—was fulfilled in Aedan's day.

The *Life of St. Berach* says Aedan gave Aberfoyle to Berach. This is also unlikely to be true, because Christians were always saying things like that to enhance their claims to property. This reference to Aberfoyle does however give some idea of the western bounds of Manau. Arthur's boyhood and youth were spent in Manau in a world in which war was a constant threat and he was no doubt trained to arms from an early age. He was probably unable to read and write, but this would not have bothered a warrior born, as he was soon to prove to be.

KNIGHTS AND ROUND TABLES

Five years after Conall, not Aedan, became king of the Scots, Columba-Crimthann arrived in Scotland. One of the world's Top-Ten saints, he is and was commonly called Columba, the dove of the church, but when he was a young man he was also known as Crimthann, the fox, and so, just as I use the name Merlin-Lailoken, I use the name Columba-Crimthann.

Columba-Crimthann is usually portrayed as a gentle monk, who came to the island of Iona to set up a community in which learning could thrive and from which a beneficent Christianity could be introduced to an all but barbarian Scotland. In reality he was a ruthless political operator determined to promote his personal interests by using his new religion to obliterate the Old Way of the druids.

Born in Ireland around the year 521, probably to an aristocratic family of the Old Way, Columba-Crimthann was socially well connected and all too conscious of his status. The "*Old Irish Life*" says that while other trainee monks had to grind their own corn Columba-Crimthann did not, because "An angel of the Lord used to grind Columba's [corn] for him . . . 'because of his nobility above all.'"[5] It is unlikely an angel ground Columba's corn for him. It is more likely he got someone else to do it for him "because of his nobility above all."

After he became a fully-fledged priest, Columba-Crimthann took steps to build a powerbase. To do this he needed books, because with books came knowledge, and with knowledge came power. So he borrowed a book from one of his fellow monks and then, without permission, made a copy to keep as his own. The matter came before Diarmid the king for judgment. Diarmid famously said, "To every cow belongs its calf, to every book its little book," and ordered Columba-Crimthann to hand over his copy of the book to the owner of the original. Columba-Crimthann did what he was told to do but swore that he would be avenged upon Diarmid.

When the opportunity arose, Columba-Crimthann urged his Ui Neill kinsmen to war against Diarmid, a man of the Old Way, and so unleashed a new and ferocious form of war in Ireland: religious war. The gratuitous slaughter that followed Diarmid's defeat at the battle Cul Drebne in 561 shocked even Columba-Crimthann's Ui Neill allies and led to his being exiled from Ireland.

In 563 at the age of forty-two, Columba-Crimthann, a tall, striking, powerfully built man with a dominating personality, sailed in the company of an entourage of monks from Ireland into exile in Argyll, where his kinsman Conall Mac Comgall was king of the Scots of Dalriada.

Arthur was about four years old when Columba-Crimthann arrived in Scotland, probably living with his father's people in Manau or with his mother's family in Strathclyde. Columba-Crimthann arrived at the central seat of power, Dunadd-Dunardry, and immediately began to work to win Conall over to his side. His plan was to convert the king and use royal power to impose his form of Christianity on the people of Dalriada. Conall the king was a weak character compared to the strong-willed Columba-Crimthann and was soon won over. Before long Christianity spread from the top down to the people, and from the center of Argyll out to its borders.

The Christian authorities had what they said was a revealed truth, which they did not question, and, when they had the power to impose their will, neither did anyone else. They were also prepared to support whoever happened to have secular power at any given time, no matter how unworthy that person might be and even if this was contrary to the interests of the main mass of the people, provided only that they received reciprocal support when they turned against those who challenged their "religious" power. The end result was a people who did what they were told because they were afraid of real punishment in real life and of much worse imaginary punishments in life after death. In centuries to come this Church–State partnership was called Christendom. It was to last for a thousand years and more.

The Old Way did not offer similar benefits to rulers. Most of the people of the Old Way, like all of the Christians, believed in the supernatural, but they had not created a single all-important revelation and so the basis upon which their beliefs stood was more diffuse. This diffusion led people to ask questions about their world and to find answers for themselves. Most importantly, the druids had no inflexible all-pervasive power structure capable of imposing one way of thinking over another. This allowed individualism to flourish and so made the main mass of the people uneasy and unlikely "subjects," especially if they did not have a say in how they were governed.

Conall must have known that Christianity was the coming thing in Europe and that its hierarchical system of authority offered kings like him a partner in power that complemented their secular authority. This would have made Conall, like almost any ruler, susceptible to Columba-Crimthann's blandishments.

To begin with, the people of the Old Way did not see Columba-Crimthann as a threat. When, some years after he arrived in Argyll, Columba-Crimthann visited Bridei, the king of the Picts and a man of the Old Way of the druids, in Inverness, he received a tolerant hearing from the people of the Old Way. This suggests he would have received a similar broadminded reception when he first arrived in Argyll, especially since he was related to the king. The people of the Old Way would have had no good reason to harm or even hinder him, not at first. On the contrary they would have seen in the arrival of Columba-Crimthann's Christian party an opportunity to debate and learn, even if they had no intention of becoming converts.

One of the tricks Columba-Crimthann used to win over Conall and his companions was to pretend that he had supernatural powers including, according to Adamnan, the ability to describe events that were taking place far away, while they were actually happening: "At the very hour when the Battle of *Móin Daire Lothair* was fought in Ireland, the saint [Columba-Crimthann] gave a full account of it in Britain, in the presence of King Conall."[6] Of course, Columba-Crimthann had no such ability, but this would not have prevented his followers from bruiting it about that he did. Adamnan, writing generations later, promoted Columba-Crimthann's claim of magical powers and had it fixed in the written record. This led subsequent generations to believe that Columba-Crimthann was a magician or, as Adamnan had it, a miracle-worker, which was exactly what Adamnan intended. In real life Columba-Crimthann had to rely upon more prosaic powers: his intellect and his power to persuade, coupled with the fanatical certainty he shared with almost everyone excited by a new religion.

Columba-Crimthann's Christianity was authoritarian in the extreme, which made him an enticing partner for a king—particularly a weak king—trying to control a free-thinking people. Even without real magic, talk of the supernatural combined with the promise that working with Columba-Crimthann would bolster his kingship was enough to win over the gullible Conall. By the late 560s Columba-Crimthann had brought the same religious tensions to Scotland that had led to his exile from Ireland.

Being free-thinking men of the Old Way, some of Conall's chiefs were resistant to the new deal the Christians presented and became restive when steps were taken to impose it upon them. In hindsight we can see that the chiefs who favored the Old Way were certain to fail, but this would not have been clear in the 560s, because Christianity was only at the beginning of its inexorable rise.

Columba-Crimthann set his sights on the island Lismore for his headquarters, but Lismore was the base of a druid called Muluag. (It is usually said that Muluag was a Christian saint, but this claim was made only after Muluag was dead. Muluag was marchmained.) Acting in concert, Conall and Columba-Crimthann pushed too hard and too fast as they strove to extend their influence north and west. The records written by the Christian victors do not make clear what happened, but it appears that the chiefs of Angus on their outlying islands and the chiefs of Lorne in the borderlands of the north rejected the imposition of a religious system that brooked no alternatives. They rose in revolt. This revolt began in the late 560s on the islands of Islay and Seil and spread from there.

Conall was only able to put down this rebellion with the aid of foreign troops provided by the Irish king, Colmán Bec of Meath, but even then Conall and Columba-Crimthann's victory was not absolute, and they had to settle for a compromise peace. Muluag kept Lismore. Columba-Crimthann had to settle for Iona. For the first time, religious tensions had been injected into the mix of family and tribal rivalries that until then had provided the Scots with sufficient reasons for fighting.

When Conall's unhappy reign came to an end with his death in 573, the choice of the next king still involved the time-honored practices of the people of Dalriada, but for the first time a religious factor was part of the equation. This was to prove fundamentally incompatible with the traditional ways.

Until this time the choice of a king tended to favor one side of the royal family and then the other. This consensus tended to minimize the number of occasions when sons followed their fathers as king (a surefire way to end up with inadequate kings). After Columba-Crimthann became involved in politics in Dalriada, divisions appeared along religious lines. Parties came to be divided not between individual family members but between those who were Christians and those who were not. The result was civil war and the advent of a young warlord called Arthur.

THE ROUND TABLE is not a myth (well, not quite), and it is still there to be seen today (well, sort of).

There is no reason to believe that one person—Wace or anyone else—invented the idea of *The Table Round*, at least not from a standing start. Wace, Robert de Boron, and Malory were able to draw from a large body of first-millennium sources that included references to the practices of the people of the Old Way, most of which are now lost to us. These sources would have been garbled by the time they became available to Wace and others in the twelfth century, but, even if they were not, being Celtic sources they would have been alien to writers of English adventures and French romances.

Wace, Robert de Boron, and Malory were all bound to provide stories that were acceptable to audiences steeped in the romances of the troubadours and, of course, stories that catered to the demands of the Christian Church. These audiences would not have been receptive to stories starring undiluted Celtic heroes from an unfamiliar culture, and so men like Malory invented stories involving medieval knights and their ladies, and Robert de Boron came up with his Round Table/Last Supper nonsense. Southern British and French writers reworked their sources to suit their audiences in the same way as, say, American film makers remake European films to please their audiences, using actors an American audience knows and American settings—this is just human nature.

This does not mean that all of the original source material is necessarily lost. We can still find in Malory a detail which, although slight, makes sense when looked at with reference to Scotland in the sixth century and, indeed, when looked at with specific reference to Arthur Mac Aedan.

According to Malory, Arthur married Guinevere the daughter of "Leodegrance, of the land of Camelard, the which holdeth in his house the Table Round." Leodegrance gave the Round Table to Arthur as a wedding present: "I shall send a gift [that] shall please him . . . for I shall give him the Table Round."[7]

Why would Malory say the Round Table was a gift from the family of Arthur's wife? Why say it was a gift at all? Why not just invent a miraculous origin? Why not just have the table come up out of the waters of a loch like Excalibur, or appear by magic like the sword and the stone? The answer to these questions can be found when we look at the Round Table's solid base in Scottish history.

The passage in Malory helped me to understand the historical source of the Round Table story. Gabhran, Arthur's grandfather, married into the royal house of Manau, where Pictish influences were strong. Rights passed down the female line among the Picts and so it was by right of his mother that Gabhran's son, Aedan, become king of Manau. When he became king Aedan gained control of the fortress on Stirling Castle Rock and with that came what has come to be called the Round Table. It was not actually the wedding present Malory says it was, but it was part of the package that came with the marriages of Gabhran, Aedan, and Arthur into Pictish royalty. It is easy to see how Malory, the imaginative, ingenious, commercial storyteller, got the idea for his *wedding present* story, because it fits neatly with the customs of the Celts of Scotland and indeed of the wider world.

As early as the third century BCE, the Greek writer Posidonius described Celtic warriors at a feast seated in a circle, a practice that continued for at least the next thousand years,

> When a large number [of Celts] feast together they sit around in a circle with the most influential chieftain at the centre . . . His position is accorded on whether he surpasses the others in warlike skills, or nobility of his family, or his wealth. Beside him sits the person giving the feast and on either side of them sit the others in order of their distinction or merit.[8]

The Round Table was not round to enable everyone to feel as if they were equals, nor was it akin to any table that might have been used at the Last Supper or indeed to any other table, because the Round Table was not a table. It was a round earthwork, known as Arthur's Knot or the King's Knot, the remnants of which lie to this day in the shadow of Stirling Castle rock. There, as Posidonius said of the Celts of the European mainland, Celts of Scotland sat in a circle with the most influential chief at the center.

Gabhran, his son Aedan, and Aedan's son Arthur all sat there with their fellows. This practice was the foundation upon which the much later fiction of the Round Table was built. (Of course, a raised round earth mound was too close to nature for the Church, and so, just as in the sword-and-stone episode, an anvil was placed between the sword and the stone; a manmade artifact, a table, was substituted for the earth mound.)

Arthur's Knot or the King's Knot is similar to *Dhaill*—both were meeting places set in the lees of important forts, the fort on Stirling Castle rock and Dunardry, respectively. (Making meeting places at the foot of hills avoided the need for strangers to take long walks up to the summit of a fort, but also denied strangers the opportunity to see the defenses of the fort on the top of the hill.)

We do not know what, if anything, there was at *Dhaill*. Whatever may be there today will only be seen if someone excavates the site. But at Stirling there was a raised round earthwork. We know this because the Knot at Stirling was examined by archaeologists in 2011. The headline in the Scottish newspaper, the *Herald*, was "Find unearthed in hunt for King Arthur's round table."[9] In England, the *Telegraph*[10] read, "King Arthur's round table may have been found by archaeologists in Scotland: Archaeologists searching for King Arthur's round table have found a 'circular feature' beneath the historic King's Knot in Stirling." According to the *Telegraph*, the King's Knot has been shrouded in mystery for hundreds of years:

> Though the Knot as it appears today dates from the 1620s, its flat-topped central mound is thought to be much older . . . Archaeologists from Glasgow University, working with the Stirling Local History Society and Stirling Field and Archaeological Society, conducted the first ever non-invasive survey of the site in May and June in a bid to uncover some of its secrets. Their findings show there was indeed a round feature on the site that pre-dates the visible earthworks . . . a circular ditch and other earth works. . . The finds show that the present mound was created on an older site and throws new light on a tradition that King Arthur's Round Table was located in this vicinity . . . [A]erial photographs taken in 1980 showed three concentric ditches beneath and around the King's Knot mound, suggesting an earthwork monument had preceded it.

Arthur's or the King's Knot was desecrated in the early seventeenth century to please Charles I, when stepped earthworks were added to form an ornamental garden. Then it was "restored" in the nineteenth century to the point where only modern archaeological techniques have allowed us to see what was there in the first millennium.

It appears that local tradition preserved something of what had happened at Stirling and that this echoed down over the centuries in several works by various writers. Of course there are some who will say that the local tradition was inspired by these several works by various writers but, if they do, they have to explain why, of all the places Stirling might have been chosen to be the site of the Round Table. So many writers chose Stirling when Stirling was contrary to their interests. Béroul, a twelfth-century Norman poet writing of Tristan and Isolde, said that the Round Table was in Stirling. A squire called Perenis is sent by Tristan to "King" Arthur, with a message. Béroul says Perenis,

> did not cease to spur his horse on until he reached Caerleon. He took great trouble in carrying out this errand and he deserved a fine reward. He inquired for news of the king and learned that he was at Stirling. Fair Yseut's [Isolde's] squire went along the road which led in that direction. He asked a shepherd who was playing a reed-pipe: "Where is the king?" "Sir," said he, "he is seated on his throne. You will see the Round Table which turns like the world; his household sits around it."[11]

Béroul had no reason to place the Round Table in Scotland, far less in Stirling; on the contrary, he was writing for a southern British and French audience. He must have had some source that placed the Round Table in Stirling.

In his *Oeuvres*, written in 1365, Froissart, secretary to Queen Phillipa of England, writes of a visit he made to Stirling, where he was told that Stirling was once the castle of "King" Arthur and that there resided the Knights of the Round Table. *The Brus* (*The Bruce*), a poem by the Scottish poet John Barbour written circa 1377, tells of the escape of the English king, Edward, from Stirling Castle, after the Battle of Bannockburn.

And beneuth the castell went thai sone
Rycht be the Rond Table away . . .
And towart Lythkow . . .
Beneath the castle [Stirling] they soon went
Right by the *Round Table* away . . .
And toward Linlithgow.

This describes exactly where the Round Table is today. William of Worcester, an English chronicler writing in 1478, said that "King Arthur kept the Round Table at Stirling Castle." Sir David Lindsay, an early sixteenth-century Scottish poet, wrote, "Adew, fair Snawdoun, with thy towris hie, / Thy Chapell-royal, park, and Tabyll Round . . . / Adieu, fair Stirling, with thy towers high, / Your Chapel-royal, park, and Table Round . . ."

For Malory and others who were determined to set Arthur in the south, Stirling was just far too far north, and so they simply said the Round Table was in the south—Winchester is the favorite location—but this is fiction, pure and simple. The mound beneath the Knot of Stirling that came with marriage into Arthur's family is the earthly foundation for the fabulous fiction that is the story of the Round Table.

There was once a wisp of glory at Stirling, as the song in the musical *Camelot* almost says, but this wisp of glory was not known as "Camelot." Camelot was somewhere else, far away to the west.

5

La Naissance
d'Arthur

AEDAN WAS PROBABLY LITTLE MORE THAN SIXTEEN YEARS OLD IN THE mid-540s when he married Domelch, a Pictish "princess" of Manau. Women's names rarely survive in the records. We only know the name of Aedan's wife because one of his sons, Gartnait, is also referred to as the son of Domelch. Rights passed through the female line among the Picts and so this marriage made Aedan an even more important man in Manau.

In his *Life of Columba*, Adamnan says Aedan had four sons: Arthur; Eochaid Find; Domangart and Eochaid Buide (but not who their mother was). The *Senchus* says Arthur was Aedan's grandson, but then the *Senchus* is a somewhat suspect source (it also says Aedan had two sons named Eochaid). I prefer the evidence of Adamnan, corroborated by the *Annals of Tigernach*, which says Arthur was Aedan's son. There is no real dispute in this connection.

Aedan was born circa 530 and so would probably have been in his late twenties when Arthur was born, probably around 559. There is no record of the date of Arthur's birth, because no one knew he would go on to be so celebrated. The only birthdates available tend to be for saints, and these were probably made up after they became famous.

After Arthur became famous people were not content only to know about the events that made him famous, they wanted to believe that Arthur was innately heroic. This meant there had to be something about his birth that presaged his future heroism. Of course there was nothing of this kind in reality, and so men like Geoffrey invented stories like the one in which Merlin did some shape-changing. The invention of extraordinary events at the time of the birth of heroes is a common practice. The most famous instance of this phenomenon is perhaps the stories of the birth of Jesus of Nazareth included in two of the four Christian gospels.

Geoffrey said Uther Pendragon was Arthur's father, because if he had written the truth, that Arthur's father was a Scots king called Aedan, it would have been impossible for him to maintain the fiction that Arthur was a man of the south of Britain. Geoffrey's patrons and audience lived in the south and they wanted their hero to live there too.

It is possible that Geoffrey really did not know who Arthur's father was and that he simply made a mistake when he said it was Uther Pen Dragon, but this is unlikely. It is likely that Geoffrey knew exactly what he was doing when he took history and used it to create a commercial behemoth. However he could not have known when he wrote his *History* that he had written an immortal work of genius. Nor would he have cared when he abused his sources to suit his book that he had left in enough original material to allow the historical Arthur to be rediscovered, but he did.

Geoffrey says that the crown of the kingdom was bestowed upon Arthur when "Arthur was a young man only fifteen years old."[1] The *Scotichronicon*, written by John of Fordun around 1384 and continued by Walter Bower around 1449 in Scotland, says Arthur was fifteen years old when he became "King." It is generally accepted that Arthur was fifteen years old at the time of the episode of the sword and the stone: "When Arthur was 15 years old he attended a coronation of the chiefs of the Britons who elected him their commander in chief."[2]

Several books say that Arthur Mac Aedan was born in 559, but there is no primary authority to this effect. However, given Aedan's age and the average time between generations, it makes sense to suppose that Arthur was born around 559.

If the evidence in Geoffrey and the *Scotichronicon* is accepted, then the legendary Arthur took a sword from a stone when he was fifteen years old. The historical Arthur, Arthur Mac Aedan, took a sword from a stone in 574. If he was born in 559, then he too was fifteen at this time. I know this reasoning is a bit circular but the birth date 559 just makes sense given the later career of Arthur Mac Aedan. He could not have been born any later than 559, because he would then have been too young to have been at Arderydd, and, if he had not been at Arderydd, it is unlikely he would have been given military command in time to fight the first of the twelve Nennius battles. He could, however, have been born as much as five years earlier and still have been young enough to do all that he did. Of course, fifteen years of age may well be a standard coming-of-age age. I understand that men of the Sioux Nation went into battle at this same young age. Be that as it may, circa 559 is as good a date for the birth of Arthur as any other.

The King's Knot, viewed from Stirling Castle, the round mound that inspired the story of The Round Table, lies beneath the remains of the sixteeenth-century garden.

© *Courtesy of Historic Scotland*

The Gartnait referred to as the son of the Pictish Princess Domelch is not included among Aedan's sons in any one of the three western Scots sources of evidence: Adamnan's *Life of Columba*, the *Senchus*, and the *Annals of Tigernach* (although it may be that he is included under another name). This apparent omission and the fact that Gartnait is a distinctly Pictish name (as opposed to the Scots names of Aedan's other sons) suggests a dichotomy between Aedan's offspring that can be explained if Aedan was married more than once.

Given the dangers inherent in childbirth in the sixth century, it is quite possible that Domelch did not live into her late twenties and that Aedan was married for a second time to a woman whose name we do not know. One of Aedan's daughters, Maithgemma of Manau, is said to have been the niece of a British king. Given that Aedan was not British, this suggests the British connection must have come through her mother. Domelch is identified with reference to Manau. Maithgemma's mother, whoever she was, is identified with reference to a British kingdom, probably Strathclyde (because Aedan was an ally of Strathclyde, and because there is, as we will see, reason to believe there were close family ties between Aedan's family and Strathclyde).

This lady of Strathclyde is usually called Ygerna or Igraine—that is, in Gaelic, Grainne—but this is probably a later invention. I will call her the Lady of Strathclyde. This albeit slight evidence, which suggests that Domelch was from Manau and Maithgemma's mother was from Strathclyde, points to Aedan having been married at least twice. The question arises—was Arthur Domelch's son or the son of the Lady of Strathclyde?

A second marriage to a lady of Strathclyde would have made good sense in the 550s, because at this time the main threat to Manau, after the Picts in the north, lay in the kingdom of the Gododdin to the east and in the growing threat from the Angles in the south. A political alliance with Strathclyde, cemented by a marriage to, say, a daughter of a chief, if not of a member of the royal family, would have bolstered Manau's position or Aedan's position.

There are several reasons to suppose that Arthur's mother was from Strathclyde or, at least, that she was not a Pict of Manau. In about 584 Arthur avenged his grandfather Gabhran's defeat in battle by the

Picts when he defeated Bridei Mac Maelchon, king of the Miathi Picts, near Perth. Despite this being Arthur's victory, in the aftermath of the battle Aedan made his son Gartnait, not Arthur, king of the Picts. This, taken together with the fact that Gartnait is a Pictish name, suggests that Gartnait was of Pictish blood on his mother's side and, more to the point, that Arthur, who did not have a Pictish name, was not.

If Arthur was the son of the Lady of Strathclyde, especially if she was a woman of the royal house, this would have been a factor weighing in Arthur's favor when he strove to lead the army of Strathclyde and indeed other armies, in the Great Angle War of the 580s. If Arthur was the son of the Lady of Strathclyde and so a Briton on his mother's side, in the eyes of the army of Strathclyde at least, he would have been one of their own.

If Arthur's mother was the Lady of Strathclyde this would also explain why when Aedan became king of the Scots in 574, he made Arthur his tanist—his chosen successor (besides, of course, the fact that Arthur was obviously the most able candidate). Aedan needed the support of Strathclyde to take the Scots throne. Making Arthur his tanist would have won favor in Strathclyde. Strathclyde would have wanted one of its sons in line for the throne of the Scots. The available evidence is slight, but, on the balance of probabilities, Arthur was the son of Aedan's second wife, the Lady of Strathclyde.

If Arthur Mac Aedan was born in 559, his birth would have been a year after his grandfather, Gabhran, died, probably from wounds sustained in battle against the Picts the year before. Gabhran was succeeded by his nephew, Conall Mac Comgall. Gabhran's son Aedan, Arthur's father, was overlooked. This was not necessarily a personal slight upon Aedan. The tanistry system of selecting the next king favored alternating the kingship between different houses of the royal family, and so just as Gabhran had followed his brother Comgall as king; Conall, Comgall's son, followed Gabhran. Aedan was just not the right man in the right place at the right time.

Aedan must have spent a lot of time about Dunardry-Dunadd when his father Gabhran was king, although it is likely that when Conall succeeded to the throne Aedan moved his main base of operations back to Manau; just as, in his day, Aedan's father, Gabhran, moved east to distance himself from his brother Comgall. This would have lessened the tensions inherent in having Aedan, a potential rival for the throne, present at Conall's court.

Arthur Mac Aedan was probably born in Manau, perhaps in Stirling, Manau's main capital fortress, or west of Stirling at Aberfoyle in the Trossachs, where Aedan is known to have had a base. However, if Arthur's mother was a lady of Strathclyde, it may be that Arthur was born there, perhaps even in the Royal Town of Partick where Merlin-Lailoken had a house.

Of course, whoever the historical Arthur was, there was no "wizard Merlin' present to facilitate his birth with magic, because Merlin was not a wizard and there is no such thing as magic. It is possible however that the historical Merlin-Lailoken, the son of Morken, a chief of Strathclyde, was party to the diplomatic negotiations that would have preceded a politically important marriage such as that of Aedan and a lady of Strathclyde. Although any role Merlin-Lailoken might have played would have been secondary, because Merlin-Lailoken was only nineteen years old when Arthur was born.

During Arthur's childhood Aedan was firmly based in Manau, and so despite the fact that Arthur was almost certainly fostered out into the care of another family, he probably spent much of his childhood there. As Aedan doubtless kept in touch with events and nursed his contacts in Dalriada to facilitate his accession should the throne become vacant, so it is likely that Arthur was at least an occasional visitor to Dunardry-Dunadd.

Bridei Mac Maelchon, the vastly warlike Pictish king who had defeated Arthur's grandfather Gabhran in 558, had been on the throne for only about two years when Arthur was born. Bridei was young, about twenty-nine (close to the same age as Aedan), and ambitious to expand his kingdom. It was therefore in the interests of Manau and the Scots of Dalriada to work together against this ferocious enemy. This put Aedan in a strong political position. He had a foot in one camp, Manau, and at least a toe in the other, Dalriada.

In the legends the young Arthur was the foster son of good Sir Ector because he had to be kept out of the way until the time was right for him to reappear as the "Rightful King." It may be thought that Malory invented the story that has Arthur fostered out into a family under Merlin's wing, but the historical circumstances surrounding Arthur Mac Aedan suggest that Malory might have built his fabulous fiction upon a factual foundation—fostering was a common Celtic custom in the sixth century.

No matter how unlikely it may be, Malory's *Le Morte d'Arthur* says that by the time Arthur had grown to be a young man—at the time of the episode of the sword and the stone—his identity as the son and heir of the late king, Uther Pendragon, had been forgotten by almost everyone. This part of the story is, of course, fanciful nonsense. One thing everyone in the first millennium agreed on was that a person's ancestry was important. Inaugurations of kings were only complete if a druid, and later a bard, recited the names of the king-to-be's ascendants to the people assembled. It is impossible to believe that a real king would undermine his son's chances of succeeding to the throne by putting him in a position where his identity might be forgotten. To have allowed a potential heir to be lost sight of would have been unthinkable. One thing was certain: if a historical Arthur was fostered out, he was not fostered out *incognito*.

Malory either did not understand the historical sources he had available to him, or, and this is more likely, he took actual events and re-wrote them in the interests of his fiction, because they were alien to his audience. One has only to think of the fairytale "Snow White" or the legend of Theseus to realize that a lost and unrecognized protagonist who is later found and restored to her or his rightful place is a common contrivance in fiction.

The unscrupulous Malory would not have hesitated before writing nonsense about Arthur being anonymously fostered out into Ector's family, no matter how unlikely such an event might have been, because this allowed him to have his Arthur make a grand entrance as the "rightful king" when he took the sword from the stone. However, it is possible that the passages in *Le Morte d'Arthur* in which Arthur is fostered out into Ector's family and in which Arthur takes a sword from a stone did not spring fully formed from Malory's head. It is possible that they were based on actual historical events.

According to the twelfth-century poem *The Birth of Brandub son of Eochu and of Aedán son of Gabrán,* Brandub and Aedan were twin brothers of an Irish king who were split up on the night they were born. The baby Aedan was exchanged for one of Gabhran's twin daughters, who had, by a happy and utterly amazing coincidence, been born on the same night. The result of all this was that each family ended up with a daughter and a son, and the potential for conflict that always existed between twin brothers was avoided. Much of this story may be dismissed under the category of "too good to be true," although it is possible there is some truth behind it and that Aedan, in accordance with Celtic practice, was fostered out into the family of Eochu.

As recently as the eighteenth century when the clan system was broken up, it was common practice among highland chiefs to foster out their sons to be brought up by friends and neighbors. This had the advantage of distancing vulnerable children from the dangers posed by rivals in their native clan. Fostering also allowed children an opportunity to gain a wider experience of the world and to form friendships that might be useful to them in their later lives. (For much the same reason, clan chiefs often engaged as bodyguards men from an allied clan. Such men were less likely to, quite literally, stab them in the back.)

If Aedan was fostered, it is reasonable to suppose that Arthur Mac Aedan too was fostered as a child. This Celtic fostering practice would have been alien to Malory, a man of the south of Britain, but if he read about it in one of his sources there can be no doubt he would have found it inspirational. It may be that Malory took the idea and used it to create the part of his story in which Arthur's identity is all but lost. This would have enabled Malory to have his Arthur's true identity revealed only after taking the sword from the stone. Malory's genius was that he was able to take two historical events, Arthur's fostering and Arthur's taking a sword from a stone (something Arthur Mac Aedan really did), and tie them together to create a dazzling story.

If Arthur Mac Aedan was the son of a lady of Strathclyde, he was probably fostered out into a Strathclyde family. There is no evidence to identify the specific family into which Arthur Mac Aedan was fostered (if indeed he was). However, Malory said that the legendary

Arthur's foster brother was named Kay. The family into which Arthur Mac Aedan was fostered may also have included a boy called Kay, because a man called Kay was killed in the ninth battle on the list of Nennius, a battle which, the evidence suggests, was fought in the south of Scotland by Arthur Mac Aedan.

As a child of importance Arthur Mac Aedan would have been placed with an important family if he was fostered out into a family of Strathclyde. This may have been the royal family, which included Languoreth, Merlin-Lailoken's twin-sister; Merlin-Lailoken's own immediate family; or, perhaps, the family of Anna, Arthur's older sister.

In *Finding Merlin* I said that Anna's first husband was a chieftain of Strathclyde, by whom she had three sons, Gawain, Gaheris, and Gareth: men who were always loyal to Arthur. (Anna subsequently married Lot of the Gododdin by whom she had two children: a girl Clarisant and Mordred.) If Arthur grew up with his nephews Gawain, Gareth, and Gaheris, this would explain their later loyalty. (The name Gawain is commemorated in the Glasgow district of Govan, today the home of Rangers Football Club. In the mid-nineteenth century an ornate sixth-century sarcophagus was discovered in Govan Old Parish Church and said to have been the last resting place of Arthur, although I think it is more likely it is the grave of Merlin-Lailoken's nephew, the vile Constantine, who became king of Strathclyde in 612.)

Of course, it is not necessary to claim that Arthur was fostered out into his Aunt Anna's family to explain the loyalty of the three brothers. If Arthur was in Strathclyde when he was a boy, he was still certain to have known his sister's family well.

It is not possible to say who Arthur's foster family was. There is just not enough evidence. But the most likely scenario is this: Arthur was fostered out into the family of a Chieftain of Strathclyde. Malory and others have Arthur under the eye of Merlin-Lailoken but not under his wing, which, if there is history behind this, suggests that Arthur's foster family was not Merlin-Lailoken's family. Neither is it likely that Arthur's foster family was his sister Anna's family because this would have defeated one of the main purposes of fostering—distancing a young vulnerable child from people with close family connections, who might have cause to harm him.

Given that Malory used an old Celtic name Kay (Cai) as the name of the young son of the house and not a more "modern" Anglicized name like Thomas, suggests that, just perhaps, there was history involved—that Malory had some evidence upon which to base his story, even if only a smidgen. Kay as a name worked in English. It survives today in names like MacKay.

What of Malory's name for Kay's father? If Malory used the name of the real person, Kay, for the son, then it was reasonable to suppose he would have used the actual name of the father for the father. Why not? Perhaps the name of the father did not work in English. In this event the simple thing to do would be to *make* it work, to translate it. Ector, the name Malory uses for Arthur's foster father translates to Hector in later English, which translates to Eachann in Gaelic. Malory could simply have deleted the Gaelic name Eachann and substituted the English, Ector.

It may therefore be that that Arthur was fostered out into the family of a man named Eachann, a chieftain of Strathclyde and the father of a son called Kay. I cannot say anything about the family of Eachann and Kay. I accept that their existence is based almost entirely upon my speculations. If there was an Eachann, and if his family was close to Merlin-Lailoken's family, either as neighbors or allies or both, this would allow for Malory's fictional version of history that has Merlin a close but not ever-present part of Arthur's childhood. This would also go some way toward explaining how it came to be that Merlin-Lailoken and Arthur worked together as allies—Merlin-Lailoken the politician and Arthur Mac Aedan the general—in the Great Angle War of the late 580s. This does not seem to me to stretch things too far. A scenario such as the one I have described could have provided the inspiration for Malory's version of the childhood of Arthur.

A scenario in which Arthur spent much of his boyhood in Strathclyde would explain why, in the earliest legends, the Celtic heroes Kay and Gawain were Arthur's closest companions. In the earliest stories they were relatively rounded characters, but in time, as the stories were Christianized and later Anglicized, Gawain and Kay proved to be too Celtic to survive intact. As time passed they came to be portrayed as somewhat dull figures, if not quite bumpkins—men who played second fiddle to more acceptable, less Celtic characters such as Lancelot and those two-dimensional Christian milksops Galahad and Perceval.

If Arthur was fostered out into the care of a family in Strathclyde, whoever they may have been, he would have crossed paths with Merlin-Lailoken. In the late 560s, Arthur Mac Aedan was about ten years old, and Merlin-Lailoken was in his late twenties and a champion of the people of the Old Way, who were locked in a fierce struggle with Mungo Kentigern's Christians for control in Strathclyde. The young Arthur would have seen the remarkable Merlin-Lailoken about the Royal Town of Pertnech (Partick) and on the Druid's Hill (the Glasgow Necropolis in the present day) near Mungo's church.

Street fights between rival parties escalated in numbers and ferocity until the situation became intolerable. Consequently, Tutgual, the king of Strathclyde, called Mungo Kentigern, the Christian leader, and Morken, the leader of the people of the Old Way and father of Merlin-Lailoken, to a peace conference. This ended when Morken threw Mungo onto the floor and gave him what in Glasgow is called *a kicking*.

Soon after this episode, Cathen the druid, Merlin-Lailoken's teacher, was pulled from his horse by a Christian mob and murdered. (Cathen was called "the Battler" by his friends and "the Blasphemer" by his Christian enemies, *Blaisbheum* in Gaelic. It is from this that we get *Blaise*, the name used by southern writers for Merlin's mentor and teacher.) This was the world in which Arthur grew up. It was a time of war, a time for which he was perfectly suited.

It is likely that when he came of age, probably when he was about fifteen, Arthur Mac Aedan returned to Manau and married a prominent Pictish woman and so secured his family's rights among the Picts. This marriage was to the woman known to legend as Guinevere, which, loosely translated, means "most lovely."

Mungo continued to stir up trouble in the early 570s, not just with the people of the Old Way but also with other Christians who would not accept his form of Christianity. By then Merlin-Lailoken and his twin sister, Gwyneth-Languoreth, were predominant among the people of the Old Way. (Gwyneth-Languoreth, queen of Strathclyde, was also known as the Lioness of Damnonia, and as the swan-necked woman.

She is the "adulteress queen," commemorated by the fish and the ring on Glasgow's coat of arms.) Together Merlin-Lailoken and Gwyneth-Languoreth defeated Mungo Kentigern, and in 572 they had him exiled from Strathclyde.

Mungo ended up in Wales where he met David, later the patron saint of Wales, but Mungo was not an easy man to get along with and so he soon fell out with David. He then went off to found a monastery of his own in Flintshire in north Wales, with a young man called Asaph as his lieutenant. Before long Mungo fell out with Asaph too and so headed north with his more fanatical followers, leaving Asaph to give his name to what is still today the bishopric of St. Asaph.

It seems likely that Mungo and those who followed him into exile brought with them to Wales stories of Mungo's struggle with Merlin-Lailoken and, perhaps, of the very young Arthur, although Arthur was in his teens when Mungo was in Wales and so this is unlikely. These stories, subsequently reduced to writing, would have become part of the records held by the monks of St Asaph. It is also possible that the monks of St. Asaph kept in touch with the monks who followed Mungo back to Glasgow.

It is unlikely that it is simply a coincidence that almost 600 years later Geoffrey was bishop of St. Asaph. It is unlikely in the extreme that of all the bishoprics in England and Wales, the one to which Geoffrey, the man who wrote so much about Arthur and Merlin and who did so much to popularize their legends, was appointed bishop, just happened to be the one founded by Merlin-Lailoken's mortal enemy, Mungo Kentigern. It seems more likely that Geoffrey found some source material through his St. Asaph connection and that this enabled him to, in effect, "invent" the legend of Arthur and Merlin. If this is correct, then it may be that Geoffrey was telling the truth when he said he based his stories of Arthur and Merlin upon a "certain very ancient book" given to him by his patron and friend, Archdeacon Walter. Geoffrey says Walter obtained the "certain very ancient book," "*ex Britannia.*"[3]

One eighteenth-century historian determined to fix Arthur in the south, J. S. P. Tatlock, wrote, "There can be no question at all that *ex Britannia* can only mean from Brittany."[4] This is but another example

Tatlock died in 1948.

of the tendency to wrench the stories of Arthur and Merlin-Lailoken away from their Celtic roots and "find" their origins somewhere else—anywhere except Celtic Wales or Scotland, in this instance in France.[5] Lewis Thorpe disagrees with Tatlock; he says *ex Britannia* means "out of Wales." This makes sense if the book was brought to the lands of the Anglo-Normans—that is, England—from the lands of the Britons —that is, Wales. In this event the book would properly have been described as being *ex Britannia*. If, as I have suggested, the father of Arthur—that is, Arthur Mac Aedan—was Aedan, then the question arises of why everyone else says that Arthur's father was Uther Pendragon (albeit without saying who Uther Pendragon was).

The mid-sixth century, in which Arthur Mac Aedan grew up, was a time of turmoil. The Britons of the southern Gododdin had grown soft under the shields of the legions, and so, when the Romans left, they found themselves prey to the more warlike Picts and Scots. In the following century Vortigern, the effete king of the southern Gododdin, unwilling to lead his people in battle, hired Angle mercenaries to fight for him.

The Angles, a Germanic people, came from across the North Sea in increasing numbers, until in 547 they reached critical mass, rose up against Vortigern, and expelled him from Berwick, the capital of his kingdom. Instead of rallying his people to resist the usurpers, Vortigern and his aristocratic supporters took to the hills, built fortresses, and hid. This allowed the Angles to march unhindered to the western sea where, as Gildas wrote, the Angle army licked the ocean "with its fierce red tongue."[6]

It was then that Emrys, a man of the people, a lowly captain of captains, "raised his head," inspired his people, and waged a guerrilla war that drove the Angles back to their eastern beachhead. Gildas was unable to accept this usurpation of the social status quo, and so in *De Excidio* he gave Emrys a fictional background and an upmarket name. Gildas said Emrys was the offspring of Roman Emperors no less, and called him Ambrosius Aurelianus, but Emrys was not an aristocrat. Emrys was a rough soldier, and so when he became the undisputed leader of the British resistance (after burning Vortigern's fortress with Vortigern in it) he needed a title.

Southern writers were bound to avoid any mention of Arthur's real father, Aedan, because it would have identified Arthur as a man of the north. Geoffrey and Malory decided to give Arthur a fictional father, Uther Pendragon.

Hadrian's Wall, which lay in the southlands of the Gododdin, was once the northern border of the Roman Empire and manned by cavalry auxiliaries from Sarmatia. The Sarmatians hailed from the steppes north of the Black Sea and rode into battle under Dragon-head standards tailed with windsock-like banners, which made a scary sound when they charged. So it was that just as the people of Strathclyde were the people of the Stag; the people of Caithness were the people of the Cat; and the people of Argyll, the people of the horse and later the boar; Emrys's people, many of whom were descendants of the Sarmatian auxiliaries and proud of their Sarmatian heritage, thought of themselves as the people of the Dragon.

In P-Celtic the word for "a head," as in "chief," is *Pen* and so Emrys, needing a title and being the chief of the people of the dragon, became the first *Pen Dragon*. The traditional histories have Emrys as a fifth-century man of the south because there is an empty space in the history of the south, and southern writers used Emrys to fill it. After Emrys was assassinated his second in command and Merlin-Lailoken's kinsman, Gwenddolau, became the second Pen Dragon. In later centuries Emrys was remembered as "the" Pen Dragon and Gwenddolau as the "other" Pen Dragon—in Scots, *Uthyre Pen Dragon*.

Emrys was active in the 550s and 560s, Gwenddolau in the 560s and 570s, and Arthur in the 570s, 580s, and 590s. Three great warlords: Emrys, Gwenddolau, and Arthur. All Geoffrey and his fellows had to do was take the identity of the "Other" Pen Dragon who chronologically preceded Arthur, delete references to Gwenddolau as an individual, and use the title that was left, *Uthyre Pen Dragon*, as if it were not only a name but the name of Arthur's father. *Hey presto*, they had, in its Anglicized form, Uther Pendragon, the name by which the legendary Arthur's father is known today.

The historical Pen Dragons were of the Old Way and therefore a threat to Christianity, and so memory of their actual actions was effectively eradicated as the centuries passed. This left the title they bore free and clear for Geoffrey and his like to use as they willed. There were three Pen Dragons. The third was a warrior called Mael-gwn, who fought bravely at Arderydd and ended up a pensioner in Merlin-Lailoken's home.

Of course the name Uther Pendragon was not connected with any royal house, and so it was impossible to place it in any existing royal list. This made it easy to place Arthur in some vague time (about the turn of the fifth century) and in some vague place (in the south of Britain). Everyone could claim the legendary Arthur and place him anywhere they liked, because he belonged to no one and to nowhere, at least, not in the south of Britain. There never was a historical Arthur in the south; in the south Arthur was pure fiction.

While the story of Arthur did "befall in the days of Uther Pen Dragon," Uther Pendragon was not a king, far less, as Malory said, a king of all England. Uther Pendragon was Gwenddolau, the man who led the armies of the Old Way at the Battle of Arderydd and made his name fighting Angles.

In time, as the stories of Emrys, Gwenddolau, and Arthur were gradually distanced from their historical and geographical origins, Arthur stopped being referred to as the son of Aedan, because this identified him as a man of the north, but at least the name of Arthur survived. The names Emrys and Gwenddolau, champions fit to stand with Arthur, have been all but lost to history.

When Vortigern and his coward courtiers headed for the hills to hide from the Angles, Emrys was left with too few educated people to govern the land of the Pen Dragons efficiently, and so, Gwenddolau, one of the few aristocrats to take Emrys's side, called upon his distant cousin, Merlin-Lailoken of Strathclyde, to assist him. The scholarly Merlin-Lailoken was in his late teens when he rode south to help Emrys and Gwenddolau administer the land of the Pen Dragons. In the next decade and more, Merlin-Lailoken divided his time between the peoples of the Pen Dragons and of Strathclyde.

In Strathclyde Merlin-Lailoken, his father, Morken, and his teacher, Cathen the druid, were among the leaders of the people of the Old Way, people who opposed the imposition of Christianity by Mungo Kentigern's Christians. In 572 the king of Strathclyde, exasperated by the civil unrest Mungo had engendered, sent Mungo into exile. Merlin-Lailoken must have hoped that Mungo's departure would have allowed the Old Way to become predominant again but this was not to be. The Christians, albeit the more moderate Telleyr Christians, remained in control in Strathclyde. This was too much for Merlin-Lailoken. He went against the wise counsel of his twin-sister Languoreth and recklessly sided with Gwenddolau against Strathclyde. When Strathclyde and its allies went to war against Gwenddolau and the people of the Old Way, Merlin-Lailoken found himself fighting against his native people.

The British policy was to surround the Angles with allied kingdoms that included Ebruac (York) and the kingdom of the North Pennines in the north of England; Rheged in southwest Scotland; Strathclyde in central Scotland and the Northern Gododdin in east central Scotland. The land of the Pen Dragons was the one break in this chain of allies.

Gwenddolau, son of Ceidio, son of the Sky God, the "Other" or Uther Pendragon, was a man of the Old Way, as were almost all the people of the Pen Dragons. As such he would have allowed a measure of freedom of belief and so undermined the progress Christianity had been making under the late king Vortigern. When people were free to choose they tended to revert to the Old Way, in the memorable words of Gildas, who had clearly been reading his bible, like "dogs to their vomit." Consequently the Christians of the allied British kingdoms were opposed to Gwenddolau being allowed into their circle of allies.

The Christians found ready allies in their opposition to the Pen Dragons in the established aristocracies, because Emrys and Gwenddolau had killed Vortigern, the last king of the southern Gododdin, and worse, because Emrys and Gwenddolau led their people on merit alone. These things represented a threat to the social order. For an established king to have recognized Emrys or Gwenddolau's rule or to have accepted them as an allies would have been to condone their actions, something no king could have countenanced. So it was that the Church and what passed for the State in the sixth century had common interests and powerful reasons to come together and crush

Gwenddolau and his counselor Merlin-Lailoken and the people of the Old Way.

This Church–State partnership, later called Christendom, was in an early stage of development at this time, but it must have been evident to Merlin-Lailoken that if Gwenddolau and the people of the Pen Dragons fell to an allied army marching under Christian banners, the end of the Old Way would follow swiftly.

6

The Sword in
the Stone

THE EARLIEST REFERENCE TO MERLIN-LAILOKEN IS THE *ANNAL* ENTRY
for the year 573, which tells of the "Battle of Arderydd, between the
sons of Eliffer and Gwenddolau son of Ceidio, in which battle Gwenddolau fell, Merlin went mad."[1]

The Battle of Arderydd is one of the most celebrated battles in
the poems of the late first millennium. It was the last pitched battle in
which the people of the Old Way stood in arms against the Christians.
It was a cataclysmic defeat for the people of the Old Way.

The battle was fought at Caer Gwenddolau, today the Liddel
Strength, a fort eleven miles north of Carlisle, on the Liddel Water that
forms the modern Scotland–England border. According to tradition
the legendary Arthur fought at the Battle of Arderydd. There is evidence for this, literally on the ground, in the parish of Arthuret, the
church of Arthuret, and the hills of Arthuret, all of which are near the
battlefield and Arthur Seat, seven miles to the east. The name Arthuret
has inevitably led to the area being associated with the legendary
Arthur. It has been said he was buried there, that Camelot was there,
and that Camlann, where Arthur fought his last battle, was in this area.

It is sometimes said that *Arthuret* originally meant "Arthur's
Head," although Skene says it is a modern form of *Arderydd*. However

Skene did not make the connection between *Arderydd* and the Ardrey place-names in Argyll, and so did not go on to connect *Arderydd* with Arthur Mac Aedan. If he had done so he would have seen that that Arthur Mac Aedan was connected to the place-name Arthuret because Arthur Mac Aedan's father's Men of Manau fought in the Arderydd campaign (and it is likely that Arthur was with them), and because, well, the names Arthur and Arthuret are all but the same. If this is a mere coincidence it is quite an amazing one. It is likely that the tradition that has the legendary Arthur fighting at Arderydd arose because Arthur Mac Aedan fought at Arderydd. (The young Arthur's elevation to warlord in the following year suggests he fought well.)

If the historical Arthur Mac Aedan fought at Arderydd when he was a young man, there would have been no reason for anyone to have taken any particular notice of him. If however, in later decades, the historical Arthur Mac Aedan became famous, and in later centuries became the legendary Arthur, then there would be reason for people who lived near the battlefield to remember his connection with Arderydd. It seems likely that a battle that was probably originally called the Battle of Caer Gwenddolau came to be called Arderydd because of its association with the high lord Arthur Mac Aedan, and with the high lords of war, Arthur Mac Aedan's *Ard Airighaich*.

Why would the Q-Celtic *Ard Airigh* be remembered in the P-Celtic-speaking lands in which the Battle of Arderydd was fought? Perhaps because of Q-Celtic poems that kept the memory of Arthur Mac Aedan alive for a time. Those who prefer a southern Arthur have to explain how there came to be a battle in the north in the late sixth century that involved a man called Merlin, when their southern Arthur was a man of the south in the early sixth century. It has been said there were two battles fought on the same ground, the first involving an Arthur—who this Arthur was is never made clear—in the early sixth century and the second involving a Merlin in the late sixth century. Of course, this precludes Arthur and Merlin being contemporaries and so begs the question, How come they end up together in the legends? It has been said there were two Merlins. Nothing is too much trouble for those who believe in a southern Arthur.

If Arthur was Arthur Mac Aedan, then he was about fifteen years old and Merlin-Lailoken was about thirty-three years old when they both took part in the Battle of Arderydd in 573, and there is no need for two battles at Arderydd or two Merlins. In my book there was only one Merlin and one Arthur.

Aedan, a close neighbor and ally of Strathclyde, joined the campaign against the people of the Pen Dragons, and the army of Manau fought alongside the army of Strathclyde at the Battle of Arderydd. Skene says Aedan was on the "Roman" side, that is, the side of the Christian party, in the Arderydd campaign. This does not mean Aedan was a Christian. Neither was Strathclyde a Christian land, not really. The army of Manau doubtless included Aedan's young son, Arthur, then about fifteen years old. This was to be his first campaign. Aedan and Arthur were, of course, men of the Old Way, indeed inveterate enemies of Christians like Columba-Crimthann. The Christians may have been ascendant in Strathclyde in the early 570s, and a Christian may even have been chancellor at the time of the Arderydd campaign, but the main mass of the people and Rhydderch himself were of the Old Way. Christian influence was strong, however, and growing, and so the allied army that marched against Gwenddolau (the Uther Pen Dragon), Merlin-Lailoken, and the people of the Old Way was, if not a Christian army then at least an army marching under Christian banners.

Rhydderch, prince of Strathclyde and Merlin-Lailoken's brother-in-law, led the allied army of the Britons south against the people of the Pen Dragons. The main bulk of his army was made up of the contingents of Strathclyde and the Gododdin but also included Aedan's Men of Manau and son, the young Arthur.

The motives of the various allies were mixed. Strathclyde and the Gododdin were spurred on by increasingly assertive Christian activity, and both were keen to avenge Vortigern, the leader of the southern Gododdin, who had been killed by the Pen Dragons in the 550s. Only Aedan was indifferent to these motives. He went along with the invasion simply to ensure he did not antagonize Strathclyde. He would need Strathclyde as an ally when he made his move to take the throne of Dalriada and become king of the Scots. None of this would have mattered to the young Arthur, who was only fifteen years old and about to fight in his first pitched battle—all he would have cared about was advancing fast and engaging the enemy.

The armies of Ebruac (York) and of the Pennines advanced from the south. Gwgon Gwron son of Peredur came in on the Pen Dragon's western flank. The Angles on Gwenddolau's eastern flank prudently kept out of it. Gwenddolau and his people of the Pen Dragon were effectively surrounded and vastly outnumbered.

Gwgon Gwron was the man remembered in the *Triads* as one of the "Three Prostrate Chieftains of Britain," specifically, as a man who "would not seek a dominion, which nobody could deny to [him]." When the Angles staged their coup in 547, Gwgon Gwron was one of the aristocrats who, along with their coward king, Vortigern, deserted their people and, literally, headed for the hills. It was this leadership vacuum left by these poltroons that was filled by the Pen Dragons: first by Emrys and then, after Emrys was assassinated, by Gwenddolau. The Angles chased Vortigern and the southern Gododdin aristocracy away from the seacoast into the west but did not capture and kill him. Emrys and Gwenddolau, finally frustrated by their ineffectual king, burned Vortigern to death in his fort.

Gwgon Gwron and his fellows then went further west, and there they sat and nursed their grievances until the time came when they could retake (what they thought of as) their lands. As the poem says, Gwgon Gwron was not prepared to take action to recover what was "rightfully" his (not until backed up by overwhelming force, worm that he was).

When they were sure that they would be on the winning side, Gwgon Gwron and the men of the west were the first to attack. As enemies closed in all around him, Gwenddolau had no choice but to fall back. I picture the young Arthur riding out ahead with the Men of Manau to seek out the enemy, while behind him the main force came on more slowly, pillaging as it went.

Gwenddolau fell back to his capital fortress, Caer Gwenddolau, and there turned and made a stand. He had no choice. His warriors were hardened fighting men who had won victory after victory against the Angles, but now they were vastly outnumbered and had no real chance of victory. Caer Gwenddolau is not open to attack from the north; the north wall of the fort faces onto a cliff that falls steeply down to the Liddel Water far below. Consequently, Strathclyde and her allies crossed the River Esk before joining the forces of Ebruac (York) and the Pennines and attacking from the south, from the direction of Arthur Seat and the Arthuret Hills.

Hardly had the chiefs had time to dress their lines before "the troops were fighting, falling on both sides in a miserable slaughter."[2] As the clash of armies continued, "the slaughter was terrible, Shields shattered and bloody."[3] One warrior, Maelgwn, was young, able and brave that day at Arderydd. When Maelgwn went into battle, "The host acclaimed him."[4] (Maelgwn would go on to become the third and last Pen Dragon and would end his days a pensioner at Merlin-Lailoken's fireside, where Ardery Street in Partick, Glasgow, is today.)

Merlin-Lailoken was in the shield-wall when, "Again and again, in great throngs they came . . . The savage battle was unceasing." The lines rushed together, blood flowed everywhere, and people died on both sides. Maelgwn led charge after charge against the enemy. "Swiftly came Maelgwn's men / Warriors ready for battle, for slaughter armed. / For this battle, *Arderydd*, they have made / A lifetime of preparation."

Three of Gwenddolau's brothers, chiefs in their own right, "Who had followed him through his wars, always fighting, cut down and broke the battle lines [slaying the enemy with] their hateful swords." But it was all to no avail: "[Gwenddolau's brothers] rushed fiercely through the crowded ranks with such an attack that they soon fell killed." When Merlin-Lailoken saw them fall he knew the battle was over. Sorely grieved he cried out, "You who so recently were rushing in arms through the troops, cutting down on every side those who resisted you, now are beating the ground and are red with red blood!"

Gwenddolau's army broke. "A host of spears fly high, drawing blood. / From a host of vigorous warriors— / A host, fleeing; a host, wounded— / A host, bloody, retreating." Strathclyde and her allies, including Arthur among his father's Men of Manau, launched a final attack from all quarters. "[They] wounded [Gwenddolau's warriors] and cut them down, nor did they rest until the hostile battalions turned their backs and fled through unfrequented ways."

Gwenddolau died shortly after the battle. Merlin-Lailoken, "Departed secretly, and fled to the woods not wishing to be seen as he fled."[5] The allied cavalry set out in pursuit, no doubt with the young Arthur among their number. They hunted Merlin-Lailoken across the rivers, over the hills, and through the trees of the southwest quarter of the Caledonian Wood.

The scattered remnants of Gwenddolau's army kept up a running fight that was later commemorated in the *Triads*. The *Triad of the Faithful Warbands* tells of the war-band of "Gwendoleu son of Ceidyaw at Arderydd, who maintained the contest forty-six days after their lord was slain." This long aftermath of battle suggests Merlin-Lailoken's people were hunted down with exceptional determination and ferocity. Be that as it may, Merlin-Lailoken and his fellow escapees found safety in the Caledonian Wood. "Sweet appletree in the glade, / Trodden is the earth around its base. / The men of Rhydderch see me not."[6]

Merlin-Lailoken eluded his hunters and, "For a whole summer after this, hidden like a wild animal, he remained buried in the woods, found by no one and forgetful of himself and of his kindred." "A whole summer" is poetic license. In reality Merlin-Lailoken hid out in the forest for seven years, during which time even the influence of his twin sister, Languoreth, a princess of Strathclyde, was not enough to bring him safely back.

Tutgual, king of Strathclyde, the man Merlin-Lailoken had betrayed when he deserted Strathclyde to fight for the Pen Dragons, died circa 580. He was succeeded by his son Rhydderch and so Languoreth, Merlin-Lailoken's twin-sister, became queen. It was only then that Merlin-Lailoken was able to return to favor in Strathclyde.

The "sons of Eliffer" referred to in the 573 Arderydd entry in the *Annales Cambriae*, included Rhydderch, son of Tutgual, the king of Strathclyde, and Eliffer, daughter of a chief called Peredur who was based in southwest Scotland. This Rhydderch, the husband of Languoreth, was the commander of the army of Strathclyde and its allies at Arderydd.

There were three other sons of Eliffer. The eldest, Morcant the Wealthy, is all but unknown. He probably died before the Battle of Arderydd because it was Rhydderch, the second born, who commanded the army of Strathclyde in that campaign. The third son has no part to play in this history but the fourth and youngest son does, because, his name, Ardderchddrud, is unique.

I said in *Finding Merlin* that Ardderchddrud is "a name with the same root as Arderydd," that is, it is derived from *Ard Airigh*. There is, however, an alternative. In Welsh P-Celtic, as we have seen, *dd* can be pronounced "th," and so Arderyth, two miles north of the town of Airdrie, is not only synonymous with Arderydd, it can sound the same. It follows that if *Ardderchddrud* stands to be pronounced "Artherchddrud," then, it may be, this name is not derived from *Ard Airigh* but from the name Arthur itself.[7]

As always it is all but impossible to tell exactly to what extent a name has been warped and whether this warping happened because it was misheard or misread or deliberately changed. We can only do what we can to make sense of the evidence we have, and must accept that, sometimes, there can be no definitive answer.

The only Arthur known to have lived at the same time as Ardderchddrud is Arthur Mac Aedan. They lived near each other and must have known each other. Ardderchddrud was also closely connected to Merlin-Lailoken. His brother, Rhydderch, was married to Merlin-Lailoken's sister, Languoreth. It is possible that, like Coriolanus and Scipio Africanus, Ardderchddrud was given his name because he excelled at the Battle of Arderydd, but this is unlikely. It would have taken until at least the end of the Great Angle War, in which Arthur won his main fame, and probably until after Arthur's death before Arthur's first battle, the Battle of Arderydd, came to be associated with him and his famous war-band—this would have been too late for the battle-name Arderydd to be attached to Ardderchddrud. Besides, Ardderchddrud was the brother of Rhydderch, the prince who led the army of Strathclyde at the Battle of Arderydd, and Rhydderch was a generation older than Arthur. If Ardderchddrud too was a generation older than Arthur it would be unlikely that he would be named after Arthur, a man who was not much more than a boy at the time of the battle.

I think it is most likely that Ardderchddrud was given this name because he was later associated with Arthur Mac Aedan, the high lord, and with Arthur's war-band, the high lords or *Ard Airighaich*. If Ardderchddrud was a much younger "son of Eliffer" and so closer in age to Arthur, it may be that he, like many other "younger sons," joined Arthur's war-band seeking fortune and glory. Or, perhaps he was Strathclyde's liaison officer in Arthur's camp in the Great Angle War and became associated with the *ArdAirighaich* because of this connection.

There is another possibility, although it is speculative in the *extreme*, as opposed to the preceding possibilities which are only *very* speculative. It may be that Arthur was fostered out into Ardderchddrud's house as a child and that, in later years, after Arthur became famous, Ardderchddrud was remembered with reference to this relationship and called Ardderchddrud for that reason. Who knows? I don't know. There is not enough evidence to say with any certainty what exactly led to this man having this name.

Whatever the true meaning or backstory, Ardderchddrud is a link between the legendary Arthur and Arthur Mac Aedan. The legendary Arthur is said to have fought at the Battle of Arderydd (as did Arthur Mac Aedan), and the personal name Ardderchddrud is similar to the battle-name Arderydd. Ardderchddrud's brother was Rhydderch, and so we may reasonably suppose that Ardderchddrud lived in the "Royal Town of Pertnech," present-day Partick, Glasgow, where their father was king. This was less than a mile from where Merlin-Lailoken lived from 600 until his death almost twenty years later.

The legend of Merlin-Lailoken as a wild man of the woods was inspired by his exile after the Battle of Arderydd, in the great forest that covered the south of Scotland. This legend is illustrated in a fine stained glass window in Stobo Church near his old hiding place. This window, being in a church, shows Merlin-Lailoken as a rough, hairy penitent kneeling before a gracious, good-looking Saint Mungo Kentigern. It was inspired by a meeting between Merlin-Lailoken and Mungo to negotiate Merlin-Lailoken's return that took place near Stobo, which is now called Merlindale. The exact meeting place was where the Pausayl Burn meets the River Tweed.

There is a similar stained glass window in the Chapel of Glasgow University. It shows a naked Merlin-Lailoken crouching at the feet of an exultant Mungo Kentigern. The University Chapel window is about a mile east of Merlin-Lailoken's home in the last few decades of his long life. Today this place echoes the Battle of Arderydd—it is called Ardery Street. The locations of these two windows are not just coincidental; they are both to be found close to where significant events happened in the real life of the real man called Merlin.

ARDERYDD WAS THE central point in the life of Merlin-Lailoken, who at thirty-three years of age and in the prime of his life was already a famous man in 573. The fact that Merlin-Lailoken was a leader of the people of the Old Way in 573 is the reason why he is prominent in the Arderydd cycle of poems. These poems were written by people of the Old Way for people of the Old Way. It was only later that they were recreated in the forms that have come down to us today.

The very fact that Arthur is not mentioned in the Arderydd poems lends some weight to their authority as historical sources. If they were purely fiction, it is likely, given that Merlin is prominent in these poems, that Arthur would have been included too. In reality, Arderydd did not play a major part in "Arthur's story"—it was merely the prelude to it.

It is likely that Arthur, like the teenage Alexander at the Battle of Chaeronea, fought bravely and well at Arderydd. He would not have been made warlord of the Scots of Dalriada within the year if he had been a sluggard in the charge or less than stalwart in defense. Of course, he was the son of a king so his elevation was not necessarily based on merit, but Aedan had other sons and given Arthur's later record we can safely assume he conducted himself with distinction at Arderydd.

In the years that followed, perhaps even many decades later after Arthur had become famous, it makes sense to suppose that the local people remembered and identified local sites with reference to Arthur. So we have the place-names, the Arthuret Hills and Arthur Seat, near the field where the Battle of Arderydd was fought.

It is hardly likely that a battle fought in a P-Celtic-speaking area and won by a predominantly P-Celtic speaking people would be given the Q-Celtic-Gaelic name, *Ard Airigh*. It is more likely that in the immediate aftermath of the battle it would have been called the Battle of Caer

Gwenddolau or, if the victors did not want to commemorate their defeated foe, the Battle of the Liddel Water, or some other such name, now forgotten. Then the poets, especially Arthur's friend and personal bard, Aneirin of the Flowing Verse, Prince of Poets, took a hand and began to create the legend that we know today. In time, as the fame of Arthur eclipsed that of Rhydderch, Emrys, and Gwenddolau and, indeed, everyone else, the Battle of Arderydd came to be remembered with reference to Arthur, the *Ard Airigh*, and his men, the *Ard Airighaich*. For hundreds, if not quite a thousand years, everyone seems to have worked on the time-tested basis that, if you know the truth and you know the legend, print the legend. The truth was that Arthur was not a central figure at Arderydd, but, when later he became famous, his legend overshadowed the truth.

Before long, probably within thirty years, the battle that we know as Arderydd began to be remembered, not with reference to its politico-religious significance (that was too boring), but with reference to Arthur and his famous warrior band, who had by then become famous in all of the kingdoms of the north. After the stories were taken south, Arderydd was thought of as a place-name when in fact it was a name connected to Arthur and his war-band. The fact that the majority of Arthur's warriors were Scots and Men of Manau would, of course, have been commercially unacceptable in the south, and so would have been left out of the stories. In time, the real meaning of the name was lost (because it was not a P-Celtic Welsh word) and so we have ended up with ideas like the "battle of the weapon of the oak."

The British and Scots were like the Greeks at the time of the Trojan and Persian wars; they remembered the deeds of individual warriors and bands of warriors. When, in later centuries, P-Celtic-speaking Britons from the lands of the Gododdin went south as refugees, they took stories of Arthur and the title *Ard Airigh* with them. In the south Arthur and his men, the *ArdAirighaich* were given a P-Celtic-Welsh-British twist in the P-Celtic adaptations of the stories that inspired the P-Celtic poems we know today. For example, *Ard Airigh* becomes Ardery, and with a Welsh *dd* ending we get Arderydd.

Some thirty years after the Battle of Arderydd, Merlin-Lailoken was pushed out of the Royal Town of Pertnech by the Mungo Christians and went to live in a house his sister, Languoreth the queen, had built for him, where he lived for the last years of his long life. The name of Merlin-Lailoken's house had an *Ard Airigh* connection. Even today, out of the 10,000 streets in Glasgow, only one has the name Ardery, and it is on the land where Merlin-Lailoken had his home. It is unlikely that Merlin-Lailoken called his home after Arthur or that people called Merlin-Lailoken's home after Arthur, no matter how famous Arthur had become. It is more likely that Merlin-Lailoken's home became a refuge for warriors of the Old Way, for the *Ard Airighaich*, and that through this connection it gained the name *Ard Airigh*, which still sounds in the name Ardery Street today.

Given the word *Airigh*'s special Ulster connections, the appellation *Ard Airigh* probably came from Ulster, perhaps with Fergus, Arthur's great-great-grandfather, and was brought to Manau by Gabhran, Arthur's grandfather.

Manau was located in the center of Scotland with four great powers around it: the Scots in the west; the Picts in the north; Strathclyde in the southwest; and the Gododdin in the southeast. It was border country and there was constant warring there. It was only natural that Manau would have attracted men from other places, men who were looking for a fight and the booty that successful fighting brought.

This sits comfortably beside the romantic picture painted by many medieval writers in which the best knights of all Christendom gathered at Camelot to compete with each other, to see who could do the best good deed. Reality was probably somewhat different. In reality men probably gathered in Manau because Manau was where there was fighting, and because Arthur was the most successful warlord of the day. Independent spirits; lordless men; second sons; outlaws; general roughs and toughs—these were the men who filled the rank and file of Arthur's war-band. They were the high lords of Arthur, the *Ard Airighaich*.

The war-band of the Red Branch of Ulster came to be called the Red Branch Knights. This allows some insight into what might have happened to the name of Arthur Mac Aedan's war-band. To begin with, they too may have been called a war-band and ended up being called knights: the Knights of the Round Table of the legendary Arthur.

Arthur Mac Aedan's men may have assembled in a circle around the mound that was recently found at Stirling Castle but not around a table or, at least, not a particularly special table.

I emphasize that all of the above regarding the name of Arthur Mac Aedan's war-band is speculative. All I can say is that it is consistent with the slight evidence available. This war-band of the *Ard Airighaich* probably increased in numbers when Gabhran was fighting the Picts and increased again when he went to Manau. It was this band of men that Arthur inherited when he became his father's war chief.

Aedan was politically secure at the end of the Arderydd campaign. He had answered Strathclyde's call to battle and shown the Britons that it was better to have him as an ally than as an enemy. Aedan could now expect Strathclyde to support him when he moved to take the throne of Dalriada and make himself king of the Scots. Arthur's battles, the battles in which Arthur was in command, were about to begin.

When Conall Mac Comgall, king of the Scots, died in Kintyre in 573, two candidates stepped forward ready to succeed him. The first was his nephew, Arthur's uncle, Éoganán Mac Gabhran, the tanist and so the establishment candidate. The second was Aedan Mac Gabhran, Arthur's father.

Duncan, the late king Conall's son, stepped aside in favor of Éoganán and was later to fight on Éoganán's behalf in the civil war that followed Aedan's accession as king. This was not because Duncan liked Éoganán but because he disliked Aedan; indeed, Éoganán's support from all quarters was not so much pro-Éoganán as anti-Aedan.

The two previous choices of king had alternated between the houses of Comgall and Gabhran. Comgall was succeeded by his brother Gabhran and Gabhran was succeeded by Comgall's son Conall. If this alternation were to continue the next king would come from the house of Gabhran, which would have ruled out Conall's son, Duncan.

Éoganán, however, was Gabhran's son by his second wife, a Scots princess of the house of Comgall, and so was of both the house of Gabhran and the house of Comgall. He was perfectly placed to garner support from both factions and to challenge Aedan's candidacy.

Éoganán had other advantages. He had been born and brought up in Dalriada while Aedan, the son of a Pictish princess, was an outsider from far off Manau. However Éoganán's most important advantage was that, like the late king Conall and unlike Aedan, he was a Christian sympathizer and so could depend upon the support of Columba-Crimthann and his monks. This was to be the first time religion played a significant part in the selection of a king of the Scots.

When Duncan gave his support to Éoganán he brought the house of Comgall with him and created a "dream ticket" that split the support of the house of Gabhran and weakened Aedan. Aedan, however, while something of an outsider was also a wily politician, and had doubtless cultivated support in Dalriada during Conall's reign. Aedan was far from finished.

In the late 560s the chiefs of Angus, based on the island of Islay, and the chiefs of Lorne, based on the island of Seil, rose in rebellion against Conall after he tried to impose Christianity in the outer isles. Their opposition to Conall and his Christian impositions made these chiefs natural allies of Aedan, who was, after all, a man of the Old Way. In later years Aedan and Columba, pragmatic political power-mongers both, would find ways, if not to work together, then at least not to work against each other, although they were lifelong enemies. It is likely that Aedan supported the rebel chiefs when they came out against Conall and the Christian party and that this guaranteed him their support and the support of the people of the Old Way when Aedan came to contest the throne.

Aedan had other advantages too. He came to the contest fresh from victory at the Battle of Arderydd, with a battle-hardened army at his back and with Strathclyde as an ally. He also had by his side his fifteen-year-old son, the martial wonder of the age, Arthur.

Dalriada-Argyll in the early 570s was riven between the two royal houses of Comgall and Gabhran, and between the Old Way of the druids and Columba-Crimthann's new, militant Christianity. When Conall died the slight consensus that had kept Dalriada from the abyss of civil war evaporated.

As a politician first and a soldier second, it is likely that Aedan tried to take the throne by civil means to begin with, instructing his supporters to debate with their opponents, offer bribes, and promise favors—the usual political activity that surrounded the choice of a new king. However, it must quickly have become clear to Aedan that no peaceful resolution was possible, because this time, for the first time, the matter of religion was a major factor.

Columba-Crimthann rallied his Christians in favor of Éoganán and Duncan and against Aedan. Aedan retaliated by accusing Columba-Crimthann of being a fool and a liar and by calling upon forty-seven druids to curse him.

This was an effective tactic. Columba-Crimthann's Christians may have ignored a Druid Wall at the Battle of Cul Drebne, but this had been in the heat of battle. In his quieter moments, Columba-Crimthann still believed in the existence of "Pagan" spirits and so the curses of Aedan's druids probably had some effect upon him. But whatever effect they had, they were not enough to stop him interfering in the race for the throne. So influential was Columba-Crimthann in his opposition to Aedan that Aedan tried to have him assassinated.

The second book of Adamnan's *Life of Columba* is entitled "Miracles of Power," although it is really only a fictional compilation of magic tricks Adamnan attributed to Columba-Crimthann. In this second book Adamnan writes of a man named Ioan Mac Conall Mac Donald of Aedan's house of Gabhran, who raided the lands of Colman, one of Columba-Crimthann's supporters, on the Ardnamurchan Peninsula. Of course, this is Adamnan's account, and Adamnan was a supporter of Columba-Crimthann, and so Ioan is described as "an evil man who persecuted good men."

On his third raid Columba-Crimthann chased Ioan away; probably with curses, because, as Adamnan says, shortly afterward Ioan drowned at sea as "predicted" by Columba-Crimthann: "Again the saint was proved right."[8] It is more likely that Ioan simply drowned and that Adamnan jumped on this fact and used it when he came to enhance his pretense that Columba-Crimthann had magical powers.

At about the time of Ioan's death, circa 568 to 570, Columba-Crimthann and Conall, king of the Scots, were attempting to expand Christian influence north and west by recruiting men like Colman who, in exchange for patronage and land, were prepared to pay tithes to Columba-Crimthann. As I understand Adamnan, Ioan and Colman were engaged in the Hebridean equivalent of a "range war." It was probably Conall's promotion of the likes of Colman that led to the revolt of the chiefs of Angus on Islay and Lorne on Seil, in the north and west of Argyll.

The troubles continued with Columba-Crimthann "excommunicating those men who persecuted churches, in particular the sons of Conall Mac [Donald]"; these were the brothers of Ioan, the lately drowned Aedan supporter. It is however unlikely that the sons of Conall were excommunicated, because it is unlikely they were Christians in the first place. Supporters of Aedan they were almost certainly men of the Old Way.

In any event, what follows is what I believe happened in the early 570s. When it became clear that Conall the king did not have long to live, the supporters of the two most likely contenders for the throne started to jockey for position. On one side was the house of Comgall, whose candidate was Éoganán, Aedan's half-brother. Éoganán had the support of Duncan, the son of Conall the late king, and of Columba-Crimthann and his Christian churchmen. On the other side was the house of Gabhran, represented by Aedan and the rebellious chiefs of Islay and Seil, all men who favored the Old Way.

When the curses of his druids failed to stop Columba-Crimthann, Aedan took steps to have him killed. Adamnan says someone called Lám Dess and his fellow conspirators sailed to the unidentified island of Hinba and there lay in wait for Columba-Crimthann to assassinate him. When Columba-Crimthann and his monks arrived Lám Dess confronted him and then tried to kill him with a spear.

> Now, at the devil's prompting a man from the band of these men of evil attacked St. Columba with a spear, meaning to kill him. To prevent this one of the brethren, called Findlúgan, stepped between them, ready to die instead of the saint. As it happened he was wearing St. Columba's cowl and miraculously this garment acted like a strong, impenetrable, breastplate that could not be pierced, however sharp the spear . . . The man wearing this protection was untouched and unharmed. But the wretched man, whose name means "Right Hand," thought he had pierced the saint with his spear and made off.[9]

When Adamnan says these "men of evil" were of "the royal lineage of *Cenél nGabráin* [*sic*]"—that is, of Aedan's house—he makes plain that the "devil" in this matter was Aedan himself.[10] The name Adamnan gave to the would-be assassin, Lám Dess or Right Hand, is a definite hint that this man was acting on behalf of someone else—that is, as someone else's right-hand man. This someone else was almost certainly Aedan.

Much of what Adamnan writes are lies gauged to deceive people, but, I believe, there is some truth behind this story and that there really was an attempt upon the life of Columba-Crimthann. Columba-Crimthann appears to have known he was in danger, and, just as Saddam Hussein used doubles to avoid assassination; it seems Columba-Crimthann used Findlúgan as a human shield. This caused Lám Dess to make his unsuccessful attack upon Findlúgan, thinking he was attacking Columba-Crimthann. The stuff about the miraculous cowl that acted like a breastplate is obviously untrue and simply designed to mislead the most gullible people. It is more likely that Findlúgan was a decoy and that he was given Columba-Crimthann's cowl to wear to draw the assassins to him. It appears Findlúgan was no fool and that he decided to wear a breastplate too. It also seems likely that Columba-Crimthann was tipped-off.

Lám Dess was killed a year later fighting on the unidentified Long Island. Of course, as almost always, Adamnan says Columba-Crimthann predicted the time of Lám Dess's death precisely. We do not need to take this seriously—Columba-Crimthann did not have the gift of foresight and Adamnan had the gift of hindsight.

Ioan and Colman fought small-scale fights. Chiefs, like the chiefs of Angus of Islay and Lorne of Seil, fought middling battles. Full-scale civil war had not yet broken out. This had only been avoided when Conall brought in Christian mercenaries from Ireland to quell the revolt of the chiefs of Angus and Lorne, of Islay and Seil.

Despite Adamnan's efforts to disguise the truth, a careful reading of his über-biased *Life of St. Columba* reveals what really happened at this time. Adamnan could get away with writing about miracles, but facts were a different matter. Adamnan's problem was that he was writing within 100 years of Columba-Crimthann's death

—a time when, through the oral tradition, people still knew something of what had actually happened—and so he was somewhat limited in the lies he could tell. He could invent as many miracles as he liked, no one could gainsay him there; he could "airbrush" out of history much that did not suit his book, which was a lot; and he could put a positive Columba-Crimthann-spin on everything else, but he could not mess too much with the big hard facts of history, one of which was that Columba-Crimthann opposed Aedan becoming king.

Adamnan is reduced to pretending that although Columba-Crimthann initially may have lent a tad towards the side of Éoganán, his god quickly put him right and told him he had to plump for Aedan. The most important implication of this nonsense was that this enabled Adamnan to claim that while Columba-Crimthann may have backed the wrong horse in the first place, Columba-Crimthann was still God's chosen one.

Despite Columba-Crimthann's spectacular political misjudgment, people were told that they could still rely on him to tell them what to do, because his god was always there to put him right; at least, according to Adamnan. People have believed this for centuries. In reality, Columba-Crimthann was simply determined to be on the winner's side, whomever that might be. To paraphrase a Bill Clinton campaign trope, "It's the power, stupid."

This is how it happened according to Adamnan:

> [Columba] saw one night in a mental trance an angel of the Lord sent to him. He had in his hand a glass book of the ordination of kings, which Columba received from him, and which at the angels bidding he began to read. In the book the command was given to him that he should ordain Aedan as king, which Columba refused to do because he held Aedan's brother Éoganán in higher regard.

If the supernatural elements in this passage are disregarded it comes down to this—Columba-Crimthann supported Éoganán.

Whereupon the angels reached out and struck [Columba-Crimthann] with a whip, . . . Then the angel addressed him sternly: "Know then as a certain truth, I am sent to you by God with the glass book in order that you should ordain Aedan to the kingship . . . But if you refuse to obey this command, I shall strike you again. In this way the angel . . . appeared to St. Columba on three successive nights, each time having the same glass book, and each time making the same demand that he should ordain Aedan as king. [Columba-Crimthann] obeyed the word of the Lord."[11]

If the supernatural elements in this passage are disregarded it comes down to this—Éoganán was Columba-Crimthann's preferred candidate, but when it became clear that Aedan was likely to be the winner, Columba-Crimthann backtracked. Having backed the wrong horse, Columba-Crimthann had to repair his and his god's credibility in the eyes of the people. He pretended that while he had made a mistake his god had corrected him, and that Aedan was his god's chosen one after all. Columba-Crimthann knew that his power lay in his ability to convince people that he had a direct-line to "God" and that by taking the blame himself in this way he could keep his options open for the future.

The above and what follows is based on Christian sources, because the many other sources that were once extant have been lost or destroyed.

Now Columba-Crimthann had to curry favor with Aedan. According to Adamnan, "[Columba-Crimthann] sailed from Hinba to Iona, where Aedan had arrived at this time, and he ordained him king . . . he laid his hand on Aedan's head and blessed him."[12]

This authorized version has Columba-Crimthann taking the initiative and boldly seeking out Aedan with a view to providing him with his blessing. However Cumméne, Adamnan's predecessor as Columba-Crimthann's hagiographer, says Columba-Crimthann was on Iona *when Aedan arrived*, which suggests that Columba-Crimthann was not quite so keen to see Aedan as Adamnan suggests.

It seems to me more likely that having all but secured his throne at Delgon, Aedan was traveling about his new kingdom, making himself known to the local chiefs, rewarding and penalizing as he went, until he got to Iona where he found Columba-Crimthann.

Cumméne and Adamnan agree that Columba gave Aedan his blessing on Iona. There are no independent witnesses to this event but I do not doubt it took place. If this blessing had mattered to Aedan it is likely it would have occurred in public, in front of the people of Dunadd. I do not believe that whatever ritual Columba performed on Iona was important to Aedan. This rite of ordination has been held up as the first time a king of the Scots was made king according to Christian practices, but it was nothing of the kind. This ordination was not the historical "big deal" that almost every writer on the matter has said it was. Aedan became king according to the Old Ways at Dunadd. That was what was important: that and the fact that militarily Aedan had the whip hand.

Columba-Crimthann's performance on Iona was just that, a performance, the purpose of which was to allow Columba-Crimthann and his followers to bruit it about that he, Columba-Crimthann, was a kingmaker. Aedan probably went along with it because to him it would have been mere ritual and because he was interested in doing a deal.

Columba-Crimthann's biographer, Ian Finlay, says that when Columba-Crimthann became involved in the kingship selection process, "the embers of *Cul Dreimme* [Cul Drebne] [seemed] to glow again."[13] Columba-Crimthann's blood may have been up when it looked like Éoganán might win, but the glow of the embers of Cul Drebne seem to have faded quickly because within a short time Aedan and Columba-Crimthann had agreed that Columba-Crimthann would support Aedan's political claims if Aedan would "forget" about Columba-Crimthann's earlier opposition to his kingship and allow him to remain in Dalriada. This deal suited Aedan because he had more to concern him than his animosity toward Columba-Crimthann; he was determined to secure the independence of Dalriada Scotland from Dalriada Ireland. If he had to compromise with Columba-Crimthann, who had powerful political connections in Ireland, to win over the Christians of Irish Dalriada, he would do it. Columba-Crimthann still had influence, and Aedan, ever the political operator, would not have failed to make use of this, and make use of this he did the following year at the great council of Drumceatt.

The most weighty evidence concerns the Christian Columba-Crimthann because most of it was written by his apologists or was censored by them. Consequently, there is little direct evidence of the doings of lay-people, such as Aedan and Arthur. Judging by the evidence that has survived what probably happened was this. When Éoganán, Duncan, and Columba-Crimthann proved to be immoveable—at least, by peaceful means—Aedan decided that the kingdom should go to the strongest—that is, to him. He then preempted the traditional and legitimate decision-making process by marching on Dunardry-Dunadd and occupying it, probably without much, if any opposition, given that he had struck first and so had the advantage of surprise. This did not mean that Aedan was secure in Dalriada, far from it.

Aedan had still to meet Éoganán's main force in battle, and so his position was tenuous. Anxious to add at least a veneer of legitimacy to what was, in effect, a coup d'état, Aedan took steps to have himself inaugurated king. (By ancient tradition, Scots kings were inaugurated, not crowned.) It was in his interest to ensure his inauguration was in accordance with the ways of the people of Dalriada, Picts and Scots both, and so the inauguration ceremony had to take of place on the summit of Dunadd, the place where the Scots of Scottish-Dalriada and before them the Scots and Picts and before them the Picts alone, had inaugurated their leaders. Like the rocks at Edinburgh and Stirling, Dunadd Rock is an obvious place for inauguration ceremonies, because like Edinburgh and Stirling rocks it, literally, stands out in the landscape.

Inauguration on the summit of Dunadd would have enabled Aedan to demonstrate that he was the de facto ruler of Dalriada or, at least, that he was powerful enough to command its two main capital forts, Dunardry being a short hop away, across a marsh. Inauguration on the summit of Dunadd would send out a signal to the undecided that Aedan was the man to support.

The Picts and Scots who lived in Argyll before Arthur's great-great grandfather Fergus arrived there had performed their special ceremonies on Dunadd.

> In about 500 came a fresh invasion . . . from . . . Ireland, led this time by the three sons of Erc. [Fergus Mac Erc] now established a new Scottish dynasty taking as their capital the rock-fortress of Dunadd . . . There to this day you may see, carved in the solid rock, the wild boar that was their heraldic and dynastic symbol and the footmarks where successive monarchs stood to be crowned [sic] . . .[14]

There is also, carved in the solid rock, the shape of a bowl, although the exact use to which this was put is unknown.

The Stone of Destiny, the stone upon which by ancient tradition Scots monarchs sat when they were inaugurated, had been brought to Scotland from Ireland by Fergus, Arthur's great-great grandfather.[15] Fergus kept the Stone of Destiny in the fortress town of Beregonium, modern-day Benderloch in the north of Argyll. This was the land of the chiefs of Lorne, the same chiefs who had recently rebelled against Conall and who were, by the above account, Aedan's allies, and so it would have been easy for Aedan to have the Stone of Destiny brought south. Given Aedan's easy access to the Stone of Destiny he would undoubtedly have used it at his inauguration.

In 1902, John Crichton-Stuart said, in his *Scottish Coronations*,[16] that the people in the Lordship of the Isles used a flat stone into which a footprint was cut in their ceremonies of inauguration. Apparently the chief-to-be, dressed in white, entered into a covenant with the people by placing his bare foot in the stone. He was then presented with a white wand and a sword, symbolizing his duty to do justice and defend the people. The "white" elements in this account hark of the druids and echo Pliny the Elder, who told of druids clad in white robes cutting mistletoe from oak trees and catching it in white cloths. (Merlin-Lailoken, a druid, lived outside the Royal Town of Partick, at *Ard Airigh* (modern Ardery Street) on the banks of the River Clyde, next to the White Island of the Druids, which, although it has been dredged away, is still commemorated in the modern district name, Whiteinch.) The references to white are clear, albeit inconclusive evidence that the druids of the Old Way had a part to play in these inauguration ceremonies.

Having placed his bare foot in the stone—according to John McLeod in his book *Highlanders*—the Lord of the Isles then turned "sunwise" three times, taking in the four points of the compass, while brandishing the sword to the acclaim of all. [17] It has long been supposed that footprints carved into rocks were part of pre-Christian inauguration ceremonies, symbolizing the king's union with the land and so with his people. There are two footprints at Clickhimin, Shetland; there was one outside the church at Wedale in the borders (where Arthur fought and won a battle against the Angles), and we must suppose there was a footprint somewhere in the Lordship of the Isles. It may reasonably be inferred that something similar to the events that occurred when a Lord of the Isles was inaugurated occurred at Dunadd in 574 when Aedan was made king.

In 574 Aedan was inaugurated king of the Scots when he sat on the Stone of Destiny on the summit of Dunadd before the people of Dalriada. He then placed his foot in the footprint shape carved into the stone and brandished a sword to the four points of the compass, while his supporters (and those who thought it wise to pretend to be his supporters) cheered his elevation. A bard then recited his lineage to demonstrate to all present his "right" to the throne, even though no one could have been in any doubt that Aedan's inauguration was only taking place because of his military might.

Aedan cannot have forgotten that his great-grandfather Fergus died within a year of becoming king of the Scots and that Fergus's successor, Aedan's grandfather, Domangart, was dead some six years after that. Aedan's father, Gabhran, had died soon after defeat in battle, probably of his wounds. Aedan must have known that being a king of the Scots was a dangerous business, even when that king was universally recognized and there was no internal opposition.

He must also have known that he would soon have to fight to secure his throne and so he would also have appreciated how important it was to have a recognized successor if there was to be a smooth succession in the event of his death. There was also the real danger of assassination. This could be lessened if, in the event of his death, it was accepted that his tanist would succeed and that consequently nothing would change to the advantage of the assassin's party.

Aedan could increase the chances of a smooth succession and decrease his chances of being assassinated if he appointed as tanist someone who was loyal to him and in a position to take command should he be killed. Arthur had distinguished himself at Arderydd (as evidenced by the place-names Arthuret and Arthur Seat that would in years to come be found about the battlefield) and so was an obvious choice to be tanist. Arthur was about fifteen years old when his father became king of the Scots

If Arthur was his father's tanist, his inauguration as such probably took place at the same ceremony at which his father was inaugurated king. Civil war was looming and there would have been no time to gather people together again for a separate ceremony.

Arthur would not have sat on the Stone of Destiny—that was for kings alone—but, like the Lord of the Isles and whoever used the footprints carved in the stones in Shetland and in the Borders, Arthur would have symbolized his union with the people and the land by putting his foot into the footprint carved into the stone of Dunadd and, just as his father had, by brandishing a sword to the four points of the compass. When he stepped out of the footprint carved into the stone on the summit of Dunadd, Arthur, quite literally, took a sword from a stone and, although he could not have known it at the time, stepped into legend.

All it takes is a little lateral thinking. Arthur took a sword from a stone but it was not, as Malory said, stuck in a stone or an anvil; Arthur took a sword from a stone the same way someone might take a book from a room. If one person told another person that a third person had taken a book from a room, the person who was told this would not think the book had been stuck in the floor or in the wall of the room. That would be ridiculous.

However, by the time men like Malory came to write of a legendary Arthur, the historical events upon which the legend was based had been told and retold to such an extent that much of their underlying truth had been lost. By the time Malory came to write his marvelous story of the sword in the stone, the Celtic Britons of the south had been conquered: first by the Germanic Anglo-Saxons and then by the Scandinavian-Gallic Norman-French.

These people did not understand the ways of the Celts of the sixth century or, if they did, were disinclined to propagate them. However, I suspect the broad truth that Arthur was a man of the north was generally known and that it was deliberately changed to disguise the fact that Arthur was a Celt and, worse still, a Scot.

In fairness to Malory, his telling of the story of the sword and the stone story is magnificent and it may be he simply wrote it the way he did because it was a commercial crowd-pleaser. But to the Christians who controlled almost all communications for one thousand years after the time of Arthur, the ceremony of the sword and the stone would have smacked of the Old Way. This would have been unbearable. This was a matter of choosing a "king" (at least it was according to Malory), and choosing a king was too important a matter to be left to anybody other than the Church.

Consequently, Malory went to great lengths to ensure the sword and the stone episode took place under the authority of an Archbishop of Canterbury, despite the fact that there were no Archbishops of Canterbury at that time (whenever that time is held to have been by those who favor a southern Arthur): "So the Archbishop, by the advice of Merlin, sent for all the lords of the realm . . . that they should come to London by Christmas, upon pain of cursing . . ."[18] The Christian influence in this passage is palpable. Malory clearly felt he had to make it clear that when it came to choosing a king, the Church had to be in control. Pure storytelling demanded that Merlin be the main mover in the story, but Malory was not brave enough to put storytelling first and so bowed to the power of the Church.

Even this was not good enough for Malory: he was extra-cautious. For Malory even taking a sword from a stone was too close to the truth—too close to the earth, too close to nature, too close to the Old Way. Just to be on the safe side, he added something manmade to the sword and stone story to act as a buffer between him and any suggestion of the Old Way. He had Arthur take a sword from an anvil that was set on top of the stone. This cover-up of the part the Old Way had to play in Arthur taking a sword from a stone has been effective for more than 500 years.

All it takes to see what had really happened is a little lateral thinking and a little knowledge of the time and place where Arthur Mac Aedan lived. If Arthur Mac Aedan was not inaugurated tanist at Dunadd in 574 and so did not take a sword from a stone, then quite a few coincidences exist that need to be explained, not least among them the connections between Merlin's presence at Arderydd in 573 and Arthur Mac Aedan's presence at Dunardry in 574 and at Badon in the shadow of Dunadd.

Despite the best efforts of Malory, Geoffrey, and all the other writers who favor a southern Christian Arthur, the Arthurian canon is clearly steeped in the Old Way. This has led some to tortuous lengths to explain elements that are obviously not Christian. One has written, "Whatever is pagan in the Arthurian material was knowingly put there by medieval authors. They may even have done it in jest."[19]

It is more likely that the opposite is true and that Christian writers in the thousand years that followed the time of Arthur went to extraordinary lengths to minimize references to the Old Way, to create a Christian basis for the legendary stories of Arthur. The truth is not that a few "Pagan" elements have sneaked into the Arthurian canon but that Christian propagandists have been unsuccessful in censoring all the many references to the Old Way of the druids in the early sources, despite their best efforts.

As for these references being there as jests, this is preposterous. By any reading of almost any early Christian source, it will be clear that one of the things early Christian writers lacked entirely was even a hint of a sense of humor.

TODAY MOST PEOPLE think the sword and the stone episode is pure fantasy, and, of course, in its magical details it is, but, it is also fundamentally true, as can be seen when it is set not in fiction but in history, in the place and time where it occurred: in Dalriada, Argyll, in the year 574, when Arthur Mac Aedan, the man who became the legendary Arthur truly took a sword from a stone.

Kingmaking by taking a sword from a stone is unique to the legend of Arthur. Arthur had once taken a sword from the stone on the summit of Dunadd, and I knew that sometime soon someone else would do the same thing. I wanted my son, Eliot, to be the first person known to have taken a sword from this stone since Arthur.

The only problem I had was that I did not *have* a sword. I am not a sword type of person. There are, however, several shops that sell swords to tourists on Edinburgh's Royal Mile, within a hundred yards of where I work, and so I bought a sword.

On May 25, 2002, just after dawn and in heavy rain, my then eleven-year-old son Eliot and I climbed to the summit of Dunadd. The rain and the time of day worked to ensure that there was no one about to see us, which was good because I wanted to keep the location of the stone a secret and I didn't want to be seen running about Argyll with a large sword that the police might have considered an offensive weapon.

I kept the sword a secret from my son by following him up the hill with it wrapped in a car-shawl, which I carried alongside a golf-umbrella. When we got to the top of the summit of the fort and I produced the sword, he took it in stride, although, I suspect, if he had known the story of Abraham and Isaac he might have done a runner.

I had Eliot put his foot in the footprint first to empty it of rain-water before I had a go. I am not daft. The footprint is average size. I wear a 9½ / 44 shoe, and it fit me perfectly.

My son then put his foot back in the footprint, and I gave him the sword to hold. When he stepped out of the footprint he became the first person known to me to take a sword from the stone from which Arthur once took a sword, since Arthur. (I was too self-conscious to do the same.)

As we walked back down the hill to the car park I explained that the sword was not a real sword and that I had bought it in an Edinburgh gift shop. Eliot said that did not matter, because the sword Arthur had taken out of the stone was Arthur's father's sword and the sword he had taken from the stone was *his* father's sword, and so it was just the same. The special moments come unexpectedly.

By 575 AEDAN was sufficiently secure to leave Argyll for Ireland to attend the great council of Drumceatt. Argyll was at peace or at least subdued, and so he was almost certainly accompanied by Arthur, who had a lot to learn. Columba-Crimthann too was included in Aedan's train.

The hillfort of Dunadd, the ceremonial capital of the Scots of Dalriada, Argyll. The footprint seen in the foreground is the origin of the "Sword in the Stone" legend.

The council of Drumceatt was held outside Limavady near the north coast of Ireland. All the kings and great chiefs of Dalriada-Ireland and Dalriada-Scotland were there, including the mighty Aed Mac Ainmire of the Northern Ui Neill, one of Columba's kinsmen.

The surviving sources are creations of Columba-Crimthann's propagandists or have been filtered through the censorship of his partisans for more than a thousand years, and so they tend to present Columba-Crimthann as the most important person who traveled from Scotland to Ireland for this council, but this was Aedan's expedition, arranged at his insistence, and Columba-Crimthann was only a useful fellow traveler.

Doubtless there were innumerable matters discussed at this meeting, but records of only three have come down to us: the freeing of a hostage called Scandlán More; the suppression of the bards of Ireland, and the relationship between Dalriada Scotland and Dalriada Ireland. The matter of Scandlán is not relevant to Arthur. As for the bards, unless all these people got together at Drumceatt and decided to come down hard on some popular entertainers, for bards we must read druids.

In *Finding Merlin* I argued that after the Christians suppressed the druids, they set about eradicating all memory of them by deleting direct references to them. For example, Jocelyn, Mungo Kentigern's hagiographer, wrote of "certain wicked men" when he meant druids. In time it became standard practice to avoid the word *druids* and terms like *evil men*, because evil men suggested a threat. Instead, when druids were relevant, they were referred to as bards. Any threat the memory of Merlin-Lailoken might have presented was neutered when he was reinvented in the stories as an old wizard. Arthur too was tamed when he was made a Christian, English king and, just to be sure, a cuckold too. Nothing could have been less threatening to those in power than such a man.

The druids are best pictured not just as religious men; they were interested in far more than the supernatural. They were, in effect, a professional class; individual druids, both women and men, specialized in various fields, including law, agriculture, meteorology, history, and geography. Some composed and performed poems.

As the Middle Ages approached their high point, those who practiced in these various fields found they had to do so under the auspices of the Church, except women of course—women were no longer allowed to engage in such practices. Women, quite naturally, continued to use their intelligence and skills by providing medical services, especially midwifery, the one area the Church shied away from. Almost one thousand years after the age of Arthur, during the reign of James VI, thousands of women were tortured to death as witches in Scotland alone. These were women who would have been druids when there were druids.

The idea was that only those "in the know" would know the meaning of the code-word *bard*, although most people were not daft and would have known exactly what was going on. Eventually, however, the true import of bardic references became blurred and was forgotten, until, for almost everyone, bard just meant bard.

The conventional line is that the authorities at Drumceatt were annoyed because bards were taking liberties and so had to be suppressed, but there had been bards since time immemorial, and there would be bards in one form or another for centuries to come without it ever again being felt necessary to curb them in such a drastic way. Bards taking liberties does not explain what happened.

It is no mere coincidence that this occurred at the same time that Christianity was ascendant in Ireland. Gildas himself had visited Ireland at the invitation of the recently deceased King Ainmire to promote his form of Christianity within the preceding decade. It seems likely that by the time of Drumceatt, the Christians had enough support to enable them to strike at the druids.

It is worth noting that no such agreement was reached regarding the "Bards" of Scottish-Dalriada, a clear indication that the balance of power between Aedan and Columba-Crimthann was weighted in Aedan's favor. But the main subject of agreement as far as Aedan and Arthur were concerned was recognition of Dalriada Scotland as an independent kingdom, not as a sub-kingdom of Dalriada Ireland. This was achieved. When the Council of Drumceatt came to a close in 576 Aedan was secure at home and abroad.

It was probably about this time that Arthur was married. He was only in his mid- to late teens, but marriage at this age would have been the norm in the sixth century. Of course, as everyone knows, according to the legends Arthur married Guinevere and they did not live happily ever after. It was not quite like that in real life.

When the civil war was over and the negotiations at Drumceatt concluded, Aedan and Arthur turned their attention to the threat posed by the Miathi Picts. It may be that this threat was one of the reasons Aedan had Arthur marry a Pictish princess of Manau. Such a marriage would have helped secure his family's position in the east, something that would have been especially important at a time when the Miathi Picts were threatening.

7

Camelot

THE STORY OF ARTHUR IS SO WELL KNOWN THAT IT IS NOT NECESSARY to signal it with Arthur's name—the names Merlin, Lancelot, or Guinevere will do. Even the name of Arthur's sword, Excalibur, will do, or the name of the place where he lived, Camelot. Excalibur is, without a doubt, the most famous sword there has ever been, and Camelot is, if not the most famous place there has ever been, certainly up there in the reckoning. The legendary Arthur had two swords: the sword he took from the stone and Excalibur, the sword given to him by the Lady of the Lake. This is counterintuitive. One warrior, one sword makes more sense. Rodrigo Diaz, *El Cid*, had two swords, Colada, a Spanish sword and Tizona, a Moorish sword, but then he led Spaniards and Moors and so this makes sense.

Perhaps there is some good reason why the legendary Arthur had two swords, but one reason is obvious. Malory had two good stories: the sword and the stone story and the Lady of the Lake story in which Arthur is given the magical sword Excalibur. These two stories required two different swords, and Malory was not prepared to leave either story untold. Of course Arthur could not take a sword from a stone and the same sword from a lady in a lake, and so two swords were necessary.

To begin with I dismissed both of these stories because they both involve the supernatural. There is no such thing as the divine right of kings and even if there was, it would be preposterous to suppose that the choice of a king would be left to the whim of a supposedly magical stone. Neither are there such things as a magical swords and even if there were, to believe that one might appear out of a lake in the hands of a woman who lived under the water, would be absurd.

Malory's stories are counterintuitive in one other way. It would make more sense if the sword used in the king-picking event was the most valued sword. Swords used at coronations and inaugurations are usually especially highly prized. Common sense dictates that this sword should be Excalibur. Common sense also dictates that this ceremonial sword would not be a fighting sword used day-to-day in battle.

Malory had a problem: how was he to keep both of his wonderful stories and still have the right sword in the right place at the right time? Unfortunately he did not have a wonderful solution. Malory's solution was to make the sword Arthur took from a stone an ordinary sword and have it broken in battle soon thereafter, and to make the sword taken from the lake a special sword, indeed a magical sword, Excalibur. This had to be so because Bedevere would not have hesitated before throwing a workaday sword into the lake. The sword Bedevere threw into the lake had to be Excalibur. Only the return of Excalibur to the Lady of the Lake could have provided the Big Finish Malory wanted to end his fabulous tale.

Malory had to write his story the way he did because he wanted to end *Le Morte d'Arthur* with the famous scene in which, in the aftermath of the Battle of Camlann, the mortally wounded Arthur instructs Bedevere to return Excalibur to the Lady of the Lake. Arthur had come straight from the battlefield and so this sword had to be the sword Arthur had been using in the battle, that is, his fighting sword. This sword also had to be the sword given to him by the Lady of the Lake, because the Lady of the Lake would not have been happy if she was fobbed off with some other sword. This means Excalibur had to be Arthur's fighting sword.

All that is necessary to work out what really happened is to delete the magic and look at the history that is left. Arthur is said to have taken a sword from a stone. This is usually taken to be a purely magical and so fictional event but, if Arthur was Arthur Mac Aedan, Arthur taking a sword from a stone has a non-supernatural explanation. Arthur Mac Aedan took a sword from a stone when he stepped from the stone of Dunadd.

Arthur is said to have been given a sword by the Lady of the Lake and to have returned this sword to the Lady of the Lake, but, if Arthur was Arthur Mac Aedan, this too has a non-supernatural explanation. Throwing valuables such as swords into lochs, marshes, and rivers as tribute to the spirits some people thought lived in such waters, was a common Celtic custom that still echoes in the modern practice of throwing coins into fountains and wishing wells. It was probably this Celtic custom that inspired Malory to write the wonderful ending of *Le Morte d'Arthur*.

The only part of the two sword-stories that defies sensible explanation is the part where Arthur is given a sword by an underwater female armorer, the Lady of the Lake. This is purely magical and so just did not happen. It seems likely that Malory, having decided to write about Arthur's sword being thrown into water, went too far and invented the wonderful passage that has Arthur's sword coming out of water.

Arthur Mac Aedan took a sword from a stone at Dunadd in 574 without any supernatural input. This does not mean that this sword was not a special sword. Indeed, given that it was the sword used in inauguration ceremonies, it would be reasonable to believe that it was a very special sword. It is unlikely that this ceremonial sword was the fighting sword Arthur used in his last battle. This ceremonial sword was probably too important to be used in battle, and, in any event, it is impossible to believe that any one sword would have survived more than one or two, far less a dozen battles. It is more likely that the ceremonial sword Arthur took from a stone was kept safe to be used in the next ceremony.

Given that it is quite possible that the sword Arthur used in his last battle was thrown into water after his death, the question arises, Which sword was this? Of course, if there is no need to believe the fanciful nonsense that has Arthur being given a sword by the Lady of the Lake, there is no reason to believe this sword was a particularly special sword. The sword used by Arthur in his last battle and thrown into water after his death may simply have been one of many fighting swords he used in battle.

According to the legend, Arthur was recognized as the rightful king only after he took a sword from a stone. In history Arthur Mac Aedan's right to be his father's tanist was not recognized because he took a magical sword from a magical stone. There was nothing supernatural about Arthur taking a sword from a stone on the summit of Dunadd; on the contrary, Arthur took a sword from a stone only after it was decided that he should be his father's tanist.

The inauguration ceremony in which Arthur took a sword from a stone also involved the Stone of Destiny that Arthur Mac Aedan's great-great-grandfather, Fergus Mor Mac Erc, had brought to Scotland from Ireland. Although there is no record to the effect, it would be reasonable to suppose that the sword used in inauguration ceremonies had also been brought to Scotland from Ireland at the same time. If so, the sword used to inaugurate the kings of the Scots of Scottish-Dalriada could properly be described as a sword of Scotland and of Ireland.

Over six centuries, any description of this sword is likely to have become garbled as it was passed from mouth to mouth by people unfamiliar with the culture from which it sprang. It is possible that after six centuries this sword could have been forgotten or, if remembered at all, remembered by some bland name such as "the inauguration sword," but it is also possible that it was given another name.

Geoffrey's name for the legendary Arthur's sword is Caliburn. The sword Arthur Mac Aedan took from a stone was a sword of both Scotland and Ireland—that is, in Latin, a sword of *Caledonia* and of *Hibernia*, two names that can be clearly seen to form part of Geoffrey's composite name, Caliburn. It may be that the name Caliburn sprang fully formed from Geoffrey's head, but if it did, it would be an incredible coincidence.

All that is necessary to create Excalibur is to take *Caledonia* and add *Hibernia* after deducting the aspirate. Dropping or not sounding the aspirate is common in Gaelic: the island of Iona, for example, had various alternative names, including, with an aspirate, the name Hi, and, without an aspirate, the single letter name "I." The aspirate is missing in Iberia, which includes Spain, a part-Celtic land, especially in the west, where lie Galicia and Portugal, names which hark of their Celtic Gaelic connections. Iberia has the same root as Hibernia. One euphonic end result of all this is *Cal-ibernia*, from which it is not far to Geoffrey's Caliburn.

It may be that Geoffrey had a description of "Arthur's sword" that included the names *Caledonia* and *Hibernia*, and it may be that this inspired him to invent the name Caliburn, alternatively it may be that the names Caledonia and Hibernia were already confused by the time they came to Geoffrey's notice. Who knows?

What we do know is that Geoffrey wrote within a century of the Norman-French conquest of England and was subject to Norman-French influences, and so was bound to use names that would please his Norman-French audience. Arthur Mac Aedan's special sword may have been properly described as a sword of both Scotland and Ireland, but it would not have been in Geoffrey's interest to emphasize this. *Caliburn* would have suited his purposes much better.

Wace sat down with Geoffrey's *History of the Kings of Britain* to write his *Roman de Brut* a generation after Geoffrey. Wace was Norman-French and writing in France, and so he was untrammeled by British ties and free to give Arthur's sword whatever name he chose. Wace could have built on Geoffrey's Caliburn by making Arthur's sword extra big, powerful, sharp, or frightening—*Supercalibur*, perhaps—but no, Wace, who seems to have had some idea of the origins of the name Caliburn, called Arthur's sword Excalibur. *Ex*, that is, "out of" or "from," plus Caliburn, gives us *Ex Calibur*, the sword that came out of or was from Scotland and Ireland. Geoffrey was a man of Wales and Wace a man of France, but Arthur Mac Aedan's special sword was, quite literally, a sword of Scotland and Ireland. If Arthur was Arthur Mac Aedan, then the sword name Excalibur makes sense.

The name Excalibur may have an explanation, but what about the name Arthur? In 574, the year he took Excalibur from the stone of Dunadd, Arthur would still have been viewed as an outsider in Argyll. Although many members of the house of Gabhran supported Arthur's father Aedan when he fought to win the kingship of the Scots, many others of the house of Gabhran, and almost the entire house of Comgall, favored Aedan's rival Éoganán. To most of the people of Dalriada, therefore, Arthur was not only an outsider but an unwelcome outsider and, worse, an outsider who had been party to the use of force to take control of Dalriada. It would not have boosted Arthur's popularity among the natives of Dalriada that he was made tanist, given his first independent command, and told to crush all opposition to his father's rule, and that he did exactly that.

In these circumstances it would not be surprising if Arthur had been given an uncomplimentary nickname. Nicknames were common in the sixth century. The prefix *Mor* was particularly popular among warriors. Merlin-Lailoken's father was called Morken, *Mor Ceann*, literally, Big Chief. It is, therefore, reasonable to suppose that Arthur too was a nickname.

There is another, simpler, explanation for the name Arthur: one that not only applies to Arthur Mac Aedan especially but also explains why the name Arthur became more popular about the time of Arthur Mac Aedan (although I accept this explanation is somewhat speculative).

I was picturing Arthur standing with his foot in the footprint in the stone on the summit of Dunadd, holding Excalibur high and turning to the four points of the compass, north, south, east, . . . and then it struck me: although Arthur's Scots family had come to Argyll from the west, from Ireland, Arthur as an individual had come to Argyll from the east, from Manau.

In Q-Celtic-Gaelic east is *ear*. *Ear* is derived from the Old Irish Gaelic *an-air*, which is derived from words that meant something akin to "from before," that is, facing the sun. When Arthur stood on the summit of Dunadd, with his foot in the footprint, holding Excalibur, Arthur was facing the land of the rising sun and his home in Manau.

What if the people who had been born and brought up in Argyll saw Arthur for what he was, an eastern newcomer?

Air added to the Gaelic word for land, *tir*, a word which has the same root as the English words terrain and territory, gives, in Old Irish Gaelic, *Airthir*, which roughly means east land: although MacBain, in his *Etymological Dictionary*, says *Oirthir* (a variant spelling) simply means east. However, the meanings of words are always difficult things to determine at a remove of 1,500 years, and so it is impossible to be certain of the exact provenance of any one word or formulation.

What if, just as Gary Cooper was the "Westerner" in the eponymous film, Arthur was called something like *Oirthir* or *Airthir*, because to the people of Dalriada he was an easterner, and what if a variation on this theme produced the name Arthur? (It is worth noting that in some Irish accents Arthur is pronounced as *Oirthir*.)

Arthur came to Dalriada when he was about fifteen years old and was almost immediately inaugurated as tanist and made a warlord. Given that he had been born and brought up in the east, in Manau, the native Scots of Dalriada must have viewed him as something of an outsider at this time. It is easy to see that they may have called him, somewhat disparagingly, something like, *The Easterner*, and that this name may have stuck.

Alternatively, given that so many Scots had crossed from Dalriada-Ireland in the west to Dalriada-Scotland in the east, it may be that increasing numbers of boys were called something like child of the eastlands, that is, something like *Oirthir* and *Airthir*, and that Arthur was one such child.

Arthur Mac Aedan was doubly a child of the east, because his people had gone east to Argyll and then his family had gone further east to Manau. If the name Arthur is rooted in the Gaelic for *east*, it would explain the increase in the frequency of the use of the name Arthur at the time of Arthur Mac Aedan, because at this time the Irish-Scots were increasingly raiding and settling along the west coast of Britain, that is, from the Irish point of view, the east.

It is more likely however that the name Arthur became famous and consequently more frequently used as the fame of Arthur Mac Aedan spread and later, when the historical Arthur Mac Aedan was cut out of the picture, when the fame of the legendary Arthur took off. This eastern connection would also explain why the MacArthur family originates in Argyll. It has been supposed that the MacArthurs took their name in honor of the legendary Arthur (which, of course, only works if the legendary Arthur was Arthur Mac Aedan). It may be however that they gained the name MacArthur simply because they were sons of the East Land of the Gaels, that is, Argyll.

That Arthur might also have had some "bear" connections does not detract from the above speculation, indeed, it adds to it. The resentful locals, if they were anything like us, and they were, would have enjoyed the double-edged nature of the nickname Arthur, because it would have afforded them some protection if he took umbrage.

I emphasize that my above speculations are just that, speculations. It is not a subject I am comfortable with because, if Arthur is a nickname, the question arises—what was his real name? According to Adamnan, Aedan had four sons; Arthur, Domangart, Eochaid Find, and Eochaid Buide, which is all right by me, but according to the *Annals of Tigernach* Aedan's sons had other names: "The violent deaths of the sons of Aedan, Bran and Domangart and Eochaid Find and Arthur, at the Battle of Chirchind in which Aedan was the victor and at the Battle of *Coraind*."[1]

I am probably safe because Arthur is mentioned here alongside Bran, that is, Brian, and so they are probably different people. But what if they were not? What if Arthur was a nickname and Bran-Brian was his real name? It was too awful to contemplate. I would be writing *The Life of Brian*.

IT IS SAID that "whether [Camelot] actually existed and its location are still the subject of much scholarly disagreement."[2] How can this disagreement be settled? What evidence can there be?

Camelot was the legendary Arthur's capital. If Arthur Mac Aedan was the legendary Arthur, it follows that Arthur Mac Aedan's capital may be Camelot, but where was Arthur Mac Aedan's or, more to the point, his father Aedan's capital? Aedan was king in Manau and king of the Scots of Dalriada, and so there are several possibilities. The capital of Manau was probably Stirling Castle Rock, although some sources say Aedan's capital was at Aberfoyle. In Argyll there was one obvious capital fort, Dunadd, although there is reason to believe Dunadd was the ceremonial capital and Dunardry the administrative capital. In any event, I knew of no evidence that suggested either Dunadd or Dunardry was Camelot. I had stood on the summit of Dunadd and on the slopes of Dunardry, and I had looked all about me, but I had seen nothing and

I could think of nothing that suggested Camelot. As it turned out, I couldn't see the wood for the trees.

Claudius Ptolemy, the second-century Alexandrian cartographer, called the River Add, *Longus Flavium*, the Long River, although the Add is not a particularly long river. It may be that in the second century the local people called their river something like the marshy river because that is exactly what it was, and indeed, to a lesser extent, still is. If so, and if they used the especially early Argyll-rooted word *lòn*, which means marsh, it is easy to see how Ptolemy could mistakenly have called the marshy river the long river, *Longus Flavium*. In Gaelic this is *Abhon Fhlada*, from which it is said the river name Add is derived. Different languages, the passage of time, mishearings, carelessness, mischief, and stupidity: all of these things can and have led to such confusion.

Although not particularly long, the River Add *is* particularly twisted. For its last few miles, from the village of Kilmichael Glassary west to the Sound of Jura, it meanders through the vast *Moine Mhor*, Great Moss. This wide expanse of low lying, marshy land (now a bird sanctuary) causes the river to twist and turn in large loops on its way to the sea.

At first I did not think Ptolemy was relevant to the matter of Arthur, but then I reconsidered the early Argyll-rooted word *lòn*, "marsh," with reference to the Irish-rooted Q-Celtic of Arthur Mac Aedan's Scots. Arthur Mac Aedan's Q-Celtic-speaking Scots would have rendered marsh or marshy not as the early *lòn* but as the later *loth*. I saw a possibility—one that was relevant to Arthur.

Cam means "twisted" or "crooked" and *loth* means "marsh." Put the two together and we have *Cam-Loth*, twisted or crooked marsh: a perfect description of the land about Dunardry-Dunadd.[3]

Camelot was neither Dunadd nor Dunardry, far less Stirling Castle Rock, Cadbury, Colchester, or Carlisle. Camelot was a corrupted description of the land that lay about and between Dunadd and Dunardry, the twin hillforts of Dalriada.

Even today, after centuries of drainage, the River Add still runs a crooked path through the Great Moss to the Sound of Jura. It is easy to picture the way this area would have looked in the sixth century, when the marsh was wider and deeper. In the sixth century it would have been even more likely that someone would describe the marsh as twisted by the river, or as the crooked marsh, *Cam Loth*.

My name Ardrey is written in the fourteenth-century land titles, the *Poltalloch Writs*, as *Ardarie* and *Ardare* before becoming *Ardarike* and even *Dare*, all in the space of one hundred years, and these variations were in important legal records written in the place to which these place-names referred. How much easier would it have been for *Cam Loth* to become *Camelot* over six centuries, during which descriptions of the place where Arthur Mac Aedan had lived were passed on orally from Q-Celtic speakers to P-Celtic speakers to English speakers to French speakers, with, no doubt, innumerable Latin speakers also being involved along the way? Some corroboration for this idea can be found in Maxwell's *Scottish Place-Names*. Maxwell's *camlodain*, the bend of the swamp, is close to my *cam loth*, crooked marsh.

It is unlikely that Chrétien simply invented the name Camelot—why would he? Stories of Arthur were plentiful in the vast oral tradition, and his patron Marie de Champagne had provided him with an abundance of source material, although what these sources were, whether they were "Celtic, Classical or contemporary," no one knows exactly.[4] It was quite open to Chrétien to take what he wanted from what he had, and use it to name Arthur's capital, albeit in a corrupt form.

It is very possible that some of Chrétien's source material originated hundreds of years before his time, in the form of oral accounts by people who had actually seen where Arthur Mac Aedan lived. Someone would have said something like, "Arthur's base was a fort surrounded by a marsh through which a crooked or twisted river ran." Picture this informant describing the place where Arthur lived using the words *cam* (twisted, crooked) and the Q-Celtic *loth* (marsh). Picture these words, *cam* and *loth*, being conflated by non-Gaelic speakers as Cam-Loth and ending up with a name that was more euphonic to a French speaker's ear—Camelot.

If Chrétien had no source material and just invented the name Camelot, it would be quite a coincidence if he simply hit upon a name with Gaelic roots that describes the place where Arthur Mac

Aedan lived and where Arthur's father the king of the Scots had his capital. It may be this evidence is too slight to stand alone but, of course, it does not stand alone. Even today the ideals that are exemplified by the name Camelot are inextricably linked with Arthur, but Arthur did not make his name because of idealism. Arthur made his name, and made it a legend, by war. Before he took the sword from the stone, Arthur had always fought under another's command. Soon after he took the sword from the stone he was leading his first fighting force. From then on, Arthur was in always in command, not only of armies but on occasion of kings.

8

The Scottish
Civil War

CIVIL WAR BROKE OUT AMONG THE SCOTS OF DALRIADA IMMEDIATELY after Aedan's inauguration as king, and Arthur, who had just taken a sword from a stone, soon had to wield a sword in his father's cause.

Éoganán, Aedan's half-brother and Arthur's uncle, a man of both the houses of Gabhran and Comgall, and his main supporter Duncan Mac Conall of the house of Comgall, had been caught off balance by Aedan's march on Dunardry-Dunadd, but they had not been completely defeated; they were still in the field and not prepared to give up without a fight.

The *Annals of Tigernach* tell of a decisive battle in the year 574, probably in the first few weeks or months after Aedan's inauguration, "The Battle of Delgon in Kintyre, in which Dunchad [Duncan] Mac Conall Mac Comgall and many others of the House of Gabhran were killed."[1] The house of Gabhran was divided. Some of them fought alongside Duncan for Éoganán of the house of Gabhran against their friends, neighbors, and relatives of the house of Gabhran who were on Aedan's side. Duncan "and many others of the House of Gabhran were killed," means that Duncan of the house of Comgall and many others, who were of the house of Gabhran, were killed.

The Battle of Delgon was Aedan's victory. Delgon is not among the twelve battles of Arthur listed by Nennius. This makes sense. After all, Arthur was only about fifteen years old at this time. He may not even have been present at Delgon, and present or not, he was not in command at Delgon: he was too young.

This insight allowed me to place the Battle of Glein, the first of Arthur's battles listed by Nennius, both geographically and historically. Arthur was not in command at Delgon because he was too young, but he was in command at Glein, and yet, it seemed, Delgon and Glein were fought at about the same time, perhaps in the same year. How could this be? There had to be something about the battles themselves.

I am grateful to John N. McLeod for identifying the site of the Battle of Delgon as the island *Ealain da Ghallagan* in West Loch Tarbert, south of Lochgilphead.[2] McLeod wrote in the late nineteenth century, and so he did not have access to modern maps that were available to me, which perhaps explains why he does not appear to have noticed corroborating evidence for his identification. Two miles southwest of McLeod's battle-site of Delgon is the island of *Eòghain*, that is, the island of Éoganán, a name that commemorates the man who lost the Battle of Delgon.

It seems likely that Aedan and Arthur caught Éoganán and Duncan off guard with a lightning advance to Dunardry-Dunadd in the heartlands of Dalriada and forced Éoganán and Duncan to retreat to the south, where they strove to marshal their supporters and build an army. Aedan stopped his advance only long enough to be inaugurated before setting off in pursuit. It makes sense to suppose that Arthur was not with the main body of the army that followed Éoganán and Duncan. The matter of the kingship was still an issue while Éoganán and Duncan remained undefeated in the field, and many people must have remained undecided as to where their loyalties lay, and so Aedan and Arthur's position was insecure. It seems likely that Arthur remained at Dunardry-Dunadd to ensure Éoganán's supporters did not rise against his father. In any event, it would have made sense to separate Aedan and Arthur at this time lest they go down to defeat and death together, leaving their forces without a recognized successor.

The armies met at Delgon. Aedan's army had momentum, and his men could claim they were the army of the king. Éoganán and Duncan's army had probably been hastily put together, and was probably demoralized by recent events.

It is probable that Éoganán was only an ineffectual figurehead, a *Toom Tabard*, an Empty Shirt, and that the real power lay with Duncan. In any event, when the battle was over Duncan was dead, along with many of his house of Comgall and many of the house of Gabhran who had chosen to fight for Éoganán.

Éoganán was either not with his main battle-force or, when he saw that his people were losing, he retreated to the small island further down the loch that bears his name today. The fact that this island is now called *Eòghain* suggests either that he was based there before the battle or that he held out there after the battle while he negotiated terms, or perhaps both. Éoganán was allowed to go into exile in Ireland. Aedan, ever the politician, would have seen that clemency might bring some of the house of Comgall and those of the house of Gabhran who had taken up arms against him to accept him as king.

If Aedan and Arthur separated after their inaugurations, and if Arthur, who was about fifteen years old at that time, was deemed too young to be given command of an army (although only just), and if Aedan went off to fight and win the Battle of Delgon, where did this leave Arthur?

It would be unreasonable to suppose that Arthur was given command of an army immediately after his inauguration as tanist: he was still in his mid-teens. He was however the son of the new king, and he had probably acquitted himself well at the Battle of Arderydd, and so it makes sense to suppose that he was given some form of independent command.

Éoganán's main army had been defeated at Delgon, and Éoganán himself was in exile, but there must have been many discontented men of Éoganán's faction still at large. It is likely that it was in action against these men that Arthur won his first independent victory. The battle-list of Nennius's begins, "The first battle was at the mouth of the river called *Glein*." In this one line there are three clues: "Glein" is first on the list, Glein was fought at the mouth of a river and the river was called Glein.

Glein is the first battle on the list, and so, in effect, it is on an open flank, with no earlier battle to point to where it might have been fought. I had to wait until I had identified the next five battles before I was able to work backward and find Glein. The other eleven battles turned out to have been listed in chronological order, and so it was reasonable to suppose that the Battle of Glein really was the first of twelve battles fought under the command of Arthur Mac Aedan. The other eleven battles also turned out to have been fought in close proximity to each other and in a pattern that made it possible to see that one battle naturally followed upon the one before it and led on to the one that came next.

When I found the locations of the four Douglas battles, battles two to five, and Bassas, the sixth battle, and drew a line from Bassas through the sites of the Douglas battles, I found that this took me to Argyll. This made sense. Arthur played a part in the coup that had brought his father to power in Argyll in 574, and there had been fighting soon thereafter, at Delgon. It made sense to suppose that, if Glein was fought at about the same time or soon after Delgon, that the Battle of Glein was fought in Argyll.

Arthur was in Argyll in 574, before the first of the Douglas battles was fought. Argyll was, quite literally, where the action was at this time. Everything suggested that the first battle, Glein, was fought in Argyll. This was not, of course, conclusive—far from it.

Who might Arthur have fought in Argyll? The obvious answer was, of course, supporters of Éoganán and Duncan and the House of Comgall, but they had been beaten at Delgon and so there was no reason to believe the Battle of Delgon was the Battle of Glein. On the contrary, while there are innumerable burns and rivulets in the vicinity of Delgon, there is no large river that might have given its name to the battle.

I looked for another battle in the records that might be Glein by another name but without success. Delgon had merited an entry in the annals. Glein did not. I thought, perhaps the Battle of Glein was not as important as the Battle of Delgon and so did not justify an *Annal* entry. This made sense. If Delgon was a large battle, it might have its own *Annal* entry for this reason, and, if Glein was a small battle, it might not have an *Annal* entry for this reason.

It is unlikely that Arthur, who was still very young at this stage, would have been entrusted with command in a vital battle. He may have been the titular warlord of the Scots, but I could not see that, even allowing for the fact that Arthur had proved himself at the battle at Arderydd, Aedan would have entrusted him, an untried commander, with command of an army at such a crucial time.

I looked again for a possible Glein battlefield, but given there are nearly as many river mouths as there are glens in Scotland, my prospects were not good.

I found one possible site eight miles east of Glen Airigh, across Loch Fyne in the hills of Cowal, where the River Ruel runs south through *Caol Glienn*, the slender or the steep glen, to Loch Riddon and the Kyles of Bute. Was Glein fought at the mouth of the river of the slender glen? Like the rivers Glen in Northumberland and Lincolnshire there was nothing to suggest this was the right spot. Of course, unlike those who argue for Northumberland and Lincolnshire, at least I had a historical Arthur who was at about the right time. Still *Caol Glienn* did not seem right to me.

I thought again about what was going on in Argyll at the time in question. Immediately after Arthur became warlord of the Scots, Éoganán's supporters had been defeated at the Battle of Delgon.

Where did Glein fit in? The evidence suggested that Delgon and Glein were not the same battle; that no one river gave its name to this first battle; that Glein was not important enough to justify an *Annal* entry.

I concluded that if Glein was Arthur's first command, it was unlikely that he was put in charge of an army and fought a major pitched battle; it was more likely that he was in charge of a division and involved in a relatively minor engagement or series of engagements. What probably happened was this. Aedan's main battle force defeated Éoganán and Duncan at Delgon. Duncan was killed and Éoganán fled into exile in Ireland. Arthur was not present at Delgon, having been left in command of a small force to literally "hold the fort" at Dunardry-Dunadd.

Then, after the Battle of Delgon, Arthur was given his first independent command, not a battle-army but a smaller fighting-force, and ordered to stamp out the last flames of resistance among the supporters of Éoganán and the late Duncan. This would have been an ideal opportunity to try a young man with his first independent command, because it is likely this resistance was restricted to guerrilla fighting by the rivers and in the glens of Argyll.

Nennius does not mention the Battle of Camlann, Arthur's last battle, and so it is often supposed that his battle-list was based upon a record, probably in the form of a poem, written during Arthur's lifetime. If this is correct, the battle-list provides exactly what Nennius says it does: twelve battles in which Arthur was the "leader in battle."

This explains why the battles of Arderydd and Delgon are omitted from the list. Arthur was not in command at Arderydd or at Delgon. The Battle of Camlann is not included because it did not take place until after Nennius's source-poem was completed.

When Arthur started out on his career, no one knew he would become a great hero and so no one paid particular attention to his activities at that time. Later, when the poem upon which Nennius's battle-list was based was composed, the poet would have had to ask for information about Arthur's early life from those who were there.

If, as seems likely, Aneirin of the Flowing Verse wrote the poem upon which Nennius's battle-list was based—given that Aneirin was in the south during Arthur's early years—it would have been necessary for him to ask others what had happened in the early days.

Whoever Nennius's source-poet was, if he had wanted to start his poem with one of the Douglas battles, battles two to five on Nennius's battle-list, it would have been quickly pointed out to him by men who had been there that they had followed Arthur to war before the Douglas battles. If, as seems likely, these men had fought a guerrilla campaign in the aftermath of the Battle of Delgon, it is easy to see how a poet might have taken the innumerable skirmishes of which he was told and, exercising poetic license, bundled them all together into one composite battle, a battle fought at the mouth of a river called *Glein*, that is, "glen," when, in fact, the innumerable skirmishes of which he was told had been fought at many river mouths, many river crossings and in many of the glens of Argyll. If this is correct then Arthur, Arthur Mac Aedan's first "battle" was more an anti-guerrilla campaign fought, not at a river called *glen* but by the rivers and in the glens of Argyll.

Aedan now had the upper hand—Éoganán and Duncan's army had been destroyed and their supporters routed in the glens—but not everyone in Argyll was happy with Aedan as king. Éoganán was still alive and in exile in Ireland as part of the compromise that had brought the civil war to an end. While Éoganán lived he would always be a focal point for malcontents who might stage a coup if Aedan should falter. Fortunately for Aedan he did not falter, because from then on Aedan had Arthur to fight his battles for him.

A laconic entry in the *Annals of Tigernach* records Éoganán's death in 593. Secure at home and abroad Arthur was now ready to take on the Picts.

THE BATTLES OF THE BLACK WATER

Victory at the Battle of Delgon and in the Glein campaign and success at the Council of Drumceatt left Aedan and Arthur secure in Argyll, but not without enemies. Columba-Crimthann hated them, but he was too weak to do other than pretend to cooperate with their new dispensation, at least in the short-term. If Columba-Crimthann had been sufficiently powerful at this time he would have secured for his Scottish monks the same rights to persecute the druids of the Old Way as had been allowed to the Christians of Ireland at the Council of Drumceatt, but Columba-Crimthann's position in Dalriada remained precarious and so he had to bide his time.

Although still in his late teens, Arthur had fought in two major campaigns by the late 570s. In light of his achievements in later life, it is reasonable to suppose that his abilities were evident even at the beginning of his war-filled career, and that consequently he was sent to fight where the greatest danger lay. Once all internal opposition had been crushed this danger could only have been on the borders of Dalriada where lay the Miathi Picts.

The battle-list of Nennius says, "The second, the third, the fourth and the fifth were on another river, called the Douglas [Dubglas] which is in the country of Lindsey [Linnuis]."

Square mile for square mile, the place-name Douglas is even more common in Scotland than in England. I only have to drive twenty-two miles south from my home in central Scotland to the town of Douglas on the Douglas Water (although there are no Linnuis connections in this area). W. F. Skene, wrote, "There are many rivers and rivulets of this name in Scotland; but none could be said to be 'in regione Linnuis,' except two rivers—the Upper and Lower Douglas, which fall into Loch Lomond, the one through Glen Douglas, the other at Inveruglas, and are both in the district of the Lennox, the Linnuis of Nennius."[3]

North of Loch Lomond there are to be found Lochan Srath Dubh-uisge, the small loch of the meadow of the black water, and Srath Dubh-uisage, the meadow of the black water.

There are innumerable other black-associated place-names in the Lennox, just as there are all over Scotland.

In the second century the geographer Ptolemy drew a map of Britain that showed, just north of the Clyde estuary, a place called Lindum. His source of information was probably a Q-Celtic Gaelic speaker because this name was probably derived from the early Irish Gaelic, *lind*, which means "a pool." Later in Scottish Gaelic this became *linn*. It is probably from Lind and Linn that the name Linnuis was derived and applied to the area south and west of Loch Lomond. This area is still to this day called by a name that is derived from Linnuis, the Lennox. The Lennox has innumerable Douglas place-names within its bounds.

If this is correct Linnuis was not derived from some unrecorded British-Latin words, such as *Lindenses* or *Lindensia*, as Alcock suggests, but from the Q-Celtic word *Lind*, which became the Latin *Lindum* and the Q-Celtic *Linn*, then the Latin *Linnuis*, and then, later still, the Lennox.[4] Nowhere else is there this combination of Douglas and *Linnuis*, that is, the Lennox.

However slight evidence pointing south may be, it is grasped with enthusiasm and brandished boldly. Evidence that points north, however weighty it may be, is weighed only lightly in the scales. Those who contend for a southern Arthur have no real choice but to inflate the importance of what passes for evidence of Arthur in the south if their ideas are to retain even a vestige of credibility. This is particularly so with reference to the Douglas battles, because there are four of them.

In the sixth century, even in times of relative peace, neighbors tested each other's preparedness for war by raiding each other's lands. There can be no doubt but that the Picts would have taken advantage of civil war in Dalriada to plunder along their common border with the Scots and, if possible, extend their influence on Dalriada's eastern marches. It is likely therefore that in the mid- to late 570s Arthur, Arthur Mac Aedan, who was clearly a man of action, took command where the most deadly danger threatened Dalriada, the Loch Lomond front.

Few men are remembered in history and fewer still in geography. Arthur, Arthur Mac Aedan, is remembered in both. About halfway up the west bank of the loch, five miles north of Glen Douglas and the River Douglas, a pass runs west from Loch Lomond, through Glen Croe, over the well-named height called the Rest and Be Thankful, through Glen Kinglas to Loch Fyne and the heartlands of Argyll. The eastern end of this strategically vital approach is dominated by a mountain that, even today, is called Ben Arthur. This is perfect place for any man charged with commanding an army on the Dalriada-Pictland border to have had his headquarters.

It was probably here that Arthur Mac Aedan, was based in the late 570s because . . . well, if not him, then who? The legendary Arthur of the south, whoever he was? Why would anyone connect "King Arthur of England" with a mountain in the heart of the Ghaidhealtachd, the Gaelic speaking part of Scotland? If someone did just this, for some unimaginable reason, it is likely they would have chosen the highest mountain in the vicinity to commemorate their man and not the practical, strategically-perfectly-placed Ben Arthur. Is it just a coincidence that of all the hills in all the ranges in all of Britain the one that is called Ben Arthur is adjacent to the rivers and glens of Dalriada, abutting the Pictish border, where Arthur Mac Aedan lived? Is it not more likely that Ben Arthur was a real place, where a real man defended a real country against real enemies, rather than a place named in honor of some southern king?

If, as Nennius says, there were four battles in one place, Douglas, there must have been something special about this place. In the American Civil War two battles were fought at Manassas-Bull Run because it was an important railway junction between Washington and Richmond. The lands of Douglas were special for the same reasons. To invade Dalriada the Picts would have had to cross Douglas—specifically they would have had to traverse the pass commanded by the hill Ben Arthur, because Douglas and Ben Arthur lay between Dalriada and Pictland. Arthur's army, if based at Ben Arthur, would have been in a prime position to command Loch Lomond and deny the Picts the pass that led west to Argyll.

Lomond is derived from the Scottish and Irish Gaelic word *loam*, which means a "blaze" (luminous comes from the same root). The toponymist William Watson suggested that Loch Lomond means Loch of the Beacon, although I suspect a plural version, Loch of the Beacons, is more accurate. To see why this is, one must stand on Merlin-Lailoken's lands at Cadzow Hill, fifty miles to the southeast. The information board at Cadzow shows only three hills, Drumgoyne, Ben Lomond, and Ben Arthur. People in the south looking north when the beacons on the summits of Ben Lomond and Ben Arthur were lit, although they could not have seen the loch, would have known that between these two lights lay a great loch (the biggest in Britain) and, on occasion, that battle was about to begin. I picture Merlin-Lailoken standing by his fort at Cadzow watching these two great signal-fires, thinking of Arthur and his men riding out to meet the Picts.

Given the numerous black-water sites about Loch Lomond it is possible that in the sixth century much of Loch Lomondside and indeed the loch itself were called by a black-water name and that Loch Lomond and the banks of Loch Lomond were Douglas, the black water lands.

It is probably on the Douglas lands in the Lennox on the banks of Loch Lomond that Arthur fought Nennius's second, third, fourth, and fifth battles against the Picts. Just as with Glein, it is likely there was a measure of poetic license involved in recording the second to fifth battle-entries on Nennius's list (and perhaps some garbling of source material too). The Picts were a mighty people, the most powerful in Scotland in the late sixth century, and are unlikely to have been beaten in one campaign, far less in one battle. In any event, people like clean-cut battles and that is what Nennius gave them, although it is more

Ben Arthur (Arthur's headquarters) looms over the pass that led from the land of the Picts to the heartlands of Dalriada, Argyll.

likely that the four Douglas "Battles" were in fact four campaigns fought against the Picts over four campaigning seasons in the late 570s.

In four campaigns Arthur held the Picts along the line of Loch Lomond, on the Black Water, Douglas. Four times in four years the Picts attacked and four times in four years Arthur's army fought them in the hills, in the glens, by the rivers, and on the loch itself, and beat them back, until, at the end of the four Douglas campaigns, the Picts had no more fight left in them.

If the above is correct then all four Douglas battles said to have been fought by the legendary Arthur were in reality fought on the borders of the historical Arthur Mac Aedan's Dalriada. There is no need for a southern Arthur to travel north fight four battles in one place, before returning to his southern home, as Skene has suggested.

It is generally conceded that the seventh battle, the Battle of the Caledonian Wood was fought in the Scotland, because setting it anywhere else is almost impossible, given that the name includes the word *Caledonian*, and Caledonia clearly connotes Scotland. It is sometimes conceded, somewhat grudgingly, that the eleventh battle, the Battle of Agned was fought in Scotland, in Edinburgh. If those who favor a southern Arthur were to allow that the Douglas battles, all four of them, were also fought in Scotland, this would mean that half of Nennius's twelve battles were fought in Scotland, and this would make the idea of a southern Arthur untenable.

Four campaigns in four years and Arthur won them all. In the fifth year the Picts stayed their swords and primed their warning fires, because they knew that soon Arthur would come to the land of the Picts.

CARACALLA AND THE BATTLE OF BASSAS

The sixth battle on the battle-list of Nennius was fought "on the river called Bassas." Three clues: Bassas is the sixth battle; Bassas was fought on a river; and the name, Bassas.

The historical circumstances surrounding the sites of the first five battles strongly suggested that the battles on Nennius's list were in chronological order. Glein, Arthur Mac Aedan's first battle (or rather campaign) had been fought to secure his father's throne in the Glens of Argyll. Battles two to five, the Douglas battles, in reality four campaigns, had been fought by Arthur on the eastern marches of Dalriada, to secure the borders of his father's new kingdom in the face of Pictish incursions. Bassas was the sixth battle.

Having fought the Picts to a standstill in the Douglas campaigns, Arthur had no reason to fall back and little reason to stay where he was and wait to fight on the defensive again. In similar circumstances great generals such as Alexander, Caesar, Napoleon, and Lee would have advanced, and so, if as seems likely Arthur too was a great general, Arthur too would have advanced. This meant there was a good chance that the site of Arthur's next battle, the Battle of Bassas, would be in enemy territory, in the land of the Picts.

The second clue, the river reference, is a blunt thing. While battles were frequently fought at river crossings there are too many rivers in too many places to allow any meaningful search to be based upon this second clue alone. When I came to this point I found I needed more to go on, and so I left this second clue to stand, to be used as a cross-check if I could find something to cross-check it against.

Clue three, the name Bassas, had been done to death—this was, after all, the battle that had caused scholars to despair. According to the Arthurian scholar, August Hunt, "The Bassas river is the most problematic of the Arthurian battle sites, as no such stream name survives and we have no record other than this single instance in the *Historia Brittonum* of there ever having been a river so named."[5]

Like everyone else who had tried to solve the Bassas problem, I considered the prefix *bas* or *bass*, because, like everyone else, I could not find a British place-name that contained the whole word *Bassas*. Everywhere I looked someone had been there before me; every place and name I considered was a dead end.

Like everyone else who had looked for Bassas before me I found the search long and difficult, right up to the point when everything clicked into place and I knew exactly where the Battle of Bassas had been fought and how to prove it. Then I found other *entirely separate evidence* and proved it for a second time.

The Romans divided the lands of the Miathi Picts when they built the Antonine Wall from the rivers Clyde to the Forth around the year

142 CE. The Miathi Picts who found themselves south of the wall came increasingly to accept what the Romans could do for them: roads, public health, civil security, the rule of law, that kind of thing. North of the wall the Miathi Picts were presented with a stark choice: accept this dilution of their power in the south or rise against Rome. In 207 CE they rose against Rome and forced the Roman Emperor, Septimius Severus, to come north with his legions to protect his frontier.

Severus was the model for Maximus, Russell Crowe's character in the film *Gladiator*, although, unlike Maximus, Severus did not die in the arena. Severus became emperor after the death of the vile Commodus, played by Joaquin Phoenix in the film. Commodus did not die in the arena either, as he did in the film; he was strangled in his bath in December 192.

Severus was an outsider, a self-made man from the provinces and, in the words used in the film, a soldier of Rome. He ruled the empire harshly but well until his death in 211. He married twice and had two sons, one to each wife. When his oldest son was seven years old Severus re-named him Marcus Aurelius Antoninus to lend legitimacy to his line by associating his family with the much loved philosopher-emperor, Marcus Aurelius (played by Richard Harris in the film). As so often happens with the sons of famous, successful, powerful, self-made men, Antoninus and his younger brother, Publius Septimius Antoninus Geta, were not as able as their father; on the contrary, they were ambitious, effete, dissolute, and vicious: "The fond hopes of the father, and of the Roman world, were soon disappointed by these vain youths, who displayed the indolent security of hereditary princes; and a presumption that fortune would supply the place of merit and application."[6]

Gibbon said Severus brought Antoninus and Geta with him to Britain to keep them away from the fleshpots of Rome, but it is more likely that Severus knew he did not have long to live and that if he left Antoninus and Geta behind in Rome they would cause trouble by plotting against each other to succeed him. Antoninus, who was to succeed his father as emperor, was a monster to equal the emperor Gaius, a man better known by the sobriquet Caligula (said to mean "Little Boot"). Antoninus had a nickname too, one that has gone down in history as a byword for savage excess, Caracalla.

Close to the end of his reign, sick and near to death, Severus had himself carried north in a litter to fight the Miathi Picts. His elder son Antoninus-Caracalla was given a military command and came with him. His younger son Geta was left to work at staff-headquarters in York. The Romans "passed . . . fortresses and rivers and entered Caledonia," clearing woods, laying roads, and building bridges as they went. They built a road from Falkirk to Stirling, which they extended west along the banks of the Forth before turning north and building a massive fortified camp where the River Earn joins the River Tay at a place that is now called Carpow. There, at this camp, the Roman army could be supplied from the sea.

The Romans built two bridges at Carpow. A coin of Severus, dated to the year 208, shows a fixed bridge, and a medallion, dated to Antoninus-Caracalla's twelfth Tribunical year, 209, shows a bridge of boats. It makes sense to suppose that the bridge of boats spanned the wide Tay (the remains of the bridgehead works have been found on the north bank) and that the fixed bridge was across the narrow Earn, west of Carpow fort. Antoninus-Caracalla's name continued to be connected with this area even after he left Scotland to become emperor. A tile found at Carpow dedicated to Caracalla has been dated between 212 and 217. This suggests some continuing building work at Carpow and a continuing connection with, or at least a memory of, Antoninus-Caracalla.

Coin from 209 CE showing the bridge at the site of the Battle of Bassas. "Antoninus" was an official name of the man earlier named Bassianus, although better known as Caracalla. On the reverse, Pontif refers to the office of Pontifex Maximus; "TR-P XII" refers to Bassianus's twelfth tribunate; and "COS III" to his third consulship. "Traiectus" means a crossing.

When Julius Caesar bridged the Rhine the people who lived on its banks thought their river had been captured: "*Rhenum suum sicponte quasi iugo captum.*"[7] Even if the people who lived on Tayside and Earnside were not quite so simple, they must have been impressed by the extraordinary engineering of the Romans. Given that these bridges were built under the command of Antoninus-Caracalla and that he became Roman emperor soon after they were completed, it would be reasonable to suppose his name was associated with these bridges.

The bridge of boats may not have withstood the pressure of the River Tay for long, but the fixed-bridge over the River Earn could have survived for generations. It is possible that this bridge was remembered as the bridge Antoninus-Caracalla built and that consequently his name became a place-name that survived the bridge itself.

The Miathi Picts, knowing they were no match for the Romans in the open field, offered peace, but Severus rejected their overtures. He needed a quick and decisive victory. The Picts had time. Severus did not. Severus was dying. The Miathi Picts fell back before the Roman advance and waged guerrilla war. Severus, finding himself unable to bring them to battle, took out his frustration on the civilian population. He cruelly crushed all who opposed him, and many who did not, and so despoiled the lands of the Miathi Picts that they were forced to come to terms.

Antoninus-Caracalla, quite naturally for a young man of wild disposition, resented his father for bringing him to what must have seemed to him a dank and dreary place compared to Rome and, in time-honored fashion, expressed his resentment by being as contrary as he could. Severus wanted merciless action and a quick resolution of the campaign, and so Antoninus-Caracalla took an opposite tack and became relatively sympathetic towards the Picts. Unlike Severus, Antoninus-Caracalla was no soldier; he had no interest in expending energy crushing Picts on the furthest borders of the empire. All he wanted was that his father should die and that he should be emperor of Rome. He even went as far as to plot with the Picts to have Severus assassinated while peace negotiations were ongoing.

The treatment meted out by Severus to the Miathi Picts was so severe that their neighbors, the Caledonian Picts, afraid they would be next to suffer at the hands of Severus, offered the Miathi Picts their support. With the Caledonian Picts to back them up, the Miathi Picts broke the peace they had only just made and attacked the Romans. Severus, unable to join the army in the north because of ill-health, gave orders that his army show no mercy and that resistance be met with massacre: everyone was to die, men, women, and children.

Antoninus-Caracalla, who was at least nominally in command in the north, did not follow his father's policy. His inaction was not motivated by sentiment but by self-interest: Antoninus-Caracalla was, after all, a savage. He knew that Severus would soon be dead and that if he were to become emperor in his father's place he could not be away from Rome fighting Picts in the northern fastnesses of Britain when the succession was decided. If Severus died it would have been difficult for Antoninus-Caracalla to leave the scene of battle and return to Rome with rebellious Picts still rampant on the borders of the empire, and so it was in his interest to create conditions that would allow him to leave a peaceful Scotland behind him. To achieve this end Antoninus-Caracalla did not just damn his father's orders with faint obedience, he completely ignored them; indeed, he contradicted them. Severus was for utmost war and so Antoninus-Caracalla became a craven appeaser. He did not burn villages, kill their inhabitants, and "take-no-prisoners," as his father had ordered. He made contact with the leaders of the Picts, spared their families, and negotiated a truce. At the same time he put out feelers to discover on what terms he might make peace and so facilitate the façade of an honorable withdrawal.

The Caledonians and the Miathi Picts were still in revolt when Severus died in 211, leaving Antoninus-Caracalla, who had made himself their friend, free to make peace with the Picts as he had planned. He simply received pledges of fidelity and left Scotland to become Emperor.[8]

Initially Antoninus-Caracalla became joint-emperor with his brother Geta, but within a year he had Geta assassinated. In 217, after years of viciousness, he too was assassinated when one of his bodyguards killed him while he was urinating at the side of a road. Severus and Antoninus-Caracalla had father-son problems, to say the least, and so it was likely that the son would oppose his father just because he

218 | FINDING ARTHUR

was his father. This conclusion is buttressed if those who adhere to the conventional wisdom are wrong about the name Caracalla.

The nickname Caracalla is said to have been given to Antoninus after he arrived in Britain. It is said to mean "Gaulish Cloak" and to have been given to him because he popularized a particular type of heavy-hooded cloak favored by the Gauls. This seems unlikely. It is hard to picture tough legionaries, talking among themselves about their Emperor's son, saying, "Here comes old Gaulish Cloak." (The Windsor tie-knot was named for the frightful Duke of Windsor. No one who saw him approaching ever said "Here comes old tie-knot." They probably said, "run.")

Antoninus was a playboy and probably a dandy. He may even have dressed eccentrically just to annoy his strict, military-minded father. It seems likely however that there would have to have been more to a nickname to make it stick than the mere fact that a man wore a certain type of cloak. In any event, wearing a Gaulish cloak among Celtic people would have been unremarkable, and popularizing a warm Gaulish cloak in the heat of Rome, uncomfortable. This Gaulish Cloak explanation for the name Caracalla does not make sense.

It is more likely the name Caracalla had a more sensible meaning, a meaning that is clear if the matter is approached from a Scottish point of view. I took the *Calla* suffix to be relevant to the Caledonians, the collective name by which the Romans called the Pictish people who lived north of the Antonine Wall.

As for *cara*, I thought of the Italian word *cara*, not because I speak Italian (I do not), but because I remembered the aria "O mio babbino cara" from the opera *Gianni Schicchi*. In the Italian of Puccini's opera, *cara* means dear or beloved. This worked in both Latin and in Gaelic, where "dear" is *carus* and *caraid*, respectively. When I put all this together and thought about what was going on when Antoninus was given the nickname Caracalla, it seemed obvious that the real meaning of the nickname was, "dear to" or "the beloved of the Caledonians," that is, colloquially, Caledonian-Lover.

If this is correct, then Antoninus's policy of appeasement would have been known to the men in the ranks, and, although these men might have been happy to remain in camp or lay roads and build bridges instead of hunting dangerous Picts in the glens, they would still have mocked their less-than-warlike general with a name equivalent to the nasty little soubriquet once used in the American west—*Indian Lover*.

Is it not more likely that such a derisive nickname would have appealed to the legionaries more than the insipid Gaulish Cloak? If I am right, and Antoninus was sympathetic toward the Picts, this would fit with what I had concluded was the real meaning of the name Caracalla.

This is but one more example of how a Scottish insight can throw new light on old matters. If there are Scottish insights, and there are, and if they remain unknown or are ignored, as they tend to be, we will continue on the complacent path that has led almost everyone to believe that Arthur was a man of the south of Britain, when according to the evidence he was from what is now Scotland. [9]

If I am right, Bassas was fought after the Douglas campaigns on a river in the land of the Picts. If I am right, Antoninus-Caracalla built two bridges over a river in the land of the Picts, at least one of which remained for long enough after his departure for his name to be associated with, first the bridge and then the place where the bridge had been, even after the bridge itself had disappeared.

Which of his names was remembered in connection with this bridge?

Antoninus? This was a name given for purely political purposes (to associate the family of Severus with the family of the late emperor, the highly respected Marcus Aurelius). It is unlikely this name was used in daily life, except for official purposes. This is not uncommon. Edward VIII, Nazi sympathizer and tie-knot promoter (the one who was forced to abdicate), was named Edward for official purposes, but his friends and family called him David.

Caracalla? This nickname was invented at the time when the bridges were being built but it was only a nickname and not a flattering nickname at that. If I am right about what it means, it is likely it was only popular among the legionaries and most unlikely that it would have been kept in circulation among the Picts after the legions left.

It is almost certain, in my opinion, that the name that was remembered in connection with the bridges was the name Antoninus-Caracalla used day-to-day, the name he had before his father called him

Antoninus and before the soldiers took to calling him Caledonian-Lover, that is, his original name, Lucius Septimius Bassianus.

There was ample time in the four centuries that separated Antoninus-Caracalla-Bassianus from Arthur and the six centuries that separated him from Nennius for this name to be shortened, mispronounced, misheard, miswritten, misread or simply changed to make it more euphonic. There was ample time for Bassianus to become Bassas.

I believe the bridges at Carpow, and when they were gone their successors, or simply the Earn and Tay crossings, were remembered in connection with Antoninus-Caracalla by his familiar name Bassianus, a name that was later shortened to Bassas.

Of course, it is always possible that Bassianus was *deliberately* shortened to cover up the fact that Arthur's sixth battle was fought in Scotland, although it is more likely that by the time Nennius came to list the sixth battle fought by the legendary Arthur, all he knew about the battle was that it was fought "on the river at Bassas."

In the river crossing at Carpow I had found a vital strategic site that fitted the three clues in Nennius's battle entry. Carpow was in the right place to be a follow-up to the Douglas campaigns: it was on a river, and it had a Bassas connection in the name Bassianus. I took the view that the Battle of Bassas was fought at Carpow fort and that I had the evidence to prove it.

Then I found other, entirely separate, evidence that proved, again, that the Battle of Bassas was fought at Carpow.

CARPOW AND THE BATTLE OF BASSAS

In 558 Bridei Mac Maelchon, king of the Picts, defeated Arthur Mac Aedan's grandfather, Gabhran Mac Domangart, in a battle fought at Circenn. This was the first of three battles of Circenn.

Just over twenty years later the house of Gabhran was avenged when Aedan's army (with Arthur in command) defeated and killed Bridei at the second Battle of Circenn.

The third Battle of Circenn was in 596. On this occasion Aedan was officially said to have been victorious although the annals also mention his sons, including Arthur. While the victory was ascribed to Aedan this was only because he was the king: the victorious general was Arthur.

Three generations of Arthur Mac Aedan's family, all engaged in battle at a place called Circenn. What it may be asked has any of this to do with Bassas? Circenn was one of seven Pictish provinces that according to legend were named after the seven sons of Cruithne, a fabled Pictish king. This is just the ancient equivalent of modern celebrity culture, which demands that things are personalized as much as possible. In fact Cruithne is a generic name for the Picts. Bridei, for example, was designed *rig Cruithneach*, king of the Picts.

Circenn has been identified as Coupar Angus, north of Perth; Kincardine, south of Stirling; and somewhere between the rivers Tay and Dee. According to the information provided to tourists by the local council for Angus (the area about Perth), "The Pictish name for the area is known, however, and *Circhenn* or *Circenn* as the Picts knew it seems to embrace Angus and Mearns in the 9th century. The name may well be a Gaelic translation, for it is readily translated as the 'crested head,' meaning the premier province of the Picts."

Why would the Picts choose *Circenn* as the name of their premier province, if *Circenn* meant "Crested Head"? I thought this unlikely. It seemed to me that *Circenn* was taken to mean "Crested Head" only because it sounded something like the Gaelic word, *cuircinn*, which means, "A particular kind of head-dress for women."

In Scots this would be *courche* or *curges*, a covering for a woman's head, from which same root we get the English word *kerchief*. In any event, this struck me as too far-fetched.

The location of and the meaning of the name Circenn puzzled me for some time before I realized the solution had been in front of me all along, and that *Circenn* was where Carpow is today, because *Circenn* and Carpow are but two names for the same place.

The prefix *cir* in *Circenn* is the equivalent of the *car* in Carpow— the difference in the vowel is insignificant after so many centuries. What does this prefix mean? *Carn*, according to O'Brien, is a province. The language of the Picts has been all but lost but it is thought to have been, like Welsh, a form of P-Celtic. In Welsh, *caer* meant "fortress."

We have, therefore, *cir* or *car* meaning "a province" or "a fortress."

It does not matter much which it was, province or fortress, because it is quite reasonable to suppose that the premier province of the Picts and the main fortress of the premier province of the Picts, might both be called by the same name. Just as we have New York, New York, we might have had a fort called *Circenn* in a province called *Circenn*.

The suffix *cenn* was obviously the Q-Celtic-Gaelic *ceann*, "head," which made *Circenn* the head fort or province (in effect, headquarters), a name that makes sense when applied to a place that actually was a main province or fortress. Certainly this makes more obvious sense than Crested Head.

This left me with the suffix *pow*. Where did that come in? I knew the poem *John Anderson, My Jo*, by Robert Burns:

> But now your brow is beld, John,
> Your locks are like the snaw;
> But blessings on your frosty pow,
> John Anderson, my jo.

There it was—*pow*, like *ceann*, meant "head" and so there was no difference between *Circenn* and *Carpow*, they were synonymous. Both meant, in user-friendly terms, headquarters. If this is right then there is no need for tortuously defined Crested Head place-names.

Circenn and Carpow are the same name and demark the same place, the place where Arthur Mac Aedan battled against the Picts on two occasions, first in the 580s and then in the 590s. They are also where Bassianus built his bridges and gave the name Bassas to the area. They are where, according to Nennius's battle-list, the legendary Arthur did battle. The Battle of Bassas, it appears, was fought where the Rivers Tay and Earn meet, where once there was a Roman Fort and two bridges.

Before the Romans arrived at Circenn, it was a Pictish capital. Then the Romans arrived and built their great fort at Carpow, where the rivers Tay and Earn meet, because it was an ideal strategic site for a fortress. After the Romans left the Miathi Picts reoccupied this site and made it their capital again. The reason there were so many battles in this one place is obviously because of its strategic importance.[10]

After his victories in the civil war in the glens of Argyll, commemorated by Nennius as the Battle of Glein, around 574 or 575, Arthur Mac Aedan fought and won four campaigns against the Miathi Picts, Nennius's four Douglas battles. These four battles were fought on the Dalriada–Pictish border, near Loch Lomond, between approximately 577 to 580.

Despite all these victories Arthur knew the Picts were still strong enough to present a threat in the future and so he decided to attack them and defeat them on their own ground. The war of the Scots against the Picts that followed was waged both on land and at sea. According to the *Annals of Ulster*, in the year 580 there was an "expedition to *Innsi Orc* by Aedán son of Gabrán," that is, an attack on the Orkney Islands by Aedan's navy.

Nennius's battle-list does not include this naval expedition among Arthur's—that is, Arthur Mac Aedan's—battles, because Arthur was not in command of this expedition. He was in the south on the Pictish border with the Scots army.

Following his father's naval victory in the Orkneys, Arthur invaded the lands of the Picts, marched to the gates of their capital, and there in circa 584 his army met and defeated the army of the Pictish king, Bridei Mac Maelchon (the man who had defeated Arthur's grandfather in that same place some twenty-six years before, at the first Battle of Circenn).

In this, the second Battle of Circenn, sometimes called the Battle of Bassas, fought in the vicinity of the old Roman fort at Carpow, Arthur avenged his grandfather. Bridei the king of the Picts was killed, and Arthur's half-brother Gartnait was made king in his place.

There were three battles of Bassas-Circenn-Carpow. In the first battle, in 558, Gabhran, Arthur's grandfather, was defeated by the Picts. In the second battle, in circa 584 Arthur defeated the same Picts; this was the battle known as the Battle of Bassas. In the third battle, Arthur again defeated the Picts, although it was a pyrrhic victory in which Gartnait among many others in Arthur's army were killed.

If the sixth battle on Nennius's battle-list had been named the Battle of Circenn or Carpow, its name alone would have set the scene in the far north of Britain, contrary to the interests of southern storytellers and their patrons. No one in the south would have been interested in the Picts and so the Picts were written out of the picture. Nennius or someone before him simply used the mysterious and so unproblematic name Bassas and that was that.

There are only four battle-entries in the *Annales Cambriae* between circa 447, when the entries begin, and 600, when, everyone agrees, Arthur (whoever he was) was dead. These are the Battle of Badon, the twelfth battle on Nennius's list; the Battle of Camlann, at which, according to a general consensus, Arthur died; the Battle of Arderydd, at which the entry for 573 says "Merlin went mad"; and a battle, supposedly, fought on the Isle of Man. This fourth battle is dated 584.

The legendary Arthur fought at Badon and at Camlann. Merlin fought at Arderydd and so there is at least some connection between the legendary Arthur and this battle. This leaves only the battle on the Isle of Man. It seems unlikely that this battle is the only one of the four that has no Arthurian connection.

What if this fourth battle was not fought on the Isle of Man? What if, to bolster the case for a southern Arthur, the evidence has been enhanced by "a scribe who . . . thinks he knows, more than the original, and who cannot resist the temptation to insert his knowledge"?[11]

What evidence is there to suggest that this is what happened? Skene says,

> The name of Manau was applied by the Welsh to the Isle of Man . . . the Latin form was *Eubonia*, the Cymric, *Manau*; but it appears from Nennius that this name of Manau was also applied to a district in North Britain [Manau] . . . The Irish name for the Isle of Man is *Manand* or *Manann*; and it appears from the Irish Annals that a district on the north was likewise known by that name, as they record in 711 a slaughter of the Picts by the Saxons *in Campo Manand*, or the Plain of *Manann*, as distinguished from the island. It is, of course, difficult to discriminate between the two places, and to ascertain whether an event recorded as taking place in *Manau* or *Manann* belongs to the island or the district. Events which really belong to the one are often attributed to the other.[12]

Nothing connects any historical Arthur with the Isle of Man, but there is evidence that connects Arthur Mac Aedan with Manau. His grandfather, Gabhran, lived there; his father, Aedan, lived there; and he lived there. As Skene says, it is difficult to discriminate between the Isle of Man and Manau (unless, of course, you are determined to set Arthur in the south, in which case, you will do what the compilers of the *Annales Cambriae* did: plonk for the Isle of Man).

Not only can the historical Arthur, Arthur Mac Aedan, be connected with *Manau*, he can be connected with an actual battle in Manau. An entry in the *Annals of Ulster* for the year 582 reads, "The Battle of Manu, in which Aedán son of Gabrán son of Domangart was victor." The father of Arthur Mac Aedan is said to have won a battle at "Manu," an irrelevant two years before the battle listed in the *Annales Cambriae*. This is not a simple coincidence. This is because the battles recorded in the two sets of annals are one and the same.

This means that of the four battles listed in the *Annales Cambriae*, three can be associated with the legendary Arthur and with Arthur Mac Aedan, and one, the battle said to have been fought on the Isle of Man but which was really fought in Manau, while not listed as one of the legendary Arthur's battles can be associated with Arthur Mac Aedan.

The battle-list of Nennius, the *Lives of the Saints*, and the *Annales Cambriae*, are all southern British works, written for southern British purposes, by partisans of a southern British establishment. They are all determined, either consciously or not, to set the legend of Arthur in the south.

Before Nennius wrote his *Historia*, Arthur was simply a historical figure. After the *Historia*, under the pens of southern clerics, Arthur became a legend. To exist in the south of Britain it was necessary for Arthur to become a legendary figure, because Arthur does not exist in the history of the south.

9

The Great Angle War

THE LEGEND OF ARTHUR WAS BORN IN THE GREAT ANGLE WAR THAT Arthur Mac Aedan waged and won by the 580s. Neither mainstream history nor conventional Arthurian wisdom recognizes the Great Angle War. It is not that they reject it as having nothing to do with Arthur, it is just that they had not heard about it until I found the seventh, eighth, ninth, and tenth battles on Nennius's battle-list and saw that they were all parts of one campaign.

The Great Angle War began soon after Hussa came to the Angle throne of Bernicia around 585. Hussa launched a surprise attack against the Gododdin, marching north, hard and fast, through Lauderdale, along the line of Dere Street, the old Roman road, toward Edinburgh.

The available evidence is too slight to allow a detailed exposition of the campaign that followed. The following reconstruction is consistent with such evidence as there is. The Angles planned to defeat the Gododdin before the Gododdin could get help from their fellow Britons. Then they intended to secure their western flank before regrouping and attacking Strathclyde.

As the beacons on the hills spread news of the approaching Angles, the Gododdin mobilized their army. Men were called in from far fields, marshaled, provisioned, armed, and assigned, but these were men who had not waged major war in a decade and lacked experience. The Gododdin army was not battle-ready as the Angles advanced.

The same could not be said of Arthur's Men of Manau, positioned on the border of the Gododdin lands, some twenty miles from Edinburgh. Arthur's warriors were battle-hardened veterans, fresh from the destruction of the Picts at the Battle of Bassas. They were well trained, well equipped, well led, and their morale was high because under Arthur, they were undefeated.

The obvious tactical line for Arthur to follow would have been to march east, join the Gododdin, and make ready to receive the Angles in Edinburgh. Instead, in an act of martial genius to rival Lee's flanking attack at Chancellorsville, Arthur led his cavalry south to Peebles before turning east to place his force on the western flank of the main body of the Angle army, in a position to threaten the Angle lines of communication.

Arthur's cavalry probed the flank of the Angle army as his infantry arrived from Manau and joined the ranks of his growing force. The Caledonian Wood was deep and dense, and the Angles could not have been sure how many men Arthur had, and so they sent warriors south and west as a precautionary measure, depleting the numbers they could bring to bear against the Gododdin.

Arthur, spreading his men thin and wide, moved speedily and aggressively, refusing major engagements. By this means he convinced the Angles that they were faced by far more men than in reality they were, just as the Confederate General Magruder stalled a vastly superior Union attack in 1862. The hit-and-run tactics of Arthur and his Men of Manau developed into a long running fight as they pressed on east through the woods: "With huge dark-socketed crimson spears, stern and steadfast the battle-hounds fought."[1]

This battle, like the Battle of the Wilderness in the American Civil War, was more a series of engagements fought out over several days, perhaps a week or more, in the dark fastnesses of the great wood. This is why this "Battle" was called the Battle of the Caledonian Wood, an enormously imprecise name given that the Caledonian Wood covered half of southern Scotland in the sixth century. Just as with the Glein "Battle," there was no one battlefield. The Battle of the Caledonian

The remains of the Roman Fort and the Pictish capital, where the Battle of Bassas was fought, were to the right in this photograph, above the smaller river, the River Earn.

© RCAHMS (Society of Antiquaries of Scotland Collection).
Licensor www.rcahms.gov.uk.

Wood was given that name because, as the name suggests, it was fought in the Caledonian Wood, wherever Arthur's small but growing force could advance, find enemies, kill them, and advance again. The likely line of battle runs east from Peebles to Clovenfords, through what today are the forests of Glentress, Cardrona, Elibank, and Traquair, and Yair Hill.

Arthur's tactics and aggression caused confusion in the counsels of the Angles. Soon they were looking over their shoulders unsure how many more men would be needed to quell this unquantifiable enemy which had unexpectedly appeared on their flank and threatened to endanger their supply base in the ruins of the Roman fort of Trimontium (near modern Melrose).

Arthur and the Men of Manau had seized the initiative. They could not beat the massively more numerous Angles on their own, but they had won their fights in the forest, thrown the Angles off balance, slowed the Angle advance, and bloodied them. Arthur's rapid actions took the heat out of the Angle advance and prevented the Gododdin from being crushed before the levies of Strathclyde had time to take the field.

By the end of the "Battle" of the Caledonian Wood, the Angles were up against the Gododdin to their front and Arthur's Men of Manau, newly reinforced by the army of Strathclyde, on their flank. When this first phase of the campaign came to a close the Angle army was still intact and entirely formidable. Nennius famously wrote, "Then Arthur fought against them in those days, together with the kings of the British; but he was their leader in battle."[2]

It is now generally accepted that this passage means Arthur fought in the company of kings, indeed, led them in battle, but that that he himself was not a king. It happens sometimes, when a danger is truly deadly, that established authorities will break with tradition and choose the best man for the job, as opposed to the one who best suits the individual interests of those in power. This does not happen often. It happened in 1940 at the start of the Second World War, when Winston Churchill became Prime Minister. It also happened in the mid-580s when Arthur Mac Aedan became the warlord of the Britons (and of course of his Scots and Men of Manau).

IT IS COMMONLY allowed, as I have explained, that Nennius's seventh battle, the Battle of the Caledonian Wood, was fought in Scotland, but this is only because there is no real alternative, given that Caledonia, the Roman name for the north of Britain is undeniably Scotland. However, there is no consensus as regards the eighth, ninth and tenth battles, the battles of Guinnion, the City of the Legion, and Tribruit. Who fought in these battles? Where were they fought and when? What was the reason why? These are all much disputed matters.

The allied kings recognized there was no time to debate the matter of command—the danger they faced was too great—and so they allowed Arthur, the de facto leader in the field, to continue in charge of what was now an allied army. The very fact that someone like Arthur, a Scots warlord, commanded kings, suggests an emergency measure taken in the heat of a fight and not a considered decision, coolly arrived at. If there had been time to argue the matter, it is unlikely that the kings would have allowed someone who was not a king to take command.

Arthur stayed in command for the next three battles. This suggests they were fought quickly, one after the other, without a break to allow "the natural order of kings" to reassert itself. If Arthur had faltered, halted, or suffered a defeat, he would have been immediately replaced; but Arthur, undaunted, advanced without stopping until he had beaten the Angles entirely and sent them homeward, to think again.

If the hand of Merlin-Lailoken, Chancellor of Strathclyde, was behind the decision to allow Arthur to take command of the allied army at the end of the Battle of the Caledonian Wood, this would explain why Merlin is always closely associated with Arthur. According to Nennius:

> The eighth battle was in Guinnion Fort, and in it Arthur carried the image of the holy Mary, the everlasting Virgin, on his shield, and the heathen were put to flight that day, and there was great slaughter upon them, through the power of Our Lord Jesus Christ and the power of the holy Virgin his mother.[3]

I did what I usually did with passages such as this. I put aside the purely promotional material, the reference to Mary the mother of Jesus, and looked at the evidence that remained. This left three clues: Guinnion's eighth place on the list; Guinnion the name; and the fact Guinnion was a fort.

In the sixth century there was a fort on a hill near Stow in Wedale, above the Gala Water. All that remains of this fort today is an irregular oval of walls, about 100 yards across, although all that is visible above ground are ridges of stone where walls once stood high and men looked out for danger. It was here that Arthur's allied army met and defeated the Angles in the battle Nennius called the Battle of Guinnion.

It seems likely that with Arthur now in command of a large allied army in their rear, a substantial part of the Angle army withdrew from Edinburgh along the line of the Gala Water to the fort at Stow. This placed them a mere six miles from Yair Hill, where Arthur was poised when the Battle of the Caledonian Wood was over.

Stow Fort is only a few miles from where the seventh battle, the Battle of the Caledonian Wood, ended, and so was perfectly situated to be the site of the eighth battle, the Battle of Guinnion. These factors allow the chronological order of the list to remain intact, with one battle following another just as Nennius listed them.

The first clue—Guinnion's eighth place on the list—makes sense if Guinnion is Stow Fort. Stow is but a day's march, if even that, from the Caledonian Wood. The fact that Stow Fort is, by definition, a fort, also makes sense of the third of Nennius's three clues.

Of course, perhaps, the Angles withdrew the way they had come, through Lauderdale. In this event Stow Fort would have commanded the western end of the pass that separated the Angles from Arthur, and would still be perfectly placed to have been the site of the Battle of Guinnion.

According to Skene there was corroboration for the Guinnion-Stow connection in local oral traditions, which said the Battle of Guinnion was, "connected by old tradition with the church of Wedale, in the vale of the Gala Water."[4] The church of Wedale is in Stow.

This left a clue that so far had led nowhere; the matter of the name, Guinnion, itself. The *Vatican Recension*, one of the forty-or-so versions of Nennius's *Historia* to survive, contains the following additional material.

For Arthur proceeded to Jerusalem, and there made a cross to the size of the Saviour's cross, and there it was consecrated, and for three successive days he fasted, watched, and prayed, before the Lord's cross, that the Lord would give him the victory, by this sign, over the heathen; which also took place, and he took with him the image of St. Mary, the fragments of which are still preserved in great veneration at Wedale, in English Wodale, in Latin Vallis-doloris. Wodale is a village in the province of Lodonesia, but now of the jurisdiction of the bishop of St. Andrew's, of Scotland, six miles on the west of that heretofore noble and eminent monastery of Meilros.[5]

Again the supernatural elements stand to be deleted. It is impossible to believe that Arthur went to Jerusalem and made a life-sized cross. It is more likely that these things were the invention of some Christian cleric who saw fit to expand the eighth entry on Nennius's battle-list. Given the clearly biased source of this evidence, it is highly unlikely that Arthur starved himself and did the other Christian things he is said to have done. As always with obvious promotional material, care has to be taken to identify the suspect evidence and to find whatever worthwhile evidence might lie hidden behind it.

It is possible there were pieces of wood in the church at Wedale that people said had been part of an image of Mary the mother of Jesus, but this is simply the type of thing some people have claimed and some people have believed for centuries. This information was not a helpful. I put it aside.

By contrast, the place-names in this passage point precisely to a connection between Guinnion and Stow in Wedale. Stow is said to be in *Lodonesia*, that is, in Lothian. The distance from the center of Stow to Melrose town center is twelve miles but would be less if measured from the medieval land boundaries. In any event the difference between six medieval miles and twelve modern miles is a relatively trivial point.

Wodale is the dale of the Anglo-Saxon god Woden, and so at one time Stow Fort was probably Woden's Fort (perhaps an Angle outpost before the war although it is more likely the fort-name Woden, is an Anglicization of later centuries). Anything to do with Woden would not have been pleasing to Christian ears, and so, just as Wodensday became Wednesday, places named Woden's fortification became Wednesbury, and places named Woden's open-land became Wedensfield, Wodale became Wedale.

The name Woden being unacceptable to Christians, it is likely that some cleric, having noticed that Woden sounded like the English word *woe*, decided to create a Latin version of the dale or vale and came up with the Vale of Woe: in Latin, *Vallis-doloris*. Woe was popular among the Christians. This was but one more pretense among many designed to empower the Christian Church at the expense of the truth: in this case, at the expense of truth about Arthur.

The *Vallis-doloris* invention was not used as the name of Arthur's battle, because to exorcise all Woden-associations, later Christian writers brought out their biggest gun: Mary the mother of Jesus, also known as St. Mary or the Blessed Mary. The P-Celtic for "blessed" in the adjectival form is *gwyn*, from which the name *Guinnion* eventually came.

This scenario fits neatly with Christian practice: not to eradicate sites of the Old Way but to commandeer them and use them as their own. This practice was made official by Pope Gregory I in the decade after The Great Angle War. Mary's name was frequently used when places of the people of the Old Way were taken over by Christians, particularly if the place had particular female connections.

The "Lady's Well" that once lay near St. Mary's Church in Stow was once a well of the women of the Old Way. The large stone that was to be found outside the church until about 1815 and was said to have borne Mary's footprint had nothing to do with Mary. It was almost certainly similar to the stone at Dunadd from which Arthur took a sword and probably used for the same purpose.

I picture Arthur at the Battle of Guinnion leading the combined forces of Strathclyde, together with his Scots and Men of Manau, and forcing a crossing of the Gala Water, "shattering the Angle line and scattering their columns, laying men low and making Angle wives widows." The words of Aneirin, Arthur's druid-bard, written fourteen years later, apply equally to Guinnion, "Stiff spears this splitter would slash in battle, ripping the front rank."[6]

The Angles fell back from the ford over the Gala Water, some to the fort, some eastwards through the pass to Lauderdale, and some southwards to the City of the Legions, where they would soon face Arthur again. After the Battle of Guinnion-Stow, there was nothing to stop the Gododdin army of the north from joining Arthur's army of the west and going after the Angles together.

Arthur had fought the Angles to a standstill in the Caledonian Wood and driven them back from the fort at Stow in the Battle of Guinnion. Arthur was now riding the crest of a wave of victory, and so it was not the time for the allied kings to dispute the matter of command. This was the time to use their momentum, to harry the enemy and stop them regrouping. If Arthur had not continued to advance, the kings would surely have decided that they were not after all content to be led by a Scots warlord, no matter how well he had done, and that one of their own should be appointed in his place.

Arthur must have known that although he had bested the Angles in two battles, many Angle divisions remained untested and that consequently, he had to move fast. At the head of the largest force he was ever to command, Arthur stepped up the pace and so ensured that the Angles remained off balance.

Twelve miles to the south, the Angle survivors of Guinnion-Stow met the rest of their army retiring south through Lauderdale. This reunited Angle army formed up on ground upon which they thought they could stand secure. So it was, as Nennius says, "The ninth battle was fought in the city of the Legion."

Trimontium, where the Gala Water joins the River Tweed, was the Roman capital of Scotland in the first and second centuries. By the 580s it would have been in a state of advanced disrepair, but it would still have been remembered as the City of the Legion. It was here for the first time in the campaign that the entire armies of both sides concentrated and faced each other. This was to be the Gettysburg of the first part of the Great Angle War.

Arthur did not hesitate but moved fast against his enemies. Shields clashed, men hacked with axes, cut with swords, and stabbed with spears, as both sides sought weaknesses in their enemies' shield-walls.

Again, Aneirin's words provide a taste of events at the Battle of the City of the Legion-Trimontium:

Ringed round him a rampart of shields, sharp they press the
attack, seize plunder,
Loud as thunder the crashing of shields.
Ardent man, prudent man, champion, he ripped and he
pierced with his spearpoints,
Deep in blood he butchered with blades, in the strife, heads
under hard iron.[7]

When the Angle shield-wall eventually broke, the real horror began as Arthur's men slaughtered their retreating enemies. Arthur was,

A reaper in War, he drank the sweet wine.
Mind bent on battle, he reaped battle's leeks.
Battle's bright band sang a battle song armed for battle,
Battle's pinions, his shield was sheared thin by spears in the
strife.
Comrades were fallen in battle-harness.
Stirring his war-cry, faultless his service, spellbound his
frenzy . . .[8]

The Angle stores in the fort would have made good plunder, and it cannot have been easy to maintain disciple in the ranks of Arthur's army of allies when Trimontium fell. Many other commanders would have rested secure in the knowledge that they had comprehensively defeated the enemy army, even if they had not destroyed it entirely, but not Arthur. Unlike Meade after Gettysburg, when he delayed before following Lee's defeated army to the Potomac, Arthur sprang after the Angles, looking to bring them to battle, one more time.

When I started looking for Tribruit, the tenth battle on Nennius' list, I was impressed by R. G. Collingwood's idea that the *tri* prefix meant "three." I was less impressed with his conclusion that the site of the battle might have been Chichester Harbour, where there was a triple estuary when the tide was coming in fast.[9] The nearest I got to something sensible using the "three" idea was when I considered the place where the rivers Tweed and Teviot meet. I knew these only added up to two rivers, but the Tweed at its junction with the Teviot is divided by an island that creates two streams, which, when they join the Teviot, produces three streams of rushing water. But I knew this was about as daft as Collingwood's triple-estuary-of-Chichester-Harbour suggestion, and I had scoffed at it. In my notes I wrote next to my idea, "Not confident about this." I was right not to be confident about this, because it was the wrong answer. I was, however, very close to the right answer, although, at that time, I did not know it.

Benny Hill once recited,

> They said it was an impossible task.
> Some even said they knew it.
> But I . . . I tried the impossible task,
> And I couldn't bloody do it.

I knew how he felt. Thinking "three" proved to be a pointless exercise —three what? I wasn't the first to add innumerable P- and Q-Celtic words *to tri* to see what I would get, and I was as unsuccessful as everyone else. One Welsh word however, *brwydr*, meaning "battle" or "struggle," seemed promising. It produced something like Third Battle, but this did not make sense because Tribruit was the ninth battle on the list.

Tribruit is an awkward word both euphonically and linguistically, and awkward words do not survive because users change them. I came to believe that, like many sixth century words, *Tribruit* was a corrupt form of an earlier word, one which was more awkward still. I found this earlier word in the Vatican Recension–version of Nennius's *Historia*, which contains not *Tribruit* but *Trevroit*. I was getting warmer.

As things turned out I did not have to find Tribruit. When I found the locations of the seventh, eighth, and ninth battles, the location of the tenth battle became obvious, to the very yard. The tenth battle on Nennius's list of Arthur's battles was fought, "On the banks of a river which is called Tribruit."[10] If the seventh, eighth, and ninth battles had been fought, respectively, in the Caledonian Wood, at Guinnion-Stow, and at the City of the Legions-Trimontium near Melrose, all that was necessary to find Tribruit was to draw a line through these three battle locations and keep going. It was impossible to miss Tribruit-Trevroit, because ten miles south of the City of the Legion-Trimontium is the River Teviot.

Tribruit-Trevroit-Teviot is in the right place on the battle-list, immediately after the battles of the Caledonian Wood, Guinnion-Stow, and the City of the Legion-Trimontium. Geographically the Teviot is a perfect fit, and it is of course a river, just as Nennius said. The name Tribruit and to an even greater extent the name Trevroit are close kin to the name Teviot. All three of Nennius's criteria—the place on the list, the river connection and the name—are satisfied by the River Teviot.

It may be reasonably inferred that the Angles retreated along Roman Dere Street, and so it is possible to identify the exact spot where the Battle of Tribruit took place: where the modern footbridge is today, a few yards south of Monteviot House, where the Roman Road crossed the Teviot. There is corroboration of this Tribruit-Trevroit-Teviot identification in the eleventh-century Welsh poem *Pa Gur*, which tells of a place called Tryfrwyd, generally accepted as Tribruit.

> Manawyd brought home
> A pierced shield from Tryfrwyd . . .
> By the hundreds they fell
> To Bedwyrís' four-pronged spear,
> On the shores of Tryfrwyd.

Manawyd is usually placed in the south of Britain or held to be the Isle of Man by determined southern Arthurians, but when looked at as part of the big picture, it is obvious, is it not, that Manawyd is the Manau of Arthur Mac Aedan?

To paraphrase Aneirin writing at a later date in another connection, on savage stallions Arthur and his companions leaped as one and fiercely crushed their foes in hard fighting. Together they hewed the Angle enemy. Indeed they did. Arthur and his army drove the Angles back to the Teviot, and there they routed them entirely as the panicked Angles tried to put the river between them their worst nightmare, Arthur.

The Angles, all but trapped, fought ferociously for their lives. In charge after charge Arthur's lieutenants, including his nephew Gawain, led the warriors Arthur called "the best men in the world."[12] Kay, Arthur's boyhood friend and now one of his veterans, excelled on the banks of the Teviot: according to one account he killed one in three of the enemy, although this is doubtless somewhat exaggerated: "The sword in the battle was unerring in his hand."[13]

Kay rejoiced "as long as he hewed down," and he hewed down until he was killed by arrows.

> To battle he would come
> By the hundred would he slaughter;
> There was no day that would satisfy him.
> Unmerited was the death of Cai [Kay] . . .
> Before the pang of blue shafts.[14]

Arthur's lieutenant Bedevere and an otherwise unknown officer, Bridlaw, were in command of the wings of Arthur's army:

> Nine hundred would listen to them.
> Six hundred gasping for breath,
> Would be the cost of attacking them.

Eventually, the last bloody remains of what had once been a proud and powerful Angle army escaped across the Teviot and hurried in panic south to their coastal heartlands. It was to be thirty years before they staged such a campaign again, and when they did they went south not north. The Angles were victorious in the south; there they created Angle-land, England. Had it not been for Arthur, the same thing would have happened in the north and there would have been no Scotland, only a Greater England.

Arthur led an allied army on this one occasion only. In a campaign of relentless ferocity he won four battles, in the Caledonian Wood, at Guinnion-Stow, at the City of the Legion-Trimontium and finally on the banks of Tribruit-Trevroit-Teviot river.

When and where Arthur lived and who he was have long been mysteries that have beset historians for centuries. The Great Angle War is different. It has not been a mystery because, until *Finding Merlin*, no one had said there had been a Great Angle War, and so no one was beset by its mysteries. If the above conclusions are correct then there was a Great Angle War, and it was won by Arthur.

Arthur's victory on the banks of the Teviot ended only the first Act of the Great Angle War. When next the Angles attacked, Arthur would stand alone against them and win, quite literally, endless fame.

THE BATTLE OF AGNED-BREGUOIN

The Picts were content to watch their enemies tear each other to pieces in the Great Angle War, and to wait and see who won. They knew that if the Angles were victorious they would soon have to face them in battle, and that if the Angles lost they would soon have to face Arthur again.

According to the conventional wisdom there are two alternative eleventh battles in the battle-list of Nennius. The eleventh battle most often referred to is in the Harleian-related manuscripts:[15] "The eleventh battle was on the hill called Agned." The alternative eleventh battle is in Vatican Recension–related manuscripts:[16] "The eleventh [battle] was on the mountain Breguoin, which we call Cat Bregion." The so-called Gildensian manuscript of the *Historia*,[17] effectively the Harleian manuscript with a few changes, confuses the matter further with a composite version of the Harleian- and Vatican-related manuscripts: "Mount Agned, that is Cat Bregomium [*sic*]."

Despite being predisposed to place Arthur in the south, many who favor a southern Arthur are prepared to concede that Agned-Breguoin, was fought in Edinburgh or at least that the Battle of Agned was fought there. Even J. A. Giles said Agned was fought in Cadbury, Somerset, England, but allowed that Edinburgh was a possible location.[18] This suggests that there must be really good evidence for Edinburgh.

Opinions are divided on Breguoin. Some say Agned and Breguoin were the same battle, others that they were different battles and that Breguoin was fought somewhere else. There is no consensus among those who hold that Arthur was a man of the south, but most of them hold that there were two eleventh battles, perhaps because they cannot find a convincing Agned or a convincing Breguoin in the south, far less a place that satisfies both alternatives.

It is clear from the Vatican-related manuscripts, the ones that say, "The eleventh [battle] was on the mountain *Breguoin, which we call Cat Bregion*," that the earlier name was Breguoin and that Bregion is an alternative to Breguoin in another language. If the battle name had been in Latin, the universal language of the day, it would have been the same everywhere and there would have been no need for Nennius to provide an alternative which was familiar to his audience. It is therefore unlikely that either Breguoin or Bregion are Latin names.

Nennius, a monk of Bangor in Wales, would have spoken an early form of Welsh and so, when he says, "which we call . . . Bregion," he probably means in P-Celtic Welsh. It follows, therefore, that *Breguoin* cannot also be a P-Celtic word. If *Breguoin* is not a Latin or a Welsh P-Celtic word, then it is almost certainly a Q-Celtic word, because there is no other reasonable alternative language available. If *Breguoin* was a Q-Celtic word, it was likely it originated in Q-Celtic speaking Scotland or Ireland and not in the south of Britain.

The introduction to O'Brien's 1768 *Dictionary* says,

> The other vestige of ancient Irish habitations in Anglesy [*sic*], is the name of the ruins of a great edifice in that island, which Mr Rowland thinks to have been the *Arch-Druid's* supreme court of judicature. Those ruins are to this day called *Bruyn-gwin*, as the Welsh write it: a plain Irish word which signifies a white palace or house, the same as *white hall* in London. *Bruighean*, pronounced *Brúin* or *Bruyn*, in Irish signifies a great house or palace.[19]

Here, in perfect pairing, is a Q-Celtic Irish-Scottish word, *Bruighean*, that is akin to *Breguoin* and an equivalent P-Celtic Welsh word, *Bruyn-gwin*, that is similarly akin to *Bregion*. (Irish and Scottish were interchangeable in the sixth century.) This corroborates the evidence that suggests *Breguoin* was a Q-Celtic-Gaelic word and *Bregion* a P-Celtic word. It seems unlikely that this is a mere coincidence.

Allowing for the inevitable mishearings and misunderstandings that would have occurred as these words were bandied about between innumerable people from different backgrounds, speaking different languages, over different generations, it is easy to see that the person who wrote, "*Breguoin*, which we call *Cat* Bregion," might more accurately have written "*Bruighean*, which we call *Cat Bruyn-gwin*," because the latter version has at least the virtue of making sense.

"*Breguoin*, which we call *Cat* Bregion" is meaningless. "*Bruighean*, which we call *Cat Bruyn-gwin*," means, in Scots Q-Celtic, "the battle of the great house or palace," and in Welsh P-Celtic, "the battle of the white palace or house." O'Brien has more to offer. Even if he had not written about an Arch-Druid in connection with a great or white house or palace on the island of Anglesey, he would have highlighted a druidic connection because Anglesey was the main center of the druids in Britain until it was devastated by the Romans around 60 CE: the very reference to Anglesey smacks of the druids.

The color white has been associated with the druids ever since Pliny the Elder wrote about druids dressed in white cutting mistletoe from oak trees with golden shears, and so the association of druids and a white house also makes sense. All this evidence points to a location somewhere in Q-Celtic-speaking lands, which had some great or white house or palace connection . . . and some druids.

Of course, Agned still stands to be considered. If Agned was not Edinburgh or any one of the other suggested sites—where is it? Skene provides the necessary clue. Although, in his *Four Ancient Books of Wales*, he said that Agned was Edinburgh, he also provided evidence that suggested otherwise, although, of course, he did not know that: ". . . *Agned* or *Mynydd Agned* probably comes from an obsolete word, *agneaw*, to paint, *agneaid*, painted."[20] He is more specific a few pages later when he says *Mynydd Agned* means the Painted Mount.

The Picts called themselves *Cruithne*, the people. The name Pict by which they are best known today is said to have been derived from the Latin for "Painted People" and to have been given to them by the Romans because the Picts painted their bodies with intricate symbols. The Picts also carved stones with unique, intricate patterns. It may be reasonably supposed that a people called the Painted People because they painted their bodies also painted their symbol stones and their buildings (just as the Greeks painted the statues and buildings that we only see in monochrome today).

If the hill of Agned was the Painted Mount, as Skene said, then this may have been because there were painted buildings and stones on its summit. This is more likely than the actual hill being painted—it is not easy to paint a hill. If there were painted buildings and stones on Agned, then it is likely that one or more of these buildings would have been painted white because white was one of the more readily available colors, and because it is likely that at least one building was specifically for the use of the druids.

Clearly one possible place for this painted hill, and so for Agned, was somewhere in the lands of the Picts, the painted people. If Agned has a Pictish connection this would suggest that Agned and Breguoin must be separate battles because other evidence suggested that *Breguoin*, which Nennius's P-Celtic speakers called *Bregion*, was probably a Q-Celtic word, and the Picts did not speak Q-Celtic.

But then, this isn't necessarily so.

If the eleventh battle was fought where battles tend to be fought, on a border, then, it may be that Breguoin and Agned were two names for the same place. It may be that on one side of the border the battle was named Breguoin by Q-Celtic-speaking people and that on the other side of the border the battle was named Agned by P-Celtic-speaking people. If this is correct then Agned-Breguoin would have been on a Q-Celtic–P-Celtic border. The longest such border in Britain lay between the Scots and the Picts.

Useful practical details are scanty in the extreme in the early sources, but *The Prose Lancelot* contains one specific, practical detail concerning Nennius's eleventh battle: it says Bredigan (Breguoin) was five days' march from Berwick on the east coast, on the Scotland–England border. This detail does nothing to enhance the story, and so, although *The Prose Lancelot* is twelfth century and thus a very late source, this five-day march has to be considered weighty evidence.

There are two clues—a distance and a starting point.

No one knows how far a "five days' march" was in the sixth century. Roman legions marched about ten miles a day, and so, for a

Roman legionary, a five-day march was about fifty miles. This seemed a little short to me, but then I was not the one who had to build a fortified camp at the end of each days march. In 1066 King Harold of England force-marched his army from London to York, a distance of 210 miles, in some four or five days, depending upon the source, thus averaging forty-two to fifty-two miles a day. This seemed to me to be a little too far to be a standard five-day march. I asked modern soldiers how far they could march in a day, but no one I spoke to in the modern army had an answer to that question. They said everything depended upon the conditions, the circumstances, and the soldiers themselves. In 1982 in the Falkland Islands men of the Parachute Regiment "yomped" fifty-six miles over rough terrain carrying eighty-pound packs in three days. If they had kept going at this amazing pace they would have covered about ninety miles in five days.

How far is a "five days' march"? I gave up trying to find an exact answer to this question, but the "Goldilocks" solution was to suppose that a it lay somewhere between the Roman's 50 miles and Harold's 210 miles. This made the Paratroopers' 90 miles sound about right (given that soldiers in the sixth century would not have been carrying eighty-pound packs).

The question then is, Who marched for five days from Berwick? Only the Angles lived in Berwick at the relevant time, whatever that time was, and so it had to be the Angles.

Now we come to a big question. If the Angles started in Berwick and marched for five days before they came to fight Nennius's eleventh battle, where did they march to?

They were unlikely to have marched northwest against the Gododdin again, so soon after Arthur had soundly beaten them in the campaign of the Caledonian Wood. To have tried to bypass the Gododdin and move directly against Strathclyde or Manau would have been to leave their right flank open to attack by the Gododdin, which would have been madness. There was nobody to attack in the west, except perhaps Rheged, but it makes no sense to suppose that the Angles would have attacked some new party when they had enough enemies already (and again this would have left them vulnerable to a flank attack). It seems unlikely that at this time they would have marched south and opened a second front against a new enemy, leaving their homeland open to invasion by their recent adversaries, the peoples of the Gododdin and Strathclyde. This left only the east, but if they had marched east they would have drowned because the North Sea is in the east. With hindsight, I can see how close I came to the answer when I got this far, and how I stepped away from it just before I got there.

How could the eleventh battle have been fought and won by Arthur, that is, by Arthur Mac Aedan, if his enemies were the Angles? They could not have fought each other if they could not get at each other. It makes no sense to suppose that Strathclyde and the Gododdin stood aside and let the Angles have a go at Arthur so soon after the service Arthur had rendered them in the campaign of the Caledonian Wood.

And yet . . . Berwick was ninety-four miles from Stirling, a distance that fitted the distance "five days' march" perfectly. It was frustrating. I couldn't let it go. I felt I was missing something important. There is so little practical evidence in the old sources, far less specific distances, that I was sure this distance had to mean something, but I could not see where "five days' march" from Berwick took the Angles.

As so often before when I could not find an answer, I found that I had been asking the wrong question. I had become hung-up on the question of where "five days' march" would have taken the Angles. I should have been asking, Why was this distance important?

The obvious answer was that this distance was important simply because this distance is one of the few distances to have survived when innumerable other distances have been lost. Of course, before it could survive in the record, it first had to exist in the record. When few distances were ever recorded, the real question, the vital question, the question I should have been asking was, Why was this distance recorded in the first place?

The Angles would have known the marching distance from their base to potential battlefields within, well . . . marching distance. Most of us have at least a rough idea of the distance from our homes to nearby places of interest. I know how long it would take me to drive from my home to Birmingham or to Newcastle. I have made both of these journeys. I do not know how long it would take me to drive from Birmingham to Newcastle, because I have not made that journey.

It seems likely that the reason the distance was recorded in the first place was because it was vital information, possibly because the Angles needed to know exactly how far they would have to march to battle through, what was for them, unfamiliar territory. This insight provided the solution to the puzzle. The journey to the eleventh battlefield may have started in Berwick and involved a five-day march, but the march itself did not start in Berwick. First they went by sea.

If the Angle expedition was a combined naval and army exercise involving a journey first by sea and then by land, across unfamiliar terrain, everything made sense. There was only one place the Angles could have gone.

The evidence is this: The eleventh battle involved Arthur and enemies from Berwick, who could only be the Angles. The Angles sailed *somewhere* before they marched for five days to fight Nennius's eleventh battle. Where could they have sailed to? Where else but to join Arthur's other enemies, the Picts?

Arthur's father Aedan had devastated the Pictish fleet in the early 580s. Around 584, Arthur had crushed the Pictish army at Bassas-Circenn-Carpow, before going on to defeat the army of the Angles in the campaign of the Caledonian Wood. It follows, therefore, that the Picts and the Angles had reason to make common cause.

The Angles must have known that if they remained on the defensive they would soon be attacked by another allied British army, but their offensive options were limited because their army had been severely mauled by Arthur in the campaign of the Caledonian Wood. However, they still had an intact fleet and a potential ally in the Picts.

The Picts knew that if they could defeat Arthur, Manau would lie open to them. Their navy had been smashed by Aedan's fleet in the early 580s, but they still had an intact army, albeit one that had suffered severe losses at Arthur's hands at Bassas-Circenn-Carpow, and they had a potential ally in the Angles.

It made sense to suppose that the Angles and the Picts agreed to combine their forces and send an army overland, west into Dalriada, and a fleet around the top of Scotland to attack Dalriada from the north. If they coordinated properly, Arthur's Scots of Dalriada would be caught in a pincer movement.

If the Angles were allied with the Picts, the most likely place for them to disembark their land forces would have been where the Romans unloaded their ships, the fort at Bassas-Circenn-Carpow, less than one hundred miles north of Berwick on the North Sea. The Anglo-Pictish navy would then have been free to sail around the north of Scotland to provide support when the allied army of Angles and Picts arrived at the western sea.

If the Anglo-Pictish land army marched west along the Roman road from Bassas-Circenn-Carpow to Lochearnhead, and carried on through Glen Ogle, Glen Dochart, Strath Fillan and Glen Lochy past the Falls of Cruachan at the head of Loch Awe and into the Pass of Brander, it would have come to the sea at Airds Bay. There they would have found that directly ahead of them lay what is now the village of Benderloch. In the sixth century Benderloch was the fortress town of Beregonium.

The marching distance from Bassas-Circenn-Carpow to Beregonium-Benderloch is about ninety-one miles, a reasonable five-day march.

It seems likely that if the Anglo-Pictish army headed west, it headed toward Beregonium-Benderloch. Of course, Beregonium is obviously a possible Latin version of Breguoin and Bregion.

I said earlier that Agned and the Castle of the Maidens had become confused with Edinburgh because Geoffrey said Mount Agned was "the Maidens' Castle," and Edinburgh was called Castle of the Maidens. It only follows that Edinburgh was Agned if there was only one Castle of the Maidens. However there were and indeed still are innumerable Maiden connections all over Scotland, including Maiden Island, south-west of Beregonium-Benderloch, across Ardmucknish Bay. It is quite possible, therefore, that there was a Maiden connection with the fort at Beregonium-Benderloch.

The evidence suggests that Nennius's eleventh battle, named both Agned and Breguoin, was fought at the fort of Beregonium, modern-day Benderloch. If so it was there that Arthur, Arthur Mac Aedan, met and defeated a combined land force of Angles and Picts.

It is likely that Agned and Breguoin were but two names for one battle.

Beregonium-Benderloch and only Beregonium-Benderloch is consistent with all the evidence concerning Nennius's eleventh battle, "On the mountain *Breguoin*, which we call *Cat Bregion*." The name Beregonium is in all probability a Latinized version of the Q-Celtic *Bruighean* from which we get *Breguoin*, and the P-Celtic Welsh *Bruyn-gwin* from which we get *Bregion*. It is likely that in the past these Celtic names were adjusted to make them more euphonic to non-Celtic ears and that a Latin ending was added. The *b* and *g* sounds of both Breguoin and Bregion are echoed in Beregonium. Besides, Gildensian-related manuscripts that say, "Mount Agned, that is *Cat Bregomium*," seem to me to be too close to *Beregonium* to be coincidental.

One name, Bruighean from which we get Breguoin, is Scots Q-Celtic, and the other *Bruyn-gwin* from which we get *Bregion*, is in the P-Celtic of the Picts. In the sixth century Beregonium was on the Scots–Pict border and often changed hands. The very fact that Beregonium was on a border lends weight to the argument that this was where the eleventh battle was fought, because, for obvious reasons, battles were often fought on borders. Being on the border between P- and Q-Celtic speakers also lends weight to the argument that there were two names for the same battle, one in Q- and one in P-Celtic.

It may be that Nennius's source came with two names for the one location because the site of the battle was on a P-Celtic–Q-Celtic border. This makes sense because it explains why Nennius did not provide alternatives for other battle-names on his list: they were not on borders. It is also possible that Nennius had more than one source, one which referred to Breguoin-Bregion and another to Agned. This is simpler and so, perhaps, more likely.

According to Skene in his *Chronicles of the Picts and Scots and Other Early Memorials*, Arthur's great-great-grandfather, Fergus Mor Mac Erc, brought the Stone of Destiny with him from Ireland to Scotland and installed it in a town he built near Dunstaffnage Castle. Dunstaffnage lies across Ardmucknish Bay, three miles south of Beregonium-Benderloch and three miles is pretty near.

Boece, a Scottish historian who flourished around the year 1,500

CE, says, "Fergus . . . brought the chair [the Stone of Destiny] from Ireland to Argyll, and was crowned upon it. He built a town in Argyll called Beregonium, in which he placed it."[21]

It would be reasonable to suppose that Fergus installed the Stone of Destiny in a suitably impressive building; indeed, if we are to accept Boece at face value, Fergus built a whole new town to house it. It is more likely, however, that Fergus fortified and added to buildings that were already there. It would be surprising if this specially built or at least improved town did not have one grand building constructed in the traditional manner and painted either in Pictish multicolor or druidic white. Such a building would fit the great white house criteria that gave rise to the Breguoin-Bregion names.

Beregonium-Benderloch had been Pictish for centuries, on and off, and so it would also be surprising if most of its buildings were not painted. A hillfort surrounded by painted buildings fits Skene's *agneaid*, "painted mount," and points directly to the battle-name Agned. The very fact that there was a fort Agned-Breguoin-Benderloch lends weight to this argument because, for obvious reasons, battles were often fought at forts. The details of this eleventh battle are not known: who did what and when, how the two sides engaged each other, we do not know. We only know that Arthur won. As far as can be gathered from the evidence, what happened was something along the following lines.

The Scots of Dalriada under Fergus Mor, Arthur's great-great-grandfather, had taken Beregonium-Benderloch in the early sixth century. Some eighty years later the Picts wanted it back, but they were not strong enough to do this on their own, as they had just lost much of their fleet to Aedan's navy. The Angles too had just been heavily defeated at the hands of an allied army under Arthur's command in the Great Angle War. They knew that if they were to be successful in any future war in the lowlands of Scotland that they would first have to neutralize Arthur. However they were not strong enough to do this on their own.

The Angles and the Picts formed an alliance and agreed to attack Arthur together. The Angles sailed north from Berwick to Carpow, near modern Perth, and there disembarked before marching west to meet their Pictish allies near Beregonium-Benderloch. This ground was unfamiliar to the Angles, but they knew their march to battle would take five days, because the Picts had provided them with this information. As the Angles marched west, their fleet sailed north around the top of Scotland to fall on Arthur from the sea.

It was always possible that the Anglo-Pictish army and fleet might have headed south from Carpow to attack Stirling. Arthur would not have known where the attack would fall until his enemies were on the move. When the Scots scouts and glen-watchers told Arthur that the Anglo-Pictish army was heading west he rode north from his base at what is now Ben Arthur at the head of a flying-force of cavalry. He would have had time to get ahead of the advancing Angles and Picts and could have met them in the field at any time, but his men were not all mustered and so he fell back before the Angles and the Picts as they advanced. He needed time to allow the Scots of Dunardry-Dunadd to assemble and march north to join him.

The advancing Angles and Picts were also determined to avoid contact with the Scots until they joined the main Pictish army near the west coast. It was there, about the fort of Beregonium-Benderloch, that the opposing armies met. The eleventh battle on Nennius's battle-list, the battle called both Agned and Breguoin, was fought on and about the hillfort of Beregonium-Benderloch. We do not have details of this battle, but we do know Arthur won, because Nennius says he won, and that he and his men chased the Angles and the Picts back into the glens and to their ships.

If Nennius's eleventh battle, Agned-Breguoin, was fought at Beregonium-Benderloch, then this eleventh battle was fought only some forty miles north of Dunardry-Dunadd and the battlefield of Badon-Badden. When I visited Benderloch with my son in 2003, we came across a living example of the way names change. We asked the young woman serving at the petrol station how to get to the fort and she gave us perfect directions to, what she correctly called, Beregonium. We still got lost however, and so when we met an older woman out walking her dog we asked her if we were on the right path to Beregonium. She told us the fort was right ahead, but she called it Ben Gonium. The young woman in the service station had probably both heard and read the name at school. The older woman had probably only heard the name as she grew up, and, as she was familiar with the word *ben*, which means "a hill," and as the fort was situated on a hill, she made the understandable mistake of thinking *Beregonium* was *Ben Gonium*.

Today the hillfort at Agned-Breguoin-Beregonium-Benderloch is heavily overgrown, with only a stub of a ruin on its summit, but in the sixth century it was a substantial place, standing above a sizable settlement. The fort was strategically vital because it lay on the border between the Scots and the Picts and because it commanded the bay of Selma, Ardmucknish Bay, and the main west coast seaways, several sea-lochs, and access to the Great Glen.

We did not make it to the top of the hill—it was too heavily overgrown—but from halfway up it was easy to see that the view over the crescent beach of the bay is largely unspoiled and easy to picture what Arthur saw when he stood there.

THE BATTLE OF BADON

Gildas's *De Excidio*, which contains the earliest reference to the Battle of Badon, is generally taken to have been written in the early sixth century. "Gildas wrote his main work, the *Ruin of Britain*, about A.D. 540 or just before," says one authoritative editor, but it is more likely that *De Excidio* was compiled by Gildas from earlier writings and completed around 598, some ten years after the Battle of Badon.

The second record of the Battle of Badon to survive is in Nennius's battle-list: "The twelfth battle was on Badon Hill and in it nine hundred and sixty men fell in one day, from a single charge of Arthur's, and no one laid them low save he alone."[22]

All the other records, including the *Annales Cambriae*, which places the Battle of Badon in 516, are based to some degree upon Gildas and Nennius; although it is likely some other source, now lost, informed the compilers of these *Annales*, because the *Annales* include an extra detail: the period of time over which the battle took place: "The Battle of Badon in which Arthur carried the Cross of our Lord Jesus Christ for three days and three nights on his shoulders and the Britons were the victors."[23]

Three days would make for a short siege. This would have been barely enough time to invest a fortress and launch an attack upon its fortifications, and certainly too little time to starve out besieged defenders. So where did *three days and three nights* come from? What happened during these three days and nights?

Use of the number three is a common device in Western tales: the story of Jesus rising from the dead after three days, the story of "The Three Bears." It may be that the matter of three days in Gildas's *De Excidio* is only a device and no more.

Gildas hints that his god was toying with the people over this period of three days to see if they really liked him, "So that in this people the Lord could make trial (as he tends to do) of his latter-day Israel to see whether it loves him or not."[24]

This is a bit bizarre. If the obviously spurious material in Nennius, the stuff that has Arthur killing everyone on his own, is disregarded, and if the passage in the *Annales* that has Arthur carrying a wooden cross about the battlefield on his shoulders is put aside (because that is just daft—holy product placement, pure and simple), then the material that remains can be looked at to see if it contains evidence that might confirm that Badon was fought at Badden. The most important item of evidence that remains is the fact that the *Annales Cambriae* say that the battle extended over three days and three nights, which is usually taken to mean that a siege was involved. When I got this far I found I had nothing more to work with. The matter of three days and three nights had to wait until they could be seen as part of a bigger picture.

The evidence suggests that the eleventh battle on Nennius' battle-list, the Battle of Agned-Breguoin, was fought at Benderloch. Badon was the twelfth battle on the list. In the land of Badden at the foot of Dunardry, forty miles south of Benderloch, there is a likely site for the Battle of Badon. Given that Dunardry and Badden are contiguous, it is also likely that Dunardry is Badon Hill.

Once I had found the sites of the eleventh and the twelfth battles, the next question I had to answer was, Why do the records say that the Battle of Badon lasted three days and three nights? I had the answer to this question in the locations for the eleventh and twelfth battles, but I hadn't seen it yet.

No one can say with certainty what happened in the lead up to and in the course of the Battle of Badon; all that can be said is that what follows is consistent with the earliest historical records and with the geography of Argyll. After the Battle of Agned-Breguoin Arthur's warriors were in the glens and hills east of Benderloch hunting down the survivors of the Anglo-Pictish army who had not found refuge in their ships. Arthur Mac Aedan probably stood on the ramparts of the fort at Benderloch looking out across the Bay of Selma, Ardmucknish Bay, watching the Anglo-Pictish fleet sail west, thinking it was headed for home.

The Anglo-Pictish fleet, however, was still intact and its ships filled with angry Angles and Picts spoiling for revenge and lusting for some speedy riposte to sate their wounded pride. Instead of sailing north, back the way they had come, humiliated and disappointed with only shaming news to report, they sailed south some forty miles, intent on laying waste the fertile heartlands of Dalriada. This was not a part of a grand strategy designed to outflank the Scots and win the war. The war was already lost. This southern venture was no more than a wild hate-filled lunge born of anger and frustration. Its aim was to kill undefended people and plunder their property and to allow the Angles and Picts to go home with something to talk about other than utter failure.

The Anglo-Pictish warriors stormed ashore at Crinan and found themselves facing only Scots women and children and the wounded soldiers and veterans who had not marched north with the army. Word was sent north to Arthur, and the Scots took refuge in the forts of Dunardry and Dunadd. The Angles and the Picts were unable to capture Dunardry on its steep hill or Dunadd in the center of its deep marsh, and so they plundered and destroyed the lands of Badden, the lands that lay around the two forts.

It was while thinking through what might have happened at this time that I came to see how the matter of *three days and three nights* fit in. The Angles and the Picts had three days untrammeled by opposition before Arthur arrived.

When Arthur heard the Angle fleet had headed south he set off in pursuit with all the men he had available, without waiting for the rest of his army to return from its pursuit of the Angles and Picts who had headed for the hills.

If the Anglo-Pictish army marched ninety miles from Carpow to Benderloch in five days, then, by this same reckoning, Arthur's army would have been able to cover the forty-two miles from Benderloch to Dunardry in about two days, despite the fact that Arthur's army had only recently marched north and had only recently fought and won a major battle. Add to this the time it would have taken for the news that the Anglo-Picts had gone south to get to Benderloch, and we have a "perfect" three days from the time the Angles came ashore at Crinan to the time Arthur arrived to raise the siege.

We cannot know exactly how long it took Arthur to march south to relieve Dunardry-Dunadd; all we can say with certainty is that some time would have passed between the Battle of Agned-Breguoin and the raising of the siege of Badden-Dunadd-Dunardry, and that "three days" sounds about right.

Arthur's flying column rode south along the line of the modern-day road and met the Angles and Picts where the road meets the Badden Burn in the shadow of Dunardry Hill, Mount Badon.

Badon-Badden was not much of a battle. The Angles and the Picts headed back to their ships when they heard Arthur was approaching, and Arthur's vanguard fought only the Anglo-Pictish rearguard as they staged a fighting retreat to their ships. The Angles and Picts had staged a raid not an invasion, and they would have been foolish to engage Arthur in a pitched battle when all the time Scots reinforcements were arriving from the north. The Angles and the Picts had their plunder and had made their point, and so they sailed for home. Of course, in reality, they were beaten. As always, the victory was Arthur's.

The now famous Battle of Badon, the battle that ended the second and final part of the Great Angle War, was, in fact, a bathetic event. It is really only famous because it is the last battle on Nennius's list and the only one mentioned in the other early primary sources, Gildas's *De Excidio* and the *Annales Cambriae*.

The above, necessarily somewhat speculative, account of the Battle of Badon is consistent with the evidence of Gildas and Nennius and with the *three days and three nights* of the *Annales Cambriae*. It is also consistent with the evidence that suggests Dunadd was where Arthur took a sword from a stone, and that the marshy land through which the River Add twists was Camelot.

Dunardry hillfort is connected to Merlin-Lailoken by the Battle of Arderydd, fought in 573, and to Arthur Mac Aedan by the inauguration ceremony in the following year. Dunadd, "Camelot," and Dunardry all adjoin the land of Badden. How likely is it that all these things are mere coincidence?

It is likely that the Great Angle War was fought in the year or two that preceded 588, the year in which Arthur, Arthur Mac Aedan, fought and won the Battle of Badon. This is consistent with the non-supernatural passages in Gildas's *De Excidio*, "From then on victory went now to our countrymen, now to their enemies."

Nennius listed twelve battles in which Arthur was commander. In all twelve of these battles Arthur was victorious. Of course, life is bound to have been more complicated than that. We may safely assume there were other peripheral skirmishes, fights, engagements, and lesser battles, in which Arthur was not in command of the forces that faced the Angles and that the Angles won some of these. So it is true to say that sometimes one side won and sometimes the other.

Gildas goes on to say that Badon Hill was "pretty well the last defeat of the villains, and certainly not the least."[25] Apparently this passage is in especially tortuous Latin. It has certainly been much argued over. By my reconstruction, the Battle of Badon was indeed "pretty well" the last victory in the Great Angle War. It was also a bit of an anticlimax. We may reasonably suppose that after Badon-Badden there was the odd skirmish here and there but that, as far as The Great Angle War was concerned, the Battle of Badon-Badden as I have described it, was pretty well it.

As for the words, "certainly not the least": why would these be necessary if someone had not suggested that Badon was the least of Arthur's battles? No one ever says the Battle of Gettysburg was "certainly not the least" of the battles in the American Civil War, because no one would ever suggest it was. When someone says something is "not the least," the one thing you can be sure of is that it is not the greatest either. Clearly the fact that Badon was only a relatively minor battle had arisen and given rise to some controversy. If it had not, Gildas's denial of its lack of importance would have been otiose.

Having said that, Gildas's Latin is so obscure it is impossible to be certain what exactly he was trying to say. Gildas was not interested in wars. Gildas was interested in religion. He probably only mentioned Badon to draw a line under it as the last Battle of the War, as if to say, "Well, that's the War over with, now let us move on to more important matters," before going back to moaning because people didn't want to be Christians.

It is said that the Battle of Badon was followed by fifty years of peace. The Battle of Badon took place in about 588 (at least, by my account) and the Edinburgh of the Gododdin Britons fell to the Angles in 638: fifty years exactly. However, if there is one thing I have learned when writing this book, it is that sixth-century dates, like sixth-century names, are unreliable things and not to be trusted. Still, it is possible that the fifty years that separated the end of Great Angle War and the defeat of the Angles from the fall of Edinburgh and the victory of the Angles came to be called fifty years of peace, as if nothing had happened in between.

Before Badon, it was possible the Angles might conquer Scotland, as they were to conquer England in the next few centuries. If the Angles had conquered Scotland, Celtic-Britain as a significant entity would have ceased to exist, and today there would be only a Greater England with, perhaps, the last glimmers of Celtic culture clinging on along the western coasts.

After Badon, the danger of an Angle conquest of northern Britain ceased to exist for at least the ten years that preceded Gildas's *De Excidio*.[26] During this ten-year period, while many towns stood empty and ruined, there was, what Gildas calls, an unlooked for recovery.[27]

When next the Angles staged a full-blown invasion, in the mid-610s, they went south to what is now England, not north to Scotland, and so Scotland remained at "peace." The Angles clearly remembered what Arthur had done to them the last time they went north.

In the south the Angles won the Battle of Chester or Carlisle around 615 and so cut off the Britons of the north from their southern cousins. In the next few centuries the Angles and their Saxon cousins pressed the British west into what is now Wales. The rest of the south of Britain became Angle-land, England.

So it was that Arthur and the Great Angle War determined the future of Britain. But for Arthur there would be no Scotland today, no Wales, perhaps even no Ireland, only a Greater England.

The Great Angle War ended with the Battle of Badon-Badden, but Arthur had still another campaign to fight—his last. Earlier, we saw that the capital of Dalriada was said to be the hillfort Dunadd, an opinion shared by Skene, although, as the toponymist William J. Watson said in the early twentieth century, some of the evidence Skene used referred to another site, the mysterious and unidentified Dun Monaidh. It is possible, indeed probable, that Dunardry is the mysterious Dun Monaidh and, even more famously, Mount Badon, the hill of hills.[28]

10

The Legend Is Born

THE SOURCE NENNIUS USED TO COMPILE HIS LIST OF ARTHUR'S BATTLES was probably based on an original created by someone who knew Arthur Mac Aedan. The Men of Manau were involved in other battles in the late sixth century, and so it would have been easy to inflate the number of battles in which Arthur was said to have been involved, but Nennius, and we must suppose Nennius's source, mentions only twelve. He does not mention Arderydd or Delgon, because Arthur Mac Aedan was not in command in these battles; neither does he mention the naval action in which a Scots fleet attacked the Orkney Islands in the early 580s, because Arthur Mac Aedan, was not in command. Camlann, the legendary Arthur's last battle, is omitted too. It is generally accepted that this is because Nennius's source, whatever it was, was created before the Battle of Camlann was fought.

The twelve battles on the list are chronologically and geographically in order and lie within a sensible historical context and within literal striking distance of one another (in stark contrast to later writings, which have a southern Arthur fighting in Scandinavia, France, and Italy) provided, of course, that Arthur was Arthur Mac Aedan. All this suggests some fundamental source written in the time of Arthur

Mac Aedan. The question that arises is, Who created this source of evidence?

The most obvious candidate is Aneirin, the author of *Y Gododdin*, the poem that contains the earliest surviving reference to Arthur. There is just enough evidence to make a case for Aneirin, but that is all. There is not enough to say that the case is proved, at least not beyond reasonable doubt.

Aneirin flourished at the right time to create Nennius's source. The last battle on Nennius's list, the Battle of Badon, was fought around 588 (if Arthur was Arthur Mac Aedan). Arthur Mac Aedan died in 596. Nennius's battle-list does not tell of Arthur's last battle, and so, if Arthur was Arthur Mac Aedan, Nennius's source was written before 596. The Catterick campaign that lies at the heart of Aneirin's *Y Gododdin* was fought around the year 598. It is generally accepted that Aneirin wrote *Y Gododdin* around 600. This means it is possible Aneirin wrote the sources used by Nennius, sometime shortly before 596.

Aneirin was also in the right place to create Nennius's source. It is generally accepted that Aneirin wrote *Y Gododdin* in Edinburgh. Edinburgh is only a few miles east of Stirling's "Round Table" and a few miles north of the battlefields of the Great Angle War. Arthur's Seat is in the middle of Edinburgh. Aneirin was in the right place to have known Arthur Mac Aedan and to have written about him.

The following, although somewhat speculative, is consistent with the slight evidence that survives.

Aneirin of the Flowing Verse, Prince of Poets, is almost invariably said to have been a Welshman, indeed his name is now stereotypically Welsh, but there is reason to doubt he was ever in Wales; indeed the little evidence that has survived suggests he was not.

The Britons who lived in the north of England had grown soft under Roman rule, while the Scots, who had never been conquered by Rome, had remained practiced fighters. Consequently, when the Romans left, the Scots increasingly raided British lands, and the Britons responded by bringing in Angle mercenaries from their German homes to provide them with protection. Before long the Angles became a greater threat to the Britons than the Scots had ever been; indeed by the mid-sixth century the Angles had become a threat to

both the Britons and the Scots, and so the Britons and the Scots became allies.

Aneirin's father, the warlord Dunod Fwr or Dunawd Bwr—that
is, Dunod or Dunawd, the great or stalwart—was one of many Scots
warlords who moved south and found employment bolstering the
forces of the kingdom of Elmet in the north Pennines, against Angle
pressure (just as Arthur's grandfather Gabhran had been called upon to
lead the Men of Manau a generation before). Dunod-Dunawd died
around 593. It is hard to avoid the conclusion that the real name of
Aneirin's father has been forgotten, and that all we have left, Dunod or
Dunawd, was really "of Dunadd" or "from Dunadd," that is, Dunadd
in Argyll. If he was a Scots warlord then this would make sense.

In "The Reciter's Prologue" at the beginning of *Y Gododdin*,
Aneirin is described as the "son of Dwywei." This links him with the
royal houses of the North of England. Dwywei, a princess of Elmet,
the lands about modern Leeds, was the sister of Gwallog (r. 560–590),
one of four "kings" who fought alongside Urien of Rheged, Rhydderch
of Strathclyde, and Mordred of the Gododdin against the Angles at
Lindisfarne in the late 560s.[1] It appears that Aneirin's father married
into the royal house of the kingdom of Elmet just as Gabhran, Arthur's
grandfather, married a Pictish princess in Manau.

Dwywei was the mother of Deinioel, the patron saint of Bangor,
who according to the *Annales Cambriae* died in 584. If Aneirin was
Deinioel's younger brother, these dates would fit well with those of a
poet who flourished in the late sixth and early seventh centuries.

Aneirin probably spent most of his boyhood in the north of
England, although it may be he also spent some time among his
father's people. If he did, this would have allowed Aneirin to join
Arthur Mac Aedan's company, indeed, to have become Arthur's friend
and personal bard.

In his later years, despite many misgivings, Aneirin marched south
with the Gododdin army to Catterick, when he must have known they
were headed toward inevitable defeat. A man such as this, when he was
a young man, would almost certainly have "charged to the sound of the
guns." In the sixth century the equivalent of sounding guns was the
clash of shields, and, more often than not, this was where Arthur was

to be found. It would have been only natural if a poet like Aneirin gravitated to Arthur, because Arthur was the most fruitful source of heroic material in the sixth century (and, indeed, as things would turn out, the most fruitful source of heroic material . . . ever). They would have been a perfect match, Arthur and Aneirin, the greatest warrior of the age and the greatest poet of the age. It is not possible to say with certainty that Aneirin was actually with Arthur Mac Aedan for all or indeed much of his career, but he was certainly in the right place at the right time to have heard about it firsthand.

In *Y Gododdin* Aneirin was scathing about those in authority. He seems to have been a man who pushed the envelope of tolerance to its limits. Luckily for him those in power needed the fighting men Aneirin championed and entertained with his work, and so, like one of Shakespeare's fools, he was probably allowed some license. Arthur Mac Aedan was popular with his men because he brought them victory; Aedan, Arthur's father, probably was not. Aedan was not primarily a warrior but a politician, and so he was less likely to be held in affection.

Older men, especially politicians like Aedan, a man known as "the wily," have always been the butt of jokes made by younger men who do the fighting. A man like Aneirin probably played upon this by entertaining Arthur and his men with jokes and impersonations at the expense of the high command. Just as modern politicians have to put up with mockery, men like Aedan would have had to tolerate men like Aneirin, while pretending to enjoy the fun. Of course, given a free hand, things would be different, and when Arthur died Aedan had a free hand.

When Arthur died in 596, Aneirin lost his protector and became open to the vengeance of Aedan and the old, stolid men of the court whom he had ridiculed while he lived under Arthur's shield. How would a hard, cynical politician like Aedan deal with a man like Aneirin when he no longer had to tolerate him? The answer must have been obvious to Aneirin, because within a year of Arthur's death Aneirin was to be found hiring out his pen for cash in the dissolute court of the Gododdin. Aneirin had moved fast. He probably had to.

Of course it could be argued that Aneirin did not *go to live* among the Britons, because, as the conventional wisdom holds, he was already a man of the Britons. Until now I have always gone for the simplest explanation. Why then should I now place Aneirin with Arthur's Scots and Men of Manau and then have to move him a few miles east and place him among the British Gododdin? Why not just accept that Aneirin was always a Briton? The answer to this question is, because even the Britons thought of Aneirin as a Scot.

It is unlikely that the sixteenth-century Greek painter, Doménikos Theotokópoulos, would have been called *El Greco*, The Greek, if he had stayed at home in Greece where there were a lot of . . . well, Greeks. He was called *El Greco* because he worked for much of his life in Spain, where he stood out as a Greek and so was given the sobriquet, *El Greco*.

An is Gaelic for the indefinite article "the." *Eirin* is rooted in *Éire*, which, even today, is the Irish name for the island of Ireland.

At the turn of the sixth century, only a hundred years or so had passed since Fergus Mor's Scots-Irish had invaded Argyll, and less that twenty-five years had passed since the Council of Drumceatt, when Scottish-Dalriada gained its independence from Irish-Dalriada. During this time and for a long time afterward, until at least the union of the Scots and the Picts in the ninth century, the designations Scottish and Irish were synonymous.

And so, just as we have *El Greco*, The Greek, we have *An-Eirin*, The Irishman, and just as the Spanish only called *El Greco* "the Greek," because he was not Spanish, the Britons of the Gododdin called *Aneirin*, "the Irishman," because, in their eyes, he was not a Briton.

Of course, it is always possible that Aneirin's father's Scots background led to him being nicknamed Aneirin, and that Aneirin inherited the sobriquet, but this is unlikely. Aneirin's mother was British. If he lived for most of his life among his mother's people, it is unlikely he would have been marked out as very different. If however he spent much of his life among his father's Scots, as Arthur's friend and bard as the evidence suggests, and only came back to live among Britons late in life, it is likely he would have been distinguished as *An-Eirin*.

Aneirin was killed by an ax-blow to the head, inflicted by someone called Eidyn or, and this is more likely, by someone of or from Eidyn, that is, of or from Edinburgh (the assassin's real name has been lost). This suggests that Aneirin died in Edinburgh (or at least somewhere

where there was a man with an Edinburgh connection). This could be Wales, but this must be considered unlikely.

Those who hold to the received wisdom say that the "But he was no Arthur" verse in *Y Gododdin* is an example of how far Arthur's fame had spread in the three or four generations that *they say* separated their southern Arthur's death, somewhere in south of Britain, from the writing of *Y Gododdin* in Edinburgh, in the north of Britain. It is more likely that this verse was inspired by the recent (four years in the past) death of Arthur Mac Aedan at Camelon, Falkirk, thirty miles west of Edinburgh, where *Y Gododdin* was written around 596.

I accept that the reasons why Aneirin ended up among the Gododdin are necessarily somewhat speculative—the available evidence is too slight to justify greater certainty—but they are at least consistent with the known facts.

Aneirin mentions Merlin-Lailoken only once in *Y Gododdin*. He says, "Myrddin of song, sharing the best / Part of his wealth, our strength and support."[2] This would be a surprising thing for Aneirin to say if *Y Gododdin* was pure fiction. If it was pure fiction it would be reasonable to expect a poet with Aneirin's powers of invention to have said Merlin-Lailoken did something more exciting than provide financial-backing. This suggests that *Y Gododdin* has historical foundations. I have argued in *Finding Merlin* that Merlin-Lailoken was an old man by the time of the Catterick campaign, and that consequently it makes sense to suppose that all he was able to make was a financial contribution.

It is impossible to believe that the Aneirin only wrote one line about Arthur. By the time he came to live among the Gododdin, Aneirin must have written innumerable poems praising Arthur. This early work would have found a ready market among the Gododdin because Arthur was a Gododdin hero too: they had won their greatest victories while serving under Arthur in the Great Angle War.

Aneirin did not explain who the Arthur of *Y Gododdin* was, presumably because he expected everyone to know who he was. Was this Arthur a man who lived the best part of one hundred years before *Y Gododdin*, far away in the south of Britain without a Gododdin connection, or was this Arthur, Arthur Mac Aedan, the man who led the

Gododdin to victory in The Great Angle War twelve years before *Y Gododdin*?

We have a choice. We can have a southern Arthur, unknown to history, who died three generations before *Y Gododdin* was written, some three hundred miles south of where it was written, or a northern Arthur, Arthur Mac Aedan, who died four years before *Y Gododdin* was written, some thirty miles from where it was written. Which is more likely?

It was probably through his Gododdin connection that Aneirin's poems survived to be taken south with the wave of Gododdin refugees who fled in the face of Angle threats and incursions in the 610s and 620s and again in increasing numbers following the Angle capture of Edinburgh in 638.

Human nature is what it is, and it is impossible to believe that the defeated Britons of the north, seeking shelter in the halls of their southern cousins, would not have regaled their hosts with tales of how they had been ignominiously ejected from their lands. It is almost certain they would have told and retold tales of the time when, under Arthur and Merlin-Lailoken, they had crushed the Angles in battle after battle.

Their southern British cousins may not always have appreciated hearing of these victories, particularly as they had no Arthur of their own and so no equivalent victorious war against the Angles. It would be unsurprising therefore if these southerners took the stories of Arthur that had been brought south and gradually, over decades, over centuries, removed northern references and retold them as if they had occurred in the south.

Eventually stories of Arthur that had originated in the north, in Scotland, became rooted in the southwest and west of Britain, in Devon, Cornwall, and Wales. In time the people who lived in the south came to think of these songs and poems as their own, and so we have the modern consensus that the stories of Arthur originated in the far west and southwest of southern Britain.

Why did the people of Scotland not claim these stories? They probably did but the Scots had disadvantages.

The Picts, who united with the Scots to create the nation of Scotland in the mid-ninth century, would not have appreciated stories of Arthur, because Arthur had destroyed their armies in six battles. Neither would the Angles, well settled in the southeast of Scotland by the seventh century, have thanked a poet for stories of Arthur, because Arthur had also destroyed their armies in six battles. History weighed against stories of Arthur and Merlin-Lailoken thriving in the north.

In the south, stories of Arthur and Merlin-Lailoken had an inherent flexibility, because they had no historical or geographical roots. This allowed them to be easily adapted to local conditions. Arthur could be portrayed as a local man, which explains why Arthur has no fixed abode in the south, not in history, not in geography. Neither is he firmly fixed culturally. He starts off as a Briton, but, despite the fact that everyone agrees the historical Arthur made his name fighting Angles, he ends up as a legendary Englishman. Unencumbered by history, people in the south were free to tell whatever tale of Arthur worked for them and to set the scene wherever they wanted it to be.

The evidence that survived in Scotland, while rooted in history, was also censored and warped. In Jocelyn's *Life of Kentigern*, written in Glasgow in the twelfth century, Saint Mungo Kentigern is meant to be the hero (although he still comes across as a monster). Despite this, in the last few chapters of Jocelyn's *Life* it is Merlin-Lailoken who stands out, albeit in a passage that has been heavily bowdlerized. Jocelyn could have told us even more about Merlin-Lailoken but dared not. So it was with Arthur. The authorities wanted his name obliterated, but they could not achieve this end and so they took him up and changed his story to suit their own ends. Just as this was not completely successful with Merlin-Lailoken, it was not completely successful with Arthur.

Over the centuries English armies have invaded Scotland determined on cultural extermination, most famously at the time of the Wars of Independence at the turn of the thirteenth century, when the records of Scotland were taken south to be neglected, lost, and destroyed. This cultural denigration still goes on today, consciously or unconsciously. Places like Damnonia, Strathclyde, came to be confused with Dumnonia, Cornwall, as the legend of a southern Arthur gained momentum. Fortunately these changes do not prevent us from seeing what really happened and where and when, although it is a near run thing. Even

today *Damnonia*, Strathclyde, is simply translated as *Dumnonia*, southwest England.[3] These exercises not only diluted the Scottish national
consciousness, they also prevented much that might have thrown light
upon the historicity of Arthur being available today.

Many factors weighed against the survival of the memory of
Arthur in Scotland, but the weightiest was probably competition from
the increasingly popular southern Arthur. Stories of Arthur probably
lived on in Scotland for a while but could not survive in the long run in
the face of a burgeoning "English legend," bolstered as it was by social,
political, religious, and commercial powers. There was no room for two
Arthurs of legend. One version of the story of Arthur had to go, and
the Scottish version went.

The Aneirin–Arthur Mac Aedan connections find corroboration,
literally, on the ground in Edinburgh. To suggest that the Arthur after
whom Arthur's Seat is named was not the Arthur of legend but another
Arthur would require the *invention* of another legendary Arthur. Once
it is accepted that Arthur's Seat was named after the legendary Arthur,
questions arise. How did the man who became the legend that is Arthur
come to be associated with Edinburgh? What did he do there that made
such an impression upon the people of Edinburgh that they called the
most prominent feature in their city by his name?

There is only one reasonable answer to this question—the man
whose name and fame gave rise to the legend of Arthur, Arthur Mac
Aedan, saved the people of Edinburgh in the Great Angle War in the
580s and in the hands of Aneirin became not only the greatest hero of
the Scots, the Gododdin Britons, and Britons of the south but one of
the greatest heroes in the common ken of the western world.

Wyatt Earp only became famous when he was taken up by pulp-
fiction writers, the legend writers of their day. It seems likely that
Arthur only became as famous as he is because of Aneirin, and other
poets like Aneirin.

AVALON

Malory's *Le Morte d'Arthur* is stuffed with magic-miracles, especially
when it touches on Arthur's funeral rites and the place where he was

buried. Unable to say that Arthur died a man of the Old Way, because the Church would not have countenanced such a thing, or that Arthur was buried in Scotland, because this would have been unacceptable to his audience, Malory took events that were rooted in the Old Way and in the north of Britain, and added a Christian, southern gloss. He had no real choice in the matter—it was too dangerous to cross the Church and too expensive to disappoint readers. The result is an awkward, clumsy, contradictory (but still wonderful) story, through the cracks of which it is possible to see what really happened.

Malory's Arthur is mortally wounded fighting and killing his illegitimate son, Mordred, at the Battle of Camlann. When the battle is over, Bedevere, one of Arthur's "knights," carries the wounded Arthur from the field. Knowing he is close to death, Arthur says to Bedevere, "Take thou Excalibur, my good sword, and go with it to yonder water side and, when thou comest there, I charge throw my sword into that water, and come again and tell me what thou seest."[4]

Bedevere takes Excalibur, leaves Arthur, and goes to the nearby waterside, but he cannot bring himself to throw Excalibur into the water. Instead he hides it under a tree, goes back to Arthur, and tells him that he has obeyed his instructions. When Arthur asks him what he saw when he threw Excalibur into the water, Bedevere answers, "I saw nothing but waves and winds." Arthur knows this cannot be true. He berates Bedevere and tells him to obey his orders.

Again Bedevere goes to the waterside and takes Excalibur from the place where he has hidden it, but again he cannot bring himself to throw it into the water. Back again he goes to Arthur and again Arthur asks him what he saw. Bedevere, who is obviously as lacking in imagination as he is disobedient, tells Arthur the sword simply slipped beneath the waves.

For a third time Arthur tells Bedevere what he must do. This time, Bedevere obeys the order he has been given; he takes Excalibur and hurls it as far as he can from the shore. "And there came an arm and a hand above the water and met it, and caught it, and so shook it thrice and brandished, and then vanished away the hand with the sword into the water."[5]

By Tennyson's account the arm that came up out of the water was,

The Legend Is Born | 269

"Clothed in white samite, mystic, wonderful." This arm and hand are usually said to have belonged to the "Lady of the Lake." Malory's Bedevere goes again to Arthur, one last time, and tells him of the hand that rose from the water and took Excalibur. This time Arthur is content with Bedevere's report.

This account is almost entirely obvious fiction. Anyone who has read the children's story "The Three Bears" will recognize the triplet device that has Bedevere go to the waterside three times: this is the storytelling equivalent of cosmological constant in physics—it makes things work. To tell the tale this way, Malory had to deposit the wounded Arthur some way from the water side, despite the fact that in the next chapter he has Bedevere carry Arthur to the shore, thus begging the question, Why did Bedevere not take Arthur to the shore in the first place? If he had done so, this would have allowed Arthur to see what Bedevere did with Excalibur. Of course, this would have spoiled the story. Clearly Malory was determined to use the triplet device before his big finale: the "Lady of the Lake" reaching out of the water to take Excalibur, even if this meant Arthur had to be offstage when it happened.

Such plot devices are suspect, especially if, as in this instance, they are part of an episode that involves romance or magic-miracles. However, there is reason to believe that Malory did not invent this story in its entirety. Malory, a man of the late Middle Ages living in the heart of England, is unlikely to have invented the idea of throwing a sword into water or the idea that lakes contained something supernatural. If he had invented this, it would be an amazing coincidence, because, almost one thousand years before, in the time of Arthur Mac Aedan, it was a common practice among Celtic people of the Old Way to throw valuable objects, such as swords, into water, as tribute to the spirits that some of them believed resided there.

Malory continues, "Then Sir Bedevere took . . . [Arthur] upon his back, and so went with him to that water side."[6] Women wearing black hoods arrive in a barge into which they place Arthur before taking him away to Avalon to be healed. "Comfort thyself . . . for I will into the vale of Avilion [*sic*] to heal me of my grievous wound," Arthur says.[7]

Geoffrey, writing more than three centuries before Malory, calls

Arthur's last resting place the "Isle of Avalon."[8] Avalon is described as an island by almost everyone; the main exceptions being those who like to say Avalon was Glastonbury (which is not an island, although many people have gone to tortuous lengths to claim that at one time it was).

It was, literally, more than Malory's life was worth to write something that overtly challenged the power of the Church. He had to dilute his source material with copious dollops of Christianity, sufficient to prevent it being too obvious that the story of Arthur was steeped in the Old Way. It would have been especially dangerous for Malory if he had left Arthur in the hands of obviously capable independent women, because such women suggested the Old Way of the druids. Even if this were not so, the women were still capable and independent, and capable independent women were definitely unacceptable to the Church.

Consequently, at this point Malory sprinkles his account of the death of Arthur with some clumsy Christian symbolism. The day after Arthur is supposed to have been taken away by the women in black hoods, Malory has Bedevere come to a chapel in which he finds a tomb and a hermit, who until recently had been nothing less than the Archbishop of Canterbury.[9] This retired archbishop tells Bedevere that the night before, some women had arrived with a dead body. Bedevere tells the hermit-archbishop that the body was Arthur's—so much for Arthur being taken to Avalon to be healed of his grievous wound. Bedevere then joins the erstwhile Archbishop of Canterbury in some fasting and praying.

In this passage, written almost one thousand years after the actual death of Arthur, Christianity and the Old Way clash (although, as we will see, there is a possible historical foundation upon which both versions might stand). The matter of the Archbishop and his chapel has clearly been clumsily grafted onto an original and better story that had Arthur taken away by women in a barge to Avalon. It is impossible to believe that Malory really wanted his Arthur buried in a retired Archbishop's chapel within walking distance of the place where he had just said Arthur had gone off in a boat to a mysterious island with black-hooded women. (Malory's Bedevere should have gone in the barge with the women and saved himself a walk).

It is far more likely, because it is far more commercial, that Malory would have preferred to have his Arthur sail off to Avalon to be cured, but he had no choice—he had to introduce the Archbishop and interment in a Christian Chapel, because he had to ensure Christianity was in on the act. Malory's Bedevere and the Archbishop fasted and prayed, that is, they acted contrary to nature; they denied themselves food when they were hungry and spoke to a supernatural entity, when they could have thought things through and talked things over and decided for themselves what to do. If this had been a real event and if it had involved people of the Old Way, they would probably have arranged a feast and listened to a druid-bard give them something to think about as he sang the praises of the dead Arthur.

The Old Way version of Malory's fiction, the one that left Arthur wounded but not dead, also had the advantage of a cliffhanger ending, with Arthur being taken away to be healed: would he die, would he survive? The dead Arthur of the Christian version puts the brakes on what until then had been a good-going adventure.

Malory may have had to write what suited the authorities lest they kill him, but he still knew what made a good story and commercial sense, and so, having left Arthur with the women in the barge in chapter five and then dead in a Christian crypt in chapter six, Malory began chapter seven with, "Yet some men say in many parts of England that King Arthur is not dead . . . and men say he will come again. I will not say that it shall be so."[10]

Malory's return to the Old Way version is liberally larded with Christian references and disclaimers. I love the extra-cautious words, "Yet some men say." It is easy to picture Malory saying—*but not me, don't blame me.*

Malory was treading on dangerous ground, indeed; he had put Arthur in the same position as Jesus of Nazareth (and others)—killed but not quite dead and gone, and with the prospect of a return. Just in case someone should doubt that he is on the side of the Christians, Malory concludes, "I will not say that it shall be so."

It is clear from such passages that Malory was torn between his source material and the stuff he was bound to write because of fear of punishment by the Church. His story becomes a bit of a mess:

Thus of Arthur I find never more written in books that be authorised . . . nor more of the very certainty of his death heard [sic] I never read, but thus he was led away in a ship . . . More of the death of . . . Arthur could I never find, but that ladies brought him to his burials.[11]

Malory's specific reference to "books that be authorised" suggests the possibility that there was more about Arthur and Avalon written in books that were *not* authorized. Some translations change this passage to "books of authority" and so cleverly suggest authoritative books while avoiding any connotation of unauthorized books (heaven forbid).

The awkward "of his death heard I never read" suggests something has gone awry here. The word *heard* hints at the oral tradition. It may be that something relevant to the oral tradition has been deleted. Certainly something fishy has gone on here. It seems clear that Malory was using sources that were not authorized by the Church—it can only have been the Church because no other body had sufficient interest and authority to so frighten him.

That part of Malory that was a commercial writer caused him to favor the most potentially popular version, that is, the version that contained the most Old-Way-of-the-druids material, but human weakness caused him to write only what was authorized, for fear of punishment. Malory ended up writing a cobbled-together mixture of both versions: one that had Arthur taken away by women in a barge and another that had Arthur buried in a Christian chapel.

Circumstances in Arthur Mac Aedan's Scotland in the sixth century provide a possible historical foundation for both versions. The problem is how to work out which parts in Malory were based on history and which parts were inspired by commercial considerations or required for religious and political reasons. I was fortunate in that, like almost everyone in the twenty-first century, I was well prepared to undertake this exercise because, like almost everyone in the twenty-first century, I have seen an enormous number of films created by cynical audience-pleasers according to the dictates of "the front office," and so could readily recognize many of the telltale signs that shout out—*pure fiction*!

I decided it was unlikely that Arthur had asked Bedevere to throw his sword away into a lake three times in reality. I knew, however, that water deposition was a common cult-act among the Celts, and so I knew it was possible that someone threw Arthur's sword into a lake (or, more accurately, given that it turned out all this was happening in Scotland, into a loch).

I came to see that if I stripped away from the story the propaganda, the commercial material, and the magic (the medieval equivalent of special effects) and looked at what was left with reference to history, there was evidence that pointed toward the historical Arthur.

The legendary Arthur was taken to Avalon to be buried, or to wait there until his return when his country needed him again (the legends vary). Avalon is usually thought of as an island, especially as an island in the western sea. According to Malory there was a church there, or was there? Malory's version is not clear. I was suspicious that his reference to a church was a later accretion, because Christians often added Christian glosses to traditional stories. However, it was possible there was a church on Avalon, even if Avalon was a place of the people of the Old Way at the time of Arthur's, Arthur Mac Aedan's, death. In the early 590s Pope Gregory the Great ordered that churches be built on land that was special to people of the Old Way.

Given that Arthur Mac Aedan died around 596, there would have been little time for anyone to obey Gregory's orders, but, of course, it is quite possible that local churchmen had already acted on their own initiatives. Be that as it may, it is also possible that, even if he was a man of the Old Way, Arthur, Arthur Mac Aedan, ended up under what was then or what later became Christian ground. It is even possible that his burial place was partially of the Old Way and partially Christian: things did not always change overnight.

There had to be a reason, though, why the location of Avalon was so mysterious, why it had to be kept secret. Ideally, Avalon would be a burial place with some especial female tie-in (to explain Malory's women) and would come with an explanation for the name Avalon, preferably an explanation that had something to do with apples.

All these items of evidence and many more stood to be considered with reference to the islands off the west coast of Britain and Ireland, but I did not have time to consider any of them, because Iona pushed to the front of the queue and stayed there.

Iona is an island set in the sea off the coast of western Scotland (part of Argyll, Arthur Mac Aedan country). Iona had had a Christian church on it since at least the late 560s, some thirty years before the death of Arthur Mac Aedan. It was a famous burial place of kings and other notables of Argyll. I did not know of any particular female connection, not to begin with.

This evidence did not mean that Iona was necessarily Avalon but it did mean Iona was the first island I looked at when I started to look for Avalon. If Iona was Avalon it would have been impossible for Geoffrey or Malory to have said so without undermining their preferred southern Arthur; Iona is, after all, in the far northwest of Britain. Malory clearly knew more than he said about Avalon, because after writing about it, he went on to say, "Thus of Arthur I find never more written in books that be authorised."[12] The clear implication of this is that there was more written about Arthur's burial place in books that were not authorized. If this were not so, all Malory need have said was, "Thus of Arthur I find never more written in books"—full stop.

Things are usually unauthorized because they contradict something preferred by the authorities. If Malory had identified Iona as Avalon he would have undermined the authorized books that said Avalon was Glastonbury, this being the party line in Malory's day. Even if Malory's sources had read "Avalon is Iona!" in bold ink, there was no way Malory would have said so: there were too many commercial interests at stake.

If Avalon was in the north and not the south of Britain, that fact alone would have explained why the location of Avalon had been brushed out of history. As for the female tie-in, Malory said, "And when [Arthur and Bedevere] were at the water side, even fast by the bank hived a little barge with many fair ladies in it, and among them all was a queen, and all they had black hoods."[13] These women with black hoods take the wounded Arthur away. On the same page Malory upped the ante and made it *three* queens and some other ladies. How many women were there exactly? Malory does not say but Geoffrey does.

Geoffrey says there were nine women in total; he even names

them. Malory fudged the issue because maiden connections, especially nine maiden connections, signified the Old Way of the druids, and Malory didn't want to get into trouble. These nine-maiden associations have been almost entirely scoured from both history and geography. Relatively few are left, but they include Maiden Island near Oban, forty miles from Iona. If Malory had put nine women in his barge he would have highlighted a dangerously clear link to the Old Way of the druids and this he dared not do.[14] Geoffrey dared but Malory didn't. Things had clearly tightened up since Geoffrey's day.

There is a tradition in the Western Isles of burying people on islands. People who lived in the fortress town of Beregonium and in the surrounding areas of Appin and Lorne were buried on Lismore. There are several small island graveyards in Loch Awe. Over the centuries, however, Iona has become by far the most famous island graveyard of them all.

An inventory dated 1549 lists forty-eight Scottish, eight Norwegian, and four Irish kings said to have been buried there, including Kenneth Mac Alpine around the year 860, Macbeth in 1057, and Malcolm Canmore in 1093. John Smith, the Labour Party leader and a son of Argyll, was buried there in 1994.

There are churches and burial places everywhere though, and so, although Iona met the church and burial place criteria for Avalon, these two facts alone were not weighty enough items of evidence. But these facts did not stand alone.

Arthur Mac Aedan's great-great grandfather Fergus, his grandfather Gabhran, his great-great grand uncles Lorne and Angus, and other members of his family were buried on Iona, in Oran's graveyard, *Relig Oran*.

> The oldest traditions regarding [Oran's graveyard] seem to view it as existing in the island before the establishment of this monastery by St. Columba. Thus, our old chronicles, in stating that Kenneth M'Alpin, who died in 860, was buried in Iona, add, "where the three sons of Erc, Fergus, Loarn, and Angus, were buried." These were the founders of the Dalriadic Colony upwards of sixty years before the arrival of St

Columba, and the annals of Ulster add confirmation to it when they tell us that in 784 the relics of the sons of Erc were removed to the royal cemetery of Tailten in Ireland. Fordun also tells us that Gabhran, King of Dalriada, who died in 560, was buried in *Eelic Grain* [*sic*] [Oran's graveyard], which shows the belief in his day.[15]

Aedan, Arthur's father, is not included among those buried on Iona. This lends weight to the evidence that says that others members of Arthur's family *were* buried on Iona, because Aedan and Columba-Crimthann were enemies. Aedan would not have wanted to be buried on Iona. (Aedan was buried in Kilkerran on the southeast tip of Kintyre.)

If Fergus and Gabhran, men of the Old Way both, and other members of Arthur's family were buried on Iona, then it is possible, if not probable, that Arthur was buried there too, even after the arrival of Columba-Crimthann and despite the fact that Arthur was a man of the Old Way.

In the late sixth century Iona was not as Christian as churchmen like Columba-Crimthann's hagiographer Adamnan would have us believe. There was a thriving community there before Columba-Crimthann arrived (a little over a generation before the death of Arthur Mac Aedan), and so, unless the druids and all the other people of the Old Way had been killed, expelled, or converted to Christianity, it would be reasonable to expect that some of them would still be on Iona in 596 when Arthur's body was brought there to be buried.

Druids like Oran *were* killed and women *were* expelled, but that was in the first fanatical flush of Columba-Crimthann's occupation. When Aedan came to power in 574 he protected the people of the Old Way on Iona (even if only because this diluted the power of Columba-Crimthann).

Even if there were no people of the Old Way on Iona in 596, the Columba-Crimthann Christians would still have been happy to have a man of Arthur's status buried on their island with his ancestors, because this made political sense.

Malory says that Arthur was taken to Avalon to be healed of his "grievous wound" and in the next chapter, somewhat confusingly, that Arthur was buried in a chapel "where lay a hermit grovelling on all four [*sic*], there fast by a tomb was new graven."[16] If Arthur was taken to Iona-Avalon to be buried, then the two strands of Malory's story come together neatly, because Iona is an island and there was a church on Iona in Arthur Mac Aedan's day: Columba-Crimthann's church. The *Relig Oran* where Gabhran, Arthur's grandfather, and other members of his family were buried is only a few yards from the Abbey Church of Iona. It is impossible to be "faster by" a church than the *Relig Oran*, the place where Arthur, that is Arthur Mac Aedan, is buried.

No other possible Avalon, not Glastonbury or anywhere else, has a viable historical Arthur living anywhere near it, far less evidence that the immediate antecedents of such an Arthur were buried there. The name Avalon only arrived on the scene in the twelfth century, six centuries after Arthur's, that is, Arthur Mac Aedan's death. During this time stories about Arthur that had originated in Scotland among Q-Celtic-speaking Gaels and P-Celtic-speaking Britons were taken south and subjected to Anglo-Saxon influences and later, after the Anglo-Saxons were conquered by the Norman-French in the eleventh century, to French influences. As a result we have the name Avalon, a name pleasing to French ears simply because French-influenced writers were holding the parcel when the music stopped: which is to say, when the name Avalon was finally fixed in writing.

Many people of the Old Way believed in magic cauldrons, just as many Christians believed Columba-Crimthann cast spells that imparted healing properties to bread.[17] It was said there was a magic cauldron of regeneration into which the dead were dipped before springing out to enjoy a new life on Iona. Magic cauldrons were common fictions and not exclusive to the Gaels and Picts.

The Gundestrup cauldron, found in a bog in Denmark in 1891, was probably a votive offering to the waters. The reliefs on the Gundestrup cauldron reflect the stories told of Iona's cauldron—they show people being dipped into the cauldron and brought back to life. This cauldron story fits with the later fictions that have a dead or mortally wounded Arthur taken to Avalon to be restored to active life. Iona fits these legends and more; it fits what Geoffrey says about nine women, beçause it was "By the breath of nine maidens it [the cauldron] was kindled." Unless there is some other reason for this coincidence, these are the same nine sisters we left breathing on the fire beneath the cauldron on Iona.

What probably happened was something like this. Arthur died at or shortly after the Battle of Camlann and was taken by his soldiers and by women of the Old Way (perhaps nine maidens) to Avalon-Iona to be buried alongside his ancestors, according to the Old Way of the druids. And that is that. Arthur, Arthur Mac Aedan, was probably buried according to the Old Way, because his father was still king and Aedan was anti-Christian. It may be Columba-Crimthann and his monks had a part to play, just as Columba-Crimthann was allowed a small part in Aedan's inauguration: in general, people of the Old Way were relatively tolerant.

All we can be sure about is that if Arthur's body was dipped in a *magic* cauldron it did not work (because there are no such things as magic cauldrons or magic bread).

Malory may have written of women with black hoods taking Arthur away simply because black hoods were an obvious nice touch, given that Arthur was wounded and close to death, but this matter of women in black hoods has a basis in the history of Iona. Malory was an unscrupulous man who wrote fiction for personal gain and so cannot be relied upon, except to act in his own interest. He did however have access to historical sources that are now lost to us and which provided him with ideas that he certainly used. If he knew about Iona but did not refer to it directly because it undermined his southern Arthur project, he could also have used other similar source material, provided he disguised it adequately. Malory may have avoided mentioning nine women because nine women suggested the Old Way of the druids. He may have avoided mentioning Iona, because Iona was in the north, but if he knew about Iona, it may be he also knew about black-hooded women on Iona.

The Book of Clanranald is a sporadic record of the Lords of the Isles that was kept by the family of Macvurich [*sic*]. It tells of Reginald, son of the great Somerled, Lord of the Isles, who founded a nunnery of Black Nuns on Iona in the late twelfth century. I am loathe to base any conclusion upon women's fashions, of which I know little, and so I will say no more than this—if Malory knew of the Black Nuns of Iona, even as an anachronism, even if his information was secondhand, this may have inspired his black-hooded women. All we can be sure of is that Malory said black-hooded women took Arthur to Avalon and that there were still black-hooded women on Iona as late as 1543, well after Malory wrote *Le Morte d'Arthur*.

The Church bound Malory to inject Christian material into *Le Morte d'Arthur*, but his introduction of a hermit who was once an Archbishop of Canterbury always seemed somewhat weird to me.[19] How did he come up with that one? If Iona was Avalon that question is easily answered.

Columba-Crimthann was the second most famous Christian of his day, second only to Mungo Kentigern of Glasgow, and his fame increased as time passed. By the twelfth century when Benedictine monks took charge of Iona, they understood that it was in their interest to promote the cult of Columba-Crimthann and they did just that (even though Columba-Crimthann's form of Christianity was markedly different from theirs). By Malory's day, Columba-Crimthann would have been in the running to be considered the number one Scottish Churchman. Malory must have heard of Columba-Crimthann.

There was no shortage of hermits about Iona, indeed all over the highlands, in the sixth century: one of Iona's top tourist attractions is the Hermit's Cell. Adamnan said Columba-Crimthann lived in a hut or a cell on Iona,[20] but "saints" are always said to have lived simple lives and so this may not be true (remember, this was the same Columba-Crimthann who had someone running about after him when he was a student). Of course, it does not matter whether this is true or not: what matters is that it was said to be true and people believed it.

Malory's fictional Archbishop of Canterbury, presented by Malory as a hermit, is not very different from Adamnan's fictionalized version of Abbot Columba-Crimthann, presented by Adamnan as a humble monk. All Malory needed to do was delete the main Christian player

*The Relig Oran, the graveyard where Arthur is buried, Iona-Avalon.
To the right is Oran's Chapel. To the left is Iona Abbey.*

on Iona at the time of Arthur's death, Columba-Crimthann, and insert
in his place the main English Christian player of his day, the Archbishop
of Canterbury and . . . job done.

By making his Archbishop of Canterbury a retiree and a hermit
Malory could explain how this cleric came to be away from Canterbury
in Glastonbury. Notwithstanding the fact that the church tended to
remember all its main men, right down to the most insignificant of
saints (some of whom are *only* names), Malory's Archbishop is anonymous. This anonymity was necessary because Malory's Christian Eng-

lish King Arthur is a figure of fiction (albeit one who is based upon a historical figure, Arthur mac Aedan) and because no Archbishop of Canterbury actually attended Arthur's funeral.

LANCELOT, GUINEVERE, AND MORDRED

Why is Arthur not the hero of his own legend? Almost by definition, the hero is the one who gets the girl and Arthur does not get the girl in the end of almost any of the stories. I know Ingrid Bergman flew off with Paul Henreid leaving Humphrey Bogart behind in *Casablanca*, but Humphrey could have had her if he wanted to (and probably did the night before the flight to Lisbon). In any case, Humphrey was more glamorous than Paul, which is all important. The legendary Arthur is not so blessed. He not only loses a wife he loves to Lancelot, his supposed best friend, but Lancelot is a better fighter and an all-round more exciting figure than Arthur, who is often presented as stolid and a bit dull, hardly the stuff of heroes. Why? Who was Lancelot?

Hussa of Bernicia, the Angle king at the time of the Great Angle War, died somewhere between 590 and 593, leaving his ineffectual son, Hering, to be ousted by his nephew or cousin, Aethelfrith. When Aethelfrith became king in Hering's stead, Hering escaped from Bernicia and found refuge with Aedan in Dalriada, according to most sources. This is probably because Dalriada is most famously associated with Aedan's name, but Manau makes more sense.

The evidence suggests that what happened was this. Hering sought sanctuary in Manau around 593, after he was run out of Angle-land by Aethelfrith, and there tried to convince Aedan that he still commanded substantial support in Angle-land and that, if only Aedan would put him at the head of an army, he would recover what he, Hering, continued to think of as "his" kingdom. If he succeeded, Aedan would have an ally on the southern flank of the northern Gododdin. Unfortunately for Hering, even as he tried to persuade Aedan to help him, Aedan's army, under Arthur, was engaged fighting the Picts and so action against Aethelfrith's Angles was impossible.

It is easy to see that Aedan might have ordered Arthur to accept Hering into the ranks of his men, not because Hering was worthy of such a place but because he was a prince and princes are often elevated beyond their capacities simply because they are princes. Besides, Hering was still potentially useful to Aedan. Arthur might not have been happy about this, but Hering would have been pleased to be able to preen himself as one of Arthur's *ArdAirighaich*.

After the Camlann campaign and Arthur's death, everything changed. Aedan had to regroup and restore his standing among the peoples of southern Scotland. There was no prospect of his furthering Hering's dream of a return to Angle-land, and so, again, Hering had to wait. When the Angles defeated the Gododdin at Catterick in 598, Hering must have despaired that he would ever be a king. Despite everything, five years later, Hering had his way when Aedan invaded Angle-land in Hering's name and took on Aethelfrith.

The *Anglo Saxon Chronicle* tells the tale:

> This year [603] Aedan, king of the Scots, fought with the Dalreathians, and against Ethelfrith, king of the Northumbrians, at Degaston, where he lost almost all his army. Theobald, brother of Ethelfrith, with his whole armament, was also slain. Since then no king of the Scots has dared to lead an army against this nation. Hering, the son of Hussa, led the enemy [that is, Aedan's army]. [21]

It is unlikely that Aedan would have entrusted his army to a foreign prince despite what the *Anglo Saxon Chronicle* says. It is more likely Hussa was simply a figurehead. The *Anglo Saxon Chronicle* is notoriously parochial and especially unconcerned with events in Scotland, although in fairness to the chroniclers it was probably bruited about that Hering was at the head of Aedan's army to divide the Angles and lessen the sense that this was an invasion by a foreign power.

This tactic did not work. Hering had overestimated his appeal to his "subjects," as aristocrats almost always do. Aethelfrith's army crushed Aedan's Scots at the bloody Battle of Degaston fought near Dawston near Saughtree, just north of the battlefield of Arderydd.

Aedan's men had become used to victory under Arthur, and so probably stayed too long upon the field and suffered extraordinary casualties, although not before they had destroyed one wing of the Angle army and killed Aethelfrith's brother. No one knows what happened to the historical Hering, although, given that he would have been Aethelfrith's main target, it seems likely he was killed in the battle.

Hering was from Berwick, fifteen miles from the "Holy Island" of Lindisfarne, where scholarly monks created beautiful books. Lancelot's father, Ban of Benoic, is sometimes said to have lived on an island of scholars, an island that is sometimes said to be Mont Saint-Michel off the French coast. Berwick, Benoic; Lindisfarne, Mont St Michel; Hering, Lancelot—the connections are slight but they are there.

Christian clerics did not create the story of Lancelot and Guinevere's adultery, because they did not approve of sex and would ignore it when they could. Their heroes were sexless knights like Galahad and Perceval. Secular writers created the Arthur-Guinevere-Lancelot love triangle. These Medieval storytellers, like modern storytellers, could recreate anything, and so when a southern hero was needed to dilute the legend of the Celtic Arthur and please their southern audience, they set out to find one.

Stories of Arthur had been transposed from the north to the south for centuries after Degaston, and so all southern storytellers had to do was find an Angle or a Saxon character in the world of Arthur. They found Hering, set to work, and produced Lancelot. He may never have been more than symbolically the head of Aedan's army, but this, coupled with his having been numbered among Arthur's, Arthur Mac Aedan's, men, was enough for anti-Celtic, pro-"English" clerics to insert Hering into the growing Arthurian canon.

It was also necessary that Hering-Lancelot should be a Christian or at least someone who could be passed off as a Christian. Hering probably was a Christian. He had so little else to recommend him that if he had not been a Christian, in an increasingly Christian world, someone else would probably have been chosen to be the new hero. It is ironic, but it seems likely that an incompetent waster, the historical Hering, became the foundation upon which was built that byword for glamorous heroism, the almost wholly fictional Lancelot.

Of course the name Hering had to go, not only because it sounded like the name of a fish but because it was not his real name. It seems likely that *Hering* was a derogative nickname that originated among Aethelfrith's German-speaking supporters. When Hering was pushed out of Bernicia, Aethelfrith's supporters, quite naturally, would have called this son of the late king by a disparaging name, something like "the boy." This would have fitted the little loser perfectly. The prefix *her* is from the same root as the modern German *herr*, meaning "lord," "master," or "sir." The suffix *ing* means "belonging to." *Atheling*, for example, means someone who belonged to a noble, usually royal, family; later it became a prince, the Anglo-Saxon equivalent of a Dauphin, the heir, someone who was not quite first rank. It also seems likely that *Hering* was a mocking nickname for a man who had not been tough enough to hold onto his throne in the face of the more mighty Aethelfrith and who, when he returned as a commander of someone else's army, was soundly beaten and probably killed. Hering means, in effect, "Little Master" or "Sir-ling" (a word I have just invented). In Old English and in German, a *hering* is "a herring." This fish connection would have made the nickname funnier. In time the Norman-French conquered England, and so in time Hering-Lancelot became a Frenchman, the Lancelot de Lac we know today.

The most remarkable thing about Lancelot, the one thing that makes him exceptional, is not that he was the best fighter or most noble knight (someone had to be), it is that he is said to have seduced Guinevere, Arthur's wife. How did this story come about? The obvious answer is that when it proved impossible to eradicate Arthur in the common consciousness, it was decided to neuter his legend by having Arthur cuckolded by someone who was more acceptable to a southern audience. What prompted someone to think of that?

In Malory's romance, *Le Morte d'Arthur*, Guinevere is a beautiful woman, loved first by Arthur and then by Lancelot, although, in the earlier *Alliterative Morte Arthure* and in Geoffrey's work, it is Mordred not Lancelot who is the third point of the love-triangle. (Mordred's approach involved abduction and not seduction.)

It is unlikely that Arthur, Lancelot, and Mordred all lusted after Guinevere just because she was the most attractive woman of her day. Life is just not like that. It is more likely to have been not personal but strictly business.

The *Triads*, Geoffrey, and Malory all say that "Guinevere" was the *casus belli* of the Camlann campaign in which Arthur was killed. These romanticized accounts involve either an attack on Guinevere's virtue by Mordred or her seduction by Lancelot. These accounts are probably no more than romantic audience-winning nonsense. The truth is probably more prosaic. Unless we are to believe Guinevere really was super-attractive, which, while possible, is unlikely, there must have been some other reason why Arthur, then Lancelot, and then Mordred all wanted her.

Guinevere is to the Camlann campaign what Helen is to Trojan War: a way to allow a little romance into what was really an ugly business. The *Iliad* says the Greeks attacked Troy because of Helen. The legend of Arthur says the Battle of Camlann was fought because of Guinevere. Real life does not tend to be like that. It is more likely that Agamemnon's Greeks attacked Priam's Troy and that Mordred's Gododdin attacked Arthur's Manau for more selfish reasons—for fortune and glory.

According to the ways of the Picts, rights passed through the female line, and so it makes sense to suppose that Arthur, Lancelot, and Mordred were interested in Guinevere for other than romantic reasons. Pharaohs married their sisters, because through their sisters they gained the right to rule. Caesar and Anthony did not take up with Cleopatra because she was a non-smoker with a good sense of humor, but because of the power Cleopatra brought to them.

The *Triads* have a novel take on the story. They say the Camlann campaign arose because of competition between Arthur's wife and Mordred's wife. I already knew about Cywyllog, Mordred's wife, because of the part she played in the death of Merlin-Lailoken.[22] She was Cywyllog of the House of Caw of Cambuslang, sister of both Gildas and the warlord Hueil, the man Arthur had killed in single combat in the 570s. Cywyllog, being Gildas's sister, was probably a Christian, and so even if Arthur had not killed her brother Hueil, she had reason to hate Arthur.

The idea that Guinevere and Cywyllog were rivals, however, is probably based upon something more prosaic. It is likely that Cywyllog, like her husband, simply coveted Guinevere's land, although, of course, this does not rule out personal animosity. The prize that fell to the winner of Arthur's last battle was not Guinevere's love or person but the land and power that came to her husband, and so in a way Guinevere was the cause of Arthur's last battle although only indirectly.

Arthur became increasingly famous in the eight years after Badon and before Camlann. The soldiers who had stood in the shield walls, stormed the forts, breached the enemy lines, and slaughtered the retreating Angles under his command were proud to say they had marched with Arthur as they as they sat about the fires in their halls and warmed themselves in his reflected glory. Not everyone shared these affectionate memories, however; many chiefs remembered with bitterness Arthur's usurpation of the social order when he led men of higher rank in the Great Angle War. They had allowed him to be in charge at that time only because they were afraid of the Angles, and now remembering their fear they resented Arthur even more.

The Angles were no longer a threat in the 590s. They had been chastened by their defeats in the battles of the Great Angle War. It would be a generation before they were once again poised to strike north, and even then they lost their nerve and struck south instead. Around 615, they cut across Britain and won a battle at Chester or Carlisle and drove an Angle wedge between the Britons of Scotland and their British cousins in the south.

In the 590s, with the threat of Angle invasion lifted, the chiefs of Strathclyde and the Gododdin looked apprehensively at Arthur. In the Scots of Dalriada and Men of Manau, the *ArdAirighaich*, Arthur had the most effective military force in Britain. Many of these chiefs would have been happy to see Arthur defeated, but of course not one of them was prepared to take him on.

In the years immediately after the Great Angle War most people were happy just to be alive and wanted only to enjoy life. This did not please the Christians, especially Gildas, because carefree people did not make receptive audiences for their visions of hell and damnation. He wrote,

A great multitude has been lost, as people daily rush headlong to hell; and the rest [the Gildas Christians] are counted so small a number that, as they lie in her lap, the holy mother church . . . does not see them, though they are the only true sons she has left.[23]

In the words of Gildas many people had become "slaves of the belly . . . and of the devil." that is, open to physical pleasure and non-Christian. These same people were however quite happy, and for a short time, perhaps seven or eight years, during which time Merlin-Lailoken was in the ascendant in Strathclyde, they were prosperous, although, "The cities of our land are not populated . . . as they once were."[24]

Not everyone, especially typically optimistic young people, cared about Gildas's Christianity. He said they were ignorant of past tribulations, having "experience only of the calm of the present." It was to be the calm before the storm.

Mungo Kentigern had run away to Rome and stayed there during the Great Angle War. He only returned to Strathclyde when the war was over, bringing with him the imprimatur of Pope Gregory the Great, promises of papal preferment, and money for bribes. Mungo offered the aristocrats of Strathclyde a partnership with the Church, a partnership that would be predominant in Western Europe until the Renaissance and which came to be called Christendom. Many aristocrats of Strathclyde accepted what Mungo had to offer. By the mid-590s the Mungo Christians and their new allies had undermined Merlin-Lailoken's position and were well on their way to taking control in Strathclyde.

Arthur, Arthur Mac Aedan, still had allies in Strathclyde: Merlin-Lailoken the chancellor; Rhydderch the king; and Languoreth, Merlin-Lailoken's twin sister and Rhydderch's queen. He could also call upon chiefs and warriors of Strathclyde who were resolute in the Old Way of the druids. The support of the people of the Old Way was a mixed blessing to Arthur in 596, because its corollary was that the Christian chiefs became his enemies. He also had the support of his nephews, Gawain, Gareth and Gaheris, his sister Anna's children by her first marriage, although this was counterbalanced by the children of her second marriage, Mordred and his siblings, the man and the woman who came to be called Agravain and Clarisant.

The scene was set for the Camlann campaign in which Arthur died.

In the aftermath of Camlann, Mordred controlled the eastern marches of Manau, and it would have been in his interest to marry Guinevere, or, and this is more likely, because Mordred was married to a ferocious woman called Cywyllog, to marry her off to one of his male relatives. Such a marriage to Guinevere would have legitimized Mordred's de facto authority over Guinevere's lands. He was to be disappointed.

Arthur, Arthur Mac Aedan, was killed at the Battle of Camlann, but Aedan was not and he had his own plans for Guinevere. Aedan had the now effectively landless princess, Guinevere, married to the effectively landless Hering. If Hering were to become king of the Angles in Aethelfrith's place, he would then have the power and the motive to win back Manau's eastern districts from the Gododdin and so put the border of Manau back where it was before Camlann. If Hering did not become king of the Angle-lands then no harm done: all Aedan would have lost was a landless princess. Aedan was a cynical man and a shrewd politician.

If Hering-Lancelot not only succeeded Arthur at the head of Aedan's army in the Degaston campaign, fought some seven years after Camlann, but also married Arthur's widow, Guinevere, this would explain the later, romanticized story that has Lancelot win Guinevere away from Arthur. Of course marrying someone's widow is less dramatic than seducing someone's wife, and so later writers deleted the fact that Hering-Lancelot married Arthur's widow and substituted the famous seduction of Arthur's wife. This provides a nonfictional foundation for the fictional love-triangle story, at least to the extent that Lancelot succeeded Arthur in Guinevere's bed.

Some twenty years after the Battle of Camlann, according to the twelfth-century *Vita Merlini Silvestris*, Mordred is literally lording it over Dunipace, that is, over land that had once been in Arthur's charge, including the lands about Camlann itself. Dunipace is close to what was in the sixth century the border between Manau and the lands of the Gododdin. It seems most likely that Mordred took control of these lands in the aftermath of Camlann.

The *Alliterative Morte Arthure*, which has Mordred pursuing Guinevere, makes sense if the lands Mordred took possession of in the aftermath of Camlann were lands to which Arthur had right through his marriage to Guinevere. When Guinevere was married to Arthur, it would have been his duty to hold her lands secure. When Arthur died at Camlann, Guinevere's lands were taken by Mordred. This is why romances such as the *Alliterative Morte Arthure* say Mordred tried to win Guinevere by force. It was not Guinevere Mordred was after, at least not primarily, it was her lands.

If Guinevere was married to Hering-Lancelot for political reasons, and if she knew that after the death of Hering-Lancelot at Degaston in 603 she was likely to be married off again to someone else, perhaps even someone chosen by Mordred, it would be understandable if Guinevere decided to move north where she would have been safe from the machinations of men like Mordred.

It is likely that sometime after Camlann, when her husband Arthur was killed, and after Degaston, when her second husband Hering-Lancelot was killed, that the twice widowed Guinevere retired to live with the family of her brother-in-law Gartnait near Perth. This would explain the Perthshire legend that says Guinevere died and was buried in Meigle and the eight-foot-high cross-slab stone, Meigle II, which is now in Meigle museum and which is said to have marked the place where she was buried. In isolation this oral tradition might be considered almost completely without weight, but if Arthur's wife was a woman of the Picts, in the above circumstances it fits into the big picture.

Aedan was never to be as successful in war after the death of Arthur as he was when Arthur commanded his army. After he lost the best part of his army at Degaston he must have realized that his time was up. Although Columba-Crimthann had died the year after Arthur his Christians were growing increasingly powerful in the north and west and Mungo Kentigern's Christians even more powerful in south and central Scotland, Aedan cannot have failed to remember the destruction of the people of the Pen Dragons by an army marching under Christian banners (an army in which he had played a cynical part). He must have feared the same thing happening to Dalriada and Manau. He could have changed horses and become a Christian—that is what most people did—but he was probably too old, too proud, and too stubborn to take this course, and so the year after Degaston, around 604, Aedan abdicated in favor of his son Eochaid Buide and retired to Kilkerran on the south east tip of Kintyre.

He is said to have retired to a monastery, but that is the type of thing that was invariably said of powerful men to bolster the power of the church. When he died, somewhere between 606 and 608, his body was not taken north, to be buried with his ancestors and with Arthur on Iona-Avalon. Even at the end it appears Aedan wanted nothing to do Columba-Crimthann, even though Columba-Crimthann was dead, and Columba-Crimthann's monks probably wanted nothing to do with him.

Twenty years after the Battle of Camlann, Mordred was the Lord and Cywyllog the Lady of the lands of Dunipace and Camlann, by this time no longer the eastlands of Manau but the westlands of the Gododdin. This left her perfectly placed to play a central part in the plot that would lead to Merlin-Lailoken's assassination.

In the mid-610s the Angles won a great victory over the Britons at Chester or Carlisle, and the British kings and chiefs of the north panicked, thinking they would be the Angle armies' next victims. The kings and chiefs called a conference at Dunipace that, according to the *Vita Merlini Silvestris*, was held under the aegis of the "Underking" Mordred. Merlin-Lailoken attended at Dunipace along with other political leaders, but he was unwilling to cooperate with the kings and chiefs by bringing the people of the Old Way into what was, in effect, a Christian alliance. As a result Mordred had Merlin-Lailoken imprisoned for three days to make him change his mind. Merlin-Lailoken remained obdurate, "putting off for feigned reasons what they wanted to hear."[25]

Mordred's wife, Cywyllog, encouraged Mordred to kill Merlin-Lailoken after he refused to comply with the wishes of the Christian majority, but Mordred refused for political reasons to go along with Cywyllog. Cywyllog "burst . . . into tears, because she was not able to get what she wanted and she secretly prepared snares to bring about the death of [Merlin-] Lailoken."[26]

After an exchange of insults with Cywyllog, Merlin-Lailoken "made for the trackless wastes of the wilderness. No one pursued him, but all alike began to nod significantly." They knew he had been marked for death.

Nothing came of the expected Angle invasion.

Some two or three years later, Merlin-Lailoken was again called to Dunipace to attend another conference. It was anticipated that, once again, he would be uncooperative and so it was decided to kill him as he "was passing through the fields near Drumelzier castle at sunset." Assassins, "who had been stirred up against him by the wicked woman [Cywyllog]" fell upon Merlin-Lailoken and "an end was made of him."

Mordred had, for political reasons, forbidden his wife to kill Merlin-Lailoken on his first visit to Dunipace, and so it is likely that when Merlin-Lailoken was finally assassinated it was with Mordred's approval.

The assassination of Merlin-Lailoken brought to an end the age of Arthur.

11

Finding Camlann:
The Last Battle

BY THE TIME I TACKLED THE MATTER OF CAMLANN, I KNEW THAT Arthur Mac Aedan had fought all twelve battles on the battle-list of Nennius and that all twelve of these battles had been fought in Scotland in the 570s and 580s. Therefore, it seemed sensible to suppose that Arthur's last battle was also fought in Scotland, but where? I started looking for Camlann where everyone starts, with the name. I found that *Camlann* had been variously translated as 'crooked glen" and "crooked stream," but there are innumerable crooked glens and crooked streams all over Britain—indeed they outnumber the straight glens and the straight streams—and so this translation was of little help. It did, however, prompt the question of why, if *Camlann* means "crooked glen" or "crooked stream," anyone would give such a nondescript name to such an important battle. It would have been like naming the Battle of *El Alamein*, the battle of the sandy place, accurate but not informative. I came to suspect that there was more to the name Camlann than crooked glen or stream.

Unable to find an answer to this question, I looked at the district of Camelon in the town of Falkirk, where, as long ago as the nineteenth century, Skene said there was a local tradition that Camelon was Camlann where Arthur died. The names sound so similar it would have been surprising if Camelon, Falkirk, had *not* been associated with Arthur, irrespective of any actual historical basis for this association, although, in fairness to Camelon, it did sound more like Camlann than Camboglanna, Camelford, or Cam.

Camelon, Falkirk, also fitted neatly with the other evidence I had found that pointed to Arthur Mac Aedan being Arthur. It is only fourteen miles from Arthur Mac Aedan's Stirling base, a traditional site of the "Round Table," and only a few hundred yards upstream from the one-time site of a circular beehive-shaped building known as *Arthur's O'en*, around from at least the thirteenth century until it was destroyed by "developers" in the eighteenth century.[1] On a military level, Camelon, Falkirk, lay close to the Manau–Gododdin border and being border-country was a likely place for a battle to have been fought. This alone was far weightier evidence than any evidence for any southern location. This evidence alone would have been enough to enable me to argue that the Battle of Camlann was fought at Camelon. However, as there is almost always more evidence to be found, I looked for more evidence.

I took a step back from Camelon and looked again at Geoffrey's *History of the Kings of Britain*, which, while it is mainly fiction, was based on some solid historical foundations. I looked for the history. Geoffrey says Arthur was marching on Rome to fight a Roman emperor when he heard that Mordred, whom he had appointed regent in his absence, had made himself king and taken Arthur's wife, Guinevere, as his mistress. This is obvious nonsense. There had been no emperor in Rome since 476 CE. Geoffrey's Arthur returns to Britain and frightens Guinevere into taking refuge in a nunnery but only after he has fought Mordred's army at Winchester in the far south of England.

"The fight began and immense slaughter was done on both sides."[2] Pursued by Arthur, Mordred fell back to Cornwall where, Geoffrey says, the final battle took place at the River Camblam [*sic*].[3] "Arthur, with a single division . . . charged at the squadron where he knew Mordred was. They hacked a way through with their swords and Arthur continued to advance, inflicting terrible slaughter as he went. It was at this point that the accursed traitor [Mordred] was killed and many thousands of his men with him."

Mordred's men fought on, and in the ensuing fight Arthur was mortally wounded. When the battle was over Arthur was "carried off to the Isle of Avalon, so that his wounds might be tended to."[4]

Malory's version of the Battle of Camlann in *Le Morte d'Arthur* is also mostly fiction, but again there is history to be found in his romance, magic, and propaganda. By Malory's account, Lancelot and Guinevere were engaged in a sexual affair. Mordred, Arthur's nephew, plans to break Arthur's alliance with Lancelot by telling Arthur of Lancelot's deceit and Guinevere's infidelity. Taking other knights with him as witnesses, Mordred surprises Lancelot and Guinevere when, "as the French book saith, the queen and Launcelot [*sic*] were together. And whether they were abed or at some other manner of disports, me list not hereof make no mention, for love that time was not as is nowadays."[5]

Lancelot fights his way out, killing Agravain, Mordred's brother, wounding Mordred, and leaving Guinevere behind with the promise that he will return and save her.[6] Arthur feels bound to uphold the law and so sentences Guinevere to death by burning. She is only saved when Lancelot rides to her rescue and carries her off to *Joyous Garde*, his castle in France.[7]

The sales-minded Malory knew his market well and so, as he was writing at a time when the English and French aristocracy were culturally close, he has his Arthur go to war not against a Roman Emperor in Rome but against Lancelot in France.

Malory's Mordred takes advantage of Arthur's absence in France to falsely claim that Arthur had been killed in battle, and set himself up as king in Arthur's place. He also takes steps to marry Guinevere, Arthur's "widow." Arthur returns to Britain to put down Mordred's rebellion, whereupon, "there was a great battle betwixt them, and much people were slain on both parties; but at the last Sir Arthur's party stood best, and Sir Mordred and his party fled."[8]

A truce is called and a meeting arranged. Arthur, ever wary of treachery, goes forward to meet Mordred between the armies, but only after he has told his men that if they see a sword drawn they are to, "Come on fiercely and slay that traitor . . . Mordred, for I in no wise trust him." Negotiations go well, until,

Right soon came an adder out of a little heath bush, and it stung a knight on the foot. And when the knight felt him stungen, he looked down and saw the adder, and then he drew his sword to slay the adder, and thought of none other harm. And when the host of both parties saw that sword drawn, then they blew beams, trumpets, and horns, and shouted grimly. And so both hosts dressed them together.

Arthur and his men fight bravely all day long until many on both sides are "laid to the cold earth." Still Arthur fights on "until it was near night" and all but two of Arthur's knights are dead. In despair Arthur looks for Mordred.

Then the king gat his spear in both his hands, and ran toward . . . Mordred, crying, "Traitor, now is thy death day come." And when . . . Mordred heard . . . Arthur, he ran until him with his sword drawn in his hand. And there . . . Arthur smote . . . Mordred under the shield, with the foin of his spear, throughout the body, more than a fathom. And when . . . Mordred felt that he had his death's wound he thrust himself with the might that he had up to the bur of . . . Arthur's spear. And right he smote . . . Arthur with his sword, holden in both his hands, on the side of the head, that the sword pierced the helmet and the brain pan, and therewithal . . . Mordred fell stark dead to the earth.[9]

Malory's Battle of Camlann ends with Mordred dead, and Arthur mortally wounded, ready to be taken off to Avalon.

The great thing about trying to find Arthur is that, even when you cannot find something of historical interest, the stories are still great stories. I was, however, about to find something. I felt confident that Camelon, Falkirk, was the site of the Battle of Camlann, because it was part of Manau where Arthur Mac Aedan lived and because, if Arthur Mac Aedan really was the man who became the legendary Arthur, it would be surprising if Camelon was not Camlann—the two names were just so similar.

Still, I had to stay objective. I went back to the name, *Camlann*. I knew the prefix *cam* meant "twisted" or "crooked." *Lann*, however, was more of a puzzle. One possible meaning was "blade" or "sword": *lan*, in Scottish Gaelic; *lann*, in Irish Gaelic; *llain*, in Welsh.[10] The battle of the twisted or crooked sword almost worked as a sensible name, particularly when considered along with the passage in *Le Morte d'Arthur* in which Malory makes much of the disposal of Arthur's sword Excalibur in the aftermath of Camlann. The problem with this possibility was that Excalibur was neither twisted nor crooked; on the contrary, the whole point of Malory's Excalibur episode is that Excalibur was *too perfect* to be thrown away. I decided it was unlikely that Camlann was the battle of the twisted or crooked sword.

I then considered the Scottish and Irish Gaelic meaning of *lann*, "land." *Camlann*—the battle of the twisted or crooked land? This was possible, but it did not come with any sensible context. "Twisted or crooked land" was as good a translation as any other I had found, but it was, like "twisted or crooked glen or stream," too vague to be of any real help. The landscape of Scotland is not like the Great Plains of North America, where some strangely shaped piece of land might stand out amidst the flat vastness. In Scotland it is impossible to go far without going up or down a hill, or over or through a river or a burn. Indeed almost all of Scotland could be described as "twisted or crooked land." If battle of the twisted or crooked land were to make sense, then the land in question would have to be twisted or crooked beyond even the Scottish norm.

I moved on. I had acted in legal cases in Falkirk, and so I knew Camelon because it is just across the road from the Sheriff Court. I knew that the area is now almost entirely built-up, but despite this I decided to walk the ground, because, no matter what has happened to it, I have always found walking the ground to be instructive.

On Wednesday, February 20, 2008, I was sitting in my car in Camelon, Falkirk, looking at maps and trying to find a place where I might usefully walk. Almost nothing was the way it was 150 years ago, far less 1,500 years ago. Things did not look promising. Then I imagined what Camelon would have looked like in the sixth century and focused on one of the few sixth-century features that remained: the ruins of a fort on Falkirk Golf Course. I was given permission by an officer of the golf club to walk the course, and I set off to find what was left of this fort.

A few feet from the ninth tee is a large, raised, flat area that was once a Roman Fort and which the golfers use as a practice ground because it is a protected archaeological site. I only climbed up to this Roman Fort to get a better view of the remains of the sixth-century fort near the ninth tee, but I was soon distracted by the Roman Fort itself. It was enormous, more than 1,200 feet from north to south. Standing at its northwest corner, I could see that it was now cut in two by a railway line and that much of its southern end lay under the factory buildings of an industrial estate and a gas station.

Trying to get my historical bearings, I looked at my maps and the ground in front of me, while, at the same time, trying to picture the way things had looked at the time of the Romans. I wondered what would have remained of this Roman Fort for Arthur to see almost two hundred years after the legions left. Then I remembered something and pictured land that was twisted and crooked beyond the norm. I realized I had found the battlefield of Camlann.

According to modern archaeological records, "The Roman forts at Camelon have suffered from the construction of a railway, foundries and cultivation so that virtually no remains may be seen on the surface."[11] In the late sixteenth century, when George Buchanan visited Camelon, there was more to be seen: "Only a few years before this was written remains of the ditches and walls . . . were visible; nor even yet are the walls so completely destroyed, or the vestiges so indistinct, as not to be traced in many places."[12]

In 1697 an anonymous letter-writer who had visited Camelon described, "Vestiges of two large squares of 600 feet each . . . and a ditch and a rampart around each square."[13] These Roman ditches, still visible in the seventeenth century, would have been very much more evident to Arthur, more than a thousand years earlier.

The "Plan of the Roman Station at Camelon, Stirlingshire, 1899"[14] shows a system of four giant trenches and ridges on the southern approach to the fort, created by the greatest military engineers the world has ever seen. This trench-ridge system was more than eight hundred feet from side to side and two hundred feet from front to back. In its day, and I do not doubt shortly thereafter when Arthur was active, this trench-ridge system would have looked like a section of a colossal ploughed field. It is now lost under the car park of Alexander Dennis Ltd., Glasgow Road, Falkirk; in the sixth century it must have been a remarkable, memorable feature in the landscape.

Nothing in nature could have created such twisted, crooked land; this was land that was remarkably, memorably twisted and crooked, far beyond even the Scottish norm. This, I was sure, was the twisted or crooked land that gave Arthur's last battle its name, the battle of the twisted or crooked land, the Battle of Camlann.[15]

The rim of the raised platform of the Roman fort and what remained of the ramparts that lay at the edge of the trench system would have been an obvious place for Arthur's men to form their shield wall. An attacking force would have had to approach them over unnaturally rough ground, down and up, down and up, down and up, down and up, four times before they could close with Arthur's defenders.

Camelon had always made sense as a sixth-century battlefield because of its place on the wild border country that separated Arthur's father's Manau from Mordred's Gododdin lands. As regards Arthur specifically, there was evidence that Camelon was Camlann in local tradition and in all the nearby places that had Arthurian associations. Of course, there was also the fact that Camelon and Camlann plainly and simply just sounded so very much alike.

I could have argued my Camelon-Camlann case with confidence on the strength of this evidence alone, but until I found the trench-ridge system of the Roman Fort and the meaning of the battle-name Camlann, I could not have comfortably claimed my evidence was conclusive. Now I can. Now I say the above evidence proves beyond reasonable doubt that Camelon was Camlann.

When first I came to this conclusion, I did not know that there was other, entirely separate, evidence that led to the same end by a separate way. The battle-name Camlann perfectly describes the crooked, twisted land formed by the trench and ridge defensive system of the Roman Fort of Camelon, Falkirk, as it would have been in the late sixth century of Arthur Mac Aedan and for a thousand and more years there-after. This twisted, crooked land was not only there at the right time, it was also in the right place: the east lands of Manau, where Arthur Mac Aedan's father was Chief.

The southern references to the legendary Arthur, in the *Annales Cambriae* and in the works of Geoffrey and of Malory, had led me to Camlann, and Camlann had led me to Camelon, Falkirk, where I had found the exact site of Arthur's last battle. It all made sense.

However, although I believed I had proved my case for Camlann-Camelon, I looked at the evidence again but this time, not from a southern perspective—that is, with reference to the legendary Arthur—but from a northern perspective—that is, with reference to Arthur Mac Aedan.

I went first to the *Irish Annals* that tell of the late sixth century, a time when Irish and Scots were all but synonymous, and found in the *Annals of Tigernach* that Arthur Mac Aedan died in the year 594. This was two years earlier than I believe he died, but the *Annals of Tigernach* also say that Columba died in 593, when in fact Columba died on Sun-day, June 9, 597, and so I was not too concerned about 594.

The *Tigernach* entry reads, "The violent deaths of the sons of Aedan, Bran and Domangart and Eochaid Find and Arthur, at the Bat-tle of *Chirchind* in which Aedan was the victor and at the Battle of *Coraind*."[16] Here were two battles: the first at *Chirchind* (that is, at Circenn-Carpow) and the second at somewhere called Coraind. This *Annal* entry fit neatly with the evidence in Geoffrey and Malory that said Camlann was not an isolated stand-alone battle.

This entry in *The Annals of Tigernach* presented a problem, how-ever. Arthur Mac Aedan could not have died at Chirchind-Circenn *and* at the Battle of Coraind. It had to be one or the other, but which one? I thought probably the second battle, the Battle of Coraind, because it made sense to suppose that these battles were recorded in chronological order.

I was looking for the legendary Arthur's last battle, the battle best known as Camlann, and so I supposed that if the legendary Arthur and Arthur Mac Aedan were the same person and if the legendary Arthur died at Camlann and Arthur Mac Aedan died at the Battle of Coraind, perhaps there was evidence that the battles of Camlann and Coraind were one and the same.

By this time I was satisfied that Camlann had been fought at Camelon, Falkirk, but, this did not mean I could ignore the possibility of other evidence. *The Annals of Ulster* corroborate *The Annals of Tigernach* to some extent. They tell of the deaths in battle of Aedan's sons, Bran and Domangart, in 596,[17] but, unlike *Tigernach*, they do not say Arthur and Eochaid Find died in the same battle.

In a separate entry for the same year, 596, the *Annals of Ulster* tell of, "The Battle of *Corann*."[18] Neither of these entries mentions Arthur. Reading the *Annals of Tigernach* and of *Ulster* together makes sense of the situation. It seems there were two closely connected battles. The first battle was the Battle of Chirchind-Circenn, in which Arthur's brothers, Bran and Domangart, were killed. The second battle was the Battle of Coraind or Corann, in which Arthur and his brother Eochaid Find were killed.[19]

The *Annals of Tigernach* strongly suggest that Arthur Mac Aedan died in a battle that was the culmination of a campaign. The *Annals of Ulster* tell of more than one battle in the campaigning season of 596. These two items of evidence fit in neatly with the evidence from both Geoffrey and Malory, both of whom say that the legendary Arthur's last battle was the culminating battle of a campaign. A campaign smacks of fact, because this is not something a commercial writer would obviously insert. A modern screenwriter, writing fiction, would probably write a dramatic, one-off last great battle. Why clutter up the big finish with more than one battle? That Geoffrey and Malory both wrote about more than one battle suggests that there was some history involved.

The evidence of the *Annals of Tigernach* and of *Ulster* and of Geoffrey and Malory are all consistent. However, I still had a problem. Geoffrey and Malory say Arthur died at the Battle of Camlann, which I had identified as Camelon, Falkirk, not at *Tigernach*'s Battle of Coraind or the *Ulster Annal*'s Battle of Corann.

It seemed likely that *Coraind* and *Corann* were corrupt versions of the same name. I put the more blunt *Corann* aside as the more corrupt version, because the suffix *aind*, the second part of the battle-name

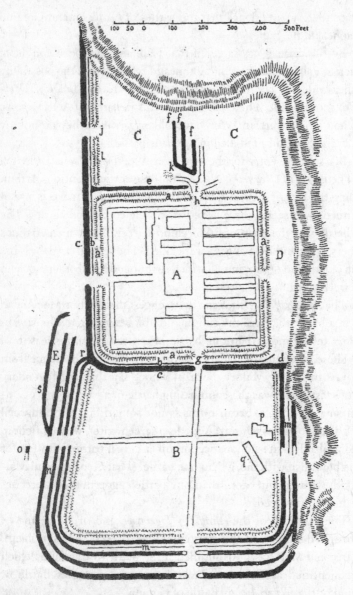

Plan from 1900–1901 excavation of Camelon Roman Fort. To the south is the trench/ditch system, the crooked ground that gave the Battle of Camlann its name.

Coraind, clearly suggested Arthur's father, Aedan. I was sure that *Coraind* was the version I should be working with. This left the prefix *cor* requiring an explanation. At first I took *cor* to be a corruption of *carn*, meaning "a province." This would make *Coraind*, "Aedan's Province." This made sense because Camelon-Camlann was in Manau where Aedan was Chief, and so Manau could reasonably be described as Aedan's Province, but then I found a more likely meaning.

I knew that on General Roy's 1793 "Plan of the Roman Fort of Camelon," there was a place called Carmuir. This lay a few hundred feet west of the Roman fort proper. I thought that because Carmuir was near a fort (*caer* in P-Celtic) and stood on what in Scots is a *muir* (in English, "a moor") *Carmuir* probably meant "Moor of the Fort" or "Fort of the Moor," something like that. Given the area in question this meaning made sense.

I went further: perhaps *Coraind* did not mean "Aedan's Province," as I had at first supposed, but "Aedan's Fort," *Caer Aedan*. This made more sense, because Manau, that is, Aedan's Province, was a relatively big place and to that extent unlikely to have been chosen as the name for a particular battle in a particular place, whereas *Coraind*, if *Coraind* meant "Aedan's Fort," made perfect sense, especially because it was the ninth tee on Falkirk Golf Course and so on the edge of the Roman Fort. Everything fit together.

If *Coraind* meant "Aedan's Fort," and if this fort lay in the shadow of the north wall of the Roman Fort at Camelon, it would have been less than 1,500 feet from the identification I had already made of the exact spot where Arthur fell in his last battle, on the crooked or twisted land that lay at the Roman Fort's southern end. Coraind, Aedan's Fort, is an alternative name for the Battle of Camlann.

The Mordred who appears in *Vita Merlini Silvestris* was the lord of Dunipace around the year 618, according to *Finding Merlin*. Given that Dunipace is only five miles from Camlann-Camelon and further from the heartlands of the Gododdin, it is reasonable to suppose that Mordred took control of both Dunipace and Camlann after the death of Arthur at Camlann.

THE NECHTANSMERE CONFUSION

It is not uncommon for one battle to have two names: Sharpsburg and Antietam; Manassas and Bull Run. The compilers of the Irish *Annals of Tigernach* and *Annals of Ulster* were like the Confederates; they used the battle-name Aedan's Fort, the P-Celtic, *Caer Aedan*. This became *Coraind* in the rendering of Q-Celtic-speaking Irish annalists and later, as the meaning of the name became even more obscure, the even more distorted *Corann*.

The people who lived near the battlefield took an opposite tack; like the Federals they stuck with the geographical name, crooked, twisted land or *Camlann*, a name that became Camelon, the modern-day name of that part of Falkirk.

The evidence suggests that the Battle of Coraind was not just fought in Aedan's Province, which is a pretty big place, but in a very specific part of Aedan's Province, exactly 1,500 feet to the south of Aedan's Fort, at the opposite end of the Roman Fort, on the crooked twisted ground that inspired the battle-name Camlann.

I had found Camelon using the southern sources, and I had found corroborative evidence in the northern sources. I was content that I had proved that the Battle of Camlann was fought in Camelon, Falkirk, and more than that, that I had identified the precise place in Camelon where it was fought and that I had proved this not once but twice.

There are three other sources of evidence all pointing to the same place, Camelon, Falkirk, as the battlefield of Camlann.

In his carefully argued *The Discovery of Arthur*, Geoffrey Ashe says,

> In 685 a battle was fought [at Nechtansmere] . . . between [the Angles] . . . and the Picts. Despite the wrong date and wrong nationalities a local legend makes this battle a clash between Arthur and Mordred, supposedly part of a feud leading up to *Camlann*.[20]

What was it that inspired this clearly distorted local legend in the area about Perth, and why was it that this local legend confused the seventh-century Battle of Nechtansmere with Arthur and Mordred, who, according to almost everyone, lived in the sixth century and far away in the south of Britain?

The detail that this battle was a prelude to Camlann tweaked my interest. The local legend noted by Geoffrey Ashe put the legendary Arthur and Mordred in the land of the Picts, where the historical Arthur Mac Aedan had also been active. It also involved them in a battle "leading up to Camlann." Geoffrey and Malory had both said exactly this: that there was campaign leading up to Camlann (except, of course, they set the scenes of their action in the far south of Britain).

I looked for a battle "leading up to Camlann." *The Annals* of *Tigernach* told of a battle fought at Chirchind (Circenn), the location of which I had identified as the fort at Carpow, in the land of the Picts. This battle was followed by a battle fought at Coraind, which I have identified as the Battle of Camlann.

The *Annals of Ulster* tell of a battle in which the sons of Aedan fought and, in a separate entry for the same year, of a battle fought at Corann, which is again Coraind and again the Battle of Camlann.

Here was evidence in a "local legend" that the legendary Arthur fought in a battle in which the historical record suggests the historical Arthur also fought. This is either an amazing coincidence or the legendary Arthur and the historical Arthur Mac Aedan were one and the same man.

If this is right, then this is how things probably happened. Arthur Mac Aedan fought and won two battles against the Picts at their capital Circenn-Carpow, outside Perth. The first of these battles, fought circa 584, is the battle best known as the Battle of Bassas. The second of these battles, fought in 596, is the battle *The Annals of Tigernach* call the Battle of Chirchind, that is, Circenn-Carpow.

It was easy to see how the legend in the Perth area came into being and became as confused as it is. The Battle of Nechtansmere, which had nothing to do with any Arthur, was fought near a place where, a century before, Arthur Mac Aedan had fought and won the Battle of Bassas-Circenn-Carpow. This connected the area around Perth with the name of Arthur.

The Battle of Nechtansmere was fought between the Picts and the Angles. The Picts and the Angles were allies when they marshaled their troops at Bassas-Circenn-Carpow before marching west to do battle with Arthur in the campaign that culminated in the Battle of Badon in circa 588. These events connected the name of Arthur with the Picts and the Angles and with the area about Perth.

After the Battle of Nechtansmere, fought between the Picts and the Angles, it is probable that Arthur's name was erroneously and confusingly injected into the Nechtansmere accounts and that this produced Geoffrey Ashe's "local legend."

I appreciate that not all of this is easy to come to grips with, but if it were easy someone else would have come up with it long ago. To make matters more confusing, in 596 Arthur Mac Aedan fought another battle on the same ground as he had fought the Battle of Bassas-Circenn-Carpow; this was the Battle of Chirchind-Circenn-Carpow, recorded in *The Annals of Tigernach*. Just as the annals say, this Battle of Chirchind-Circenn-Carpow, fought against the Picts, immediately preceded the Battle of Coraind-Camlann. Arthur's opponent at the Battle of Coraind-Camlann was Mordred. When this ingredient is added, the end result is again the "local legend" to which Geoffrey Ashe referred.

Nechtansmere was a hugely important battle, and so it was the battle best remembered in the area, because, after all, the Picts had won the Battle of Nechtansmere and they had lost every time they had come up against Arthur. No one likes remembering defeats.

If the local legend is an echo of battles fought circa 596, involving first Arthur against the Picts and second Arthur against Mordred's Gododdin, then the "wrong date" to which Geoffrey Ashe refers ceases to exist as a problem,

Geoffrey Ashe says the Angles and the Picts are the "wrong nationalities" to be involved in an Arthurian legend, but of course if Arthur was Arthur Mac Aedan, then Geoffrey Ashe's "wrong nationalities" are not wrong, because the Angles and the Picts were allies in the Badon campaign they fought against Arthur, and, not only that, they set out from the Perth area.

The most telling fact, however, is that the battle in the local legend is said to have been "a clash between Arthur and Mordred supposedly part of a feud [campaign] leading up to Camlann." This detail fits the reconstruction of the Camlann campaign that comes to light if

Arthur was Arthur Mac Aedan. There was a battle in the north, in the vicinity of Nechtansmere-Perth (Circenn-Carpow) which was part of a campaign that ended with the Battle of Camlann, a battle fought between Arthur, Arthur Mac Aedan, and Mordred of the Gododdin. It is likely that there were two battles fought, one after the other. One was lost sight of, and the participants in the second battle were simply said to have fought in the one battle that anyone remembered.

What probably happened was that Geoffrey Ashe's "local legend" of the legendary Arthur was inspired by the actions of the historical Arthur Mac Aedan, and that, in due course, anachronistic Nechtansmere references were added.

It would be a colossal coincidence if the legendary Arthur just happened to be involved in a battle near Perth, a battle that was a prelude to his death at the Battle of Camlann, when the historical Arthur Mac Aedan also just happened to have fought a battle near Perth, at Circenn-Carpow, immediately before the Battle of Coraind, that is Camlann. It is more sensible to suppose that the legendary Arthur and Arthur Mac Aedan were the same man and that he fought in a battle outside Perth immediately before he fought in his last battle at Camelon-Camlann.

LE MORTE D'ARTHUR

The Christian propagandist Adamnan, a seventh-century Abbot of Iona, favored Columba-Crimthann at the expense of warrior contemporaries such as Arthur Mac Aedan. In his historically reckless *Life of St. Columba* Adamnan recorded that what he said was an eye-witness report of the events in 596. Adamnan was gullible or deluded or just a liar, because he says that while Columba-Crimthann was on Iona, he was able to provide an account of a battle while it was happening on the other side of the country. This is nonsense, of course.

Adamnan's Columba-Crimthann says, "Let us now pray fervently to the Lord for this people and for King Aedan, for even now they are going into battle [against the Miathi Picts]."[21] Writing with the benefit of hindsight Adamnan says that a little later Columba went outside and looked at the sky (which is a nice touch) before saying, "Now the barbarians are turned in flight and victory is granted to Aedan, though it is not a happy one. From Aedan's army, three hundred and three were killed."[22]

Clearly this battle was extremely costly for the victors. Arthur, Arthur Mac Aedan, enjoyed only a pyrrhic victory at best. This was the first battle in the Camlann campaign, the Battle of Chirchind-Circenn-Carpow.

The Welsh fifteenth-century *Red Book of Hergest* contains what is left of sixth-century Scottish history after the best part of a thousand years, during which it was battered into a shape that served the purposes of those who wanted Arthur to be in the south. The writers of the *Red Book*, just like Geoffrey, said Arthur fought an unnamed Roman Emperor. This is plainly preposterous; there were no Roman emperors in the west after circa 476 CE, and even if there had been, no one from Britain could have traveled across the mainland of Europe to fight him without carving a wide swathe in history, and there is no evidence of this.

> And in the end Arthur encountered the emperor, and Arthur slew him. And Arthur's best men were slain there. When Medrawd heard that Arthur's host was dispersed, he turned against Arthur . . . And when Arthur heard that, he turned back with all that had survived of his army . . . And then there took place the Battle of Camlan . . .[23]

I dismissed the stuff about the Roman emperor as nonsense gauged to disguise the fact that Arthur was really pitched against a Pictish king, something that could not be disclosed without pointing to the fact that Arthur was a man of the north. I did however give weight to the evidence that Arthur had been involved in a debilitating battle immediately before the Battle of Camlann, because this corroborated Geoffrey, Malory, and Adamnan. The fact that, according to the *Red Book*, Camlann was preceded by another battle also corroborates the Irish-Scottish *Annals*.

The writers of the *Red Book* took care to avoid details that might identify Arthur's true place in history, but they were not careful enough because they failed to delete a passage that says the campaign against the "Emperor" was fought, "Beyond the mountain[s] of *Mynneu*."[24]

At least one writer has said this *Mynneu* refers to the Alps, but this is only because Arthur was supposed to have been fighting a Roman Emperor in Italy. No one I know of has ever come up with a name for the Alps that sounds anything like *Mynneu*. The matter is clear, Mynneu is Manau, and beyond the mountains of Mynneu means beyond the mountains of Manau. Beyond the mountains of Manau lie the mountains of Pictland, where, in the sixth century, lay the capital of the premier province of the Picts—Chirchind-Circenn-Carpow. Where else?

The *Red Book* says, "Arthur turned back" to meet Mordred at Camlann. This fits with the view that has Camlann the culmination of a campaign in which Arthur marched north against the Picts, fought and won a costly victory, and then, when he heard that Mordred's Gododdin had risen against him, marched south against Mordred with a weakened army, only to go down to defeat at Camlann.

If the *Red Book* is read with an eye on sixth century Scotland, it is clear that when it says defeated and killed an "Emperor," it means a king of the Picts. This victory was at the expense of the deaths of many of Arthur's men.

It is now possible to construct what led up to and what happened at Camlann. Arthur married Guinevere and so gained authority over her land on the eastern marches of Manau. This land and Mordred's land on the western marches of the land of the Gododdin were contiguous. Mordred was jealous of Arthur because of Arthur's reputation. Mordred knew he would have to defeat and kill Arthur and then legitimize his victory by marrying Guinevere or, and this is more likely because Mordred was already married to the fierce Cywyllog, by having one of his supporters marry Guinevere. Like other chiefs and kings who resented Arthur's past success and feared his future actions, Mordred was willing to attack Arthur but afraid to make his move until he could be sure of success.

Mordred had commanded the Gododdin contingent in an allied British army that, in the 570s, under the overall command of Taliesin's patron Urien of Rheged had pushed the Angles back to the sea at Lindisfarne. If the Britons had destroyed the Angle army there and then,

Urien would have become predominant in Scotland. Mordred found this both personally and politically intolerable. "But during this campaign, Urien was assassinated on the instigation of Morcant [Mordred], from jealousy, because his military skill and generalship surpassed that of all the other kings."[25]

Mordred, a jealous assassin in the 570s remained a jealous assassin in the 590s. This was the Mordred Arthur had at his back when he marched north against the Picts in 596. If Mordred had been jealous of Urien, how much more must Mordred have been jealous of Arthur? Cywyllog too had both personal and political reasons to hate Arthur and to plot his death.

It is impossible to say with certainty what started the Camlann campaign. It is most likely that the Miathi Picts rebelled against Gartnait, Arthur's half-brother, the man Aedan had installed as king of the Picts after the Battle of Bassas around 584. An unexpected rebellion would go some way toward explaining Arthur's heavy losses in the subsequent battle, particularly if the rebel Picts had succeeded in taking the fort at Bassas-Circenn-Carpow before Arthur arrived, thus forcing him to attack a fortified position.

In 596 Arthur advanced on the Pictish capital, where twelve years before he had defeated the Picts in the Battle of Bassas, and there engaged the Picts again. This was the battle against the Miathi Picts of which Adamnan wrote, "Now the barbarians are turned in flight and victory is granted . . . though it is not a happy one."[26]

Arthur won this battle at Carpow, but only after suffering horrific losses. Adamnan said three hundred and three of his men were killed, an enormous number, given the size of armies in the sixth century. This is the battle recorded in the *Annals of Tigernach* as the Battle of Chirchind; that is, Circenn; that is, modern Carpow.

News of this battle would have taken some days to reach Iona, ninety miles to the west. There Columba would have heard it along with everyone else. This was the battle Adamnan said Columba reported on while it was still ongoing, but this may be discounted as fiction.

According to Adamnan the dead included Arthur and his brother Eochaid Find but not Arthur's brother Domangart, who, according to Adamnan, was later killed in battle in England. This contradicts the

Irish Annals but is not surprising, because Adamnan was writing political propaganda. His only concern was to make Columba-Crimthann look good. He either did not know that Arthur survived the battle against the Miathi Picts only to be killed soon thereafter at Camlann or, and this is more likely, he confused the two battles. After all, Adamnan's main aim was to pretend that Columba-Crimthann had magical powers and so all he needed was a little historical material upon which to build his pretense.

Adamnan's omission of the Battle of Camlann can be attributed to ignorance; laziness; or cynicism, but it was probably just careless-ness, because Adamnan did not care about history—he had no reason to care, history was not his job. Alternatively, it may be that Adamnan was just being economical with the truth, using only what was neces-sary to promote the cult of Columba-Crimthann, while deleting his-torical details that were of no interest to him. Adamnan did not care whether there was one battle or two, the second being the battle at which Arthur fell, all he cared about was that he boosted Columba-Crimthann's reputation as a man of magic. He used a particular battle, Arthur Mac Aedan's Battle of Chirchind-Circenn-Carpow in 596, the first battle in the Camlann campaign, but he could just as easily have used another battle.

The historical details would have been of great interest to Columba-Crimthann the politician. He would have been disappointed that Aedan's army, under Arthur, had been victorious once more but heartened when he learned that his old enemies, Aedan and Arthur, had been weakened by the loss of so many men.

The most likely scenario is this. News of Arthur's costly victory was heard in the land of the Gododdin forty-five miles south of Carpow long before it reached Columba on Iona. Mordred, hearing of the losses sustained by Arthur's army, saw his chance to strike. While Arthur was still in the north nursing his injured army, Mordred prepared to march on Manau and, almost literally, stab Arthur in the back. When Arthur heard that the Gododdin had mobilized he turned for home, marching south to Manau to meet the threat of invasion.

The figure "three hundred and three dead" may be a stock figure meaning simply "a lot" but it sounds about right. There must have been at least as many wounded men and so the army that Arthur led home was not only drastically weakened but heavily encumbered. It must have been a sad sight to see this once great army, in its day the greatest army in Britain, limp back to Stirling, only to be told when they got there that a large Gododdin force was already massed on Manau's border, about to invade.

There was no time to call for reinforcements from Dalriada, even if there had been men available to call upon. No help could be expected from Merlin-Lailoken in Strathclyde; he had his hands full at this time dealing with the disruption caused by the recent return of Mungo Kentigern. In any event the Christians, of whom there were now many in Strathclyde, would not have wanted to take on the might of the Gododdin of Arthur's behalf, given that Arthur was the most able war leader of the people of the Old Way. It would have been impossible for Merlin-Lailoken to raise an army to fight for Arthur, even if there had been time—and there was no time.

Arthur left his wounded soldiers at Stirling and marched with the few men he had left to the fort at Caer Aedan-Coraind, the fort that stood near the ruins of the old Roman fort (at what is now Camelon).

As Mordred's army approached, Arthur moved out from the fort and formed a defensive line along what was left of the old Roman ramparts, behind the four immense Romans ditches: the crooked ground that gave the battle its name, Camlann.

Only slight and confused hints survive to provide us with some idea of the state and disposition of Arthur's forces at this time. One of the *Triads* tells of the band of Alan Fyrgan, "Who returned back by stealth from their lord, on the road at night with his servants at Camlann, and there he was slain."[27] This may be a reference to the desertion of a company of soldiers on the way to Camlann and of the death of their captain in the battle that followed.

One of the few things that can be said with some certainty is that Arthur had only a small force of exhausted men, who had only recently been engaged in a brutal battle against a fearsome foe, to pit against Mordred's vastly more numerous and fresh-in-the-field army of the Gododdin.

Hugely outnumbered, Arthur's Scots and Men of Manau fought

on until they were overwhelmed. The details of the battle are lost. All we can be sure of is that the battle was not started by a snake as Malory said and that Arthur and Mordred did not kill each other in hand-to-hand combat.

Arthur lost his last battle. He was carried from the field dead or mortally wounded and taken to Iona-Avalon and buried there. Mordred and Arthur did not kill each other at the Battle of Camlann as Malory says. That would be just too good to be true, too much the type of thing someone like Malory or a modern screenwriter would come up with. In real life heroes don't always survive to the end of the story, and when they are killed they don't always take their killers with them when they go. It is easy to see why Malory said Mordred was killed by Arthur at the Battle of Camlann: Mordred was the antihero and killing the antihero at the end of a story provides the feel-good factor that pleases audiences. Malory's version is "box-office," but it is not history.

It is generally accepted that when Nennius said the legendary Arthur fought "together with the kings of the British; but he was their leader in battle," he meant that although the legendary Arthur was a leader of kings, he himself was not a king. Arthur Mac Aedan fits this profile: he died some twelve years before his father and so did not succeed to his father's throne.

It is possible Arthur's sword was thrown into a loch in accordance with Celtic custom, perhaps into Loch Katrine, which lies almost exactly half way between Camlann and Avalon. Who knows? We do know that a woman's hand did not appear from the waters to take the sword, because Arthur lived in real life, not in myth or in legend (or in the south). Walter Scott wrote the poem *The Lady of the Lake* after he spent time with his family at Loch Katrine, but this poem is set in the time of James V's and has nothing to do with the legendary Arthur, although Walter Scott was an avid collector of traditional tales, and so it may be that he heard something in the oral tradition on the banks of Loch Katrine and that this inspired his title. I started to look for his diaries to see if there was anything to this but . . . time. There is always somewhere else to go and something else to find.

Epilogue:
Árya

I FOLLOWED O'BRIEN'S DEFINITION OF *AIRIGH*, "CERTAIN, PARTICULAR, especiall [sic], prince, nobleman &c.," and it led me to Arthur and Merlin, but there was another way I could have taken to the same end.

MacBain in his *Etymological Dictionary* expanded on O'Brien's definition of *Airigh*. He looked back to its origins in the Sanskrit of the Vedas of the Indus Valley civilization of India in the second millennium BCE.

Sanskrit is perhaps the oldest member of the Indo-European family of languages, of which Scottish Gaelic is a part. In Sanskrit *Airigh* is *Árya*, "good" or "lordly." Not lordly in the aristocratic sense but in the sense of a worthy person. It is from *Árya* that we get the word *Aryan*, meaning an honorable person. In the Vedas being *Aryan* was not a matter of rank but of character. It was certainly never a matter of race. It is ironic but perhaps not surprising that *Aryan*, a word that epitomizes all that is good in human nature, should have been stolen by the Nazis and abused for their perverted purposes. To be Aryan is not a racial thing, as the inhuman Nazi abomination would have had it, but a philosophical thing, a human thing.

According to the early-twentieth-century Indian scholar Sri Aurobindo, *Árya* was a belief in an ideal: "All the highest aspirations of the early human race, its noblest religious temper, its most idealistic velleities of thought are summed up in this single vocable [*Árya*]" In time, he says, it came to be that,

The word *Árya* expressed a particular ethical and social ideal, an ideal of well-governed life, candour, courtesy, nobility, straight dealing, courage, gentleness, purity, humanity, compassion, protection of the weak, liberality, observance of social duty, eagerness of knowledge, respect for the wise and learned, the social accomplishments . . . There is no word in human speech that has a nobler history.[1]

These are the very values exemplified by the idea that is *Camelot*.

I considered some of the complexities of the word *Airigh*, with particular reference to its Sanskrit derivation and the Indian philosophy described, and concluded that O'Brien's definition, "certain, particular, especial," and not "prince, nobleman," made most sense. This was especially so when considered with reference to Arthur, Lailoken, and Camelot because *Airigh-Árya* connotes the very values that are today associated with the Arthurian Canon.

Of course, the ideals of Camelot embody universal values to which every right-thinking person aspires. The problem is that there have always been people like Crimthann or the Taliban waiting in the wings ready to enforce an inhuman alternative. This has led to struggle between those who believe in (or say they believe in) the supernatural and those who are content with nature, especially human nature. This struggle has gone on for millennia and continues today.

I tried to follow the idea that *Árya* represents from its Sanskrit roots and came to understand a little of the Old Way—I think. I think it had relatively little to do with the supernatural, that is, relative to, say, Christianity, and that it was more, as someone in the twenty-first century might say, a people thing. Of course, the Old Way of the druids was not without supernatural elements. There is always someone who does not know how something works who comes up with a supernatural answer, and, given that this is not testable, there is always someone else who comes up with a different supernatural answer, and then the fighting starts. This is what much of our history has been about.

Crimthann and Mungo Kentigern introduced their forms of Christianity to Scotland; Augustine introduced his form of Christianity to England; and various other forms of Christianity, promulgated by other saints in the sixth and subsequent centuries, popped up in different parts of Europe. There was no place, in what came to be called Christendom, for a way of life that that allowed people to be actively curious.

Arthur and Lailoken came to personify human resistance to the new dogma. They did not become famous because they thought of the "Round Table" or of the ideal that is "Camelot." Arthur and Lailoken became famous because they were the last men holding a torch for the Old Way of the druids, in effect, for human nature, when Christianity crushed freedom of thought in the Western world for a millennium.

In the film *633 Squadron*, one officer says to another officer, "all dead, all 633 Squadron," and the other officer replies, *"you can't kill a squadron."*

You can't kill ideas either, ideas such as, "It doesn't have to be like this."

Human nature is winning.

The ideals of Camelot did not begin with Arthur. One of the greatest threats to the existence of modern Christianity was the Arian Heresy in the fourth century CE. I looked to see if I could find a connection with *Árya-Áirigh*. I got to the fourth century BCE before the trail ran cold, at least for now.

The ideals of Camelot did not end with Arthur. About 1900, an eighth- to eleventh-century stone with Celtic markings on it was found on the Swedish island of Gotland in the Baltic Sea: "The absence of the Christian cross and the context of the inscription give no indication of the stone being raised over a Christian person."[2]

This stone was raised by a man with a Scottish-Pictish name. The name of the place where this stone was found is *Ardre*.

Arthur is no more the center of the stories that bear his name than the Earth is the center of the Solar System. The battle for Heliocentricity has been won. The battle for Camelot has only just been joined.

In legend he was Arthur, *Rex Quondam Rexque Futurus*, the Once and Future King. In history he was Arthur Mac Aedan and this is the once and future history.

Selected Bibliography

Adamnan, *Life of Columba*. London: Penguin, 1995.

Alcock, Leslie. *Arthur's Britain—History and Archaeology AD 367–634*, 2nd Ed. London: Penguin, 1989.

Anderson, Marjorie. *Kings and Kingship in Early Scotland*. Edinburgh: Scottish Academic Press, 1980.

Annals of Tigernach. http://www.ucc.ie/celt/online/G100002/

Ardrey, Adam. *Finding Merlin: The Truth Behind the Legend*. New York: Overlook, 2008.

Ashe, Geoffrey. *The Discovery of Arthur*. Stroud, England: Sutton Publishing, 1985.

Bannerman, John. *Studies in the History of Dalriada*. Edinburgh: Scottish Academic Press, 1974.

Barber, Richard. *The Figure of Arthur*. London: Longman, 1972.

Barber, Richard. *The Holy Grail, The History of a Legend*. London: Penguin, 2005.

de la Bédoyère, Guy. *Eagles Over Britannia: The Roman Army in Britain*. Stroud, England: Tempus, 2001.

Béroul. *The Romance of Tristan*. London: Penguin, 1970.

The Dialogue of Merlin and Taliesin. Peniarth MS 1 National Library of Wales.

Blake, S. and S. Lloyd. *The Keys of Avalon*. London: Element, 2000.

Blake, S. and S. Lloyd. *The Lost Legend of Arthur*. London: Rider, Random House, 2004.

Boece, Hector. *The Chronicles of Scotland*. Kessinger Publishing, 2010.

Buchanan, George. *History of Scotland, Vol.1*. Blackie Fullerton & Co., 1827.

Burns, Robert. *The Complete Poems and Songs of Robert Burns*. Geddes & Grosset, 2000.

Bede. *The Ecclesiastical History of the English People*. London, Edinburgh: Penguin, revised edition, 1990.

Broun, Dauvit, and Thomas Owen Clancy, eds. "The Scottish Takeover of Pictland and the relics of Columba." In *Spes Scotorum: Saint Columba, Iona and Scotland*. Edinburgh: T. & T. Clark, 1999.

Byrne, Francis John. *Irish Kings and High Kings*. London, 1973.

Carrol, D. F. *Arthurius: A Quest for Camelot*. Privately printed, 1996.

Chadwick, Nora. "The Lost Literature of Celtic Scotland: Caw of Pritdin and Arthur of Britain." *Scottish Gaelic Studies* 7/169 (1953).

Charnock, Stephen Richard. *Local Etymology a Derivative Dictionary of Geographical Names*. London: Houlston & Wright, 1859.

Chrétien de Troyes. *Arthurian Romances*. London: Penguin, 1991.

Chrétien de Troyes. *Arthurian Romances, Lancelot or the Knight of the Cart*. London: Penguin, 2004.

Collingwood, R. G. *Roman Britain*. London: Oxford University Press, 1923; reprint with corrections, Oxford: Clarendon Press, 1959.

Collingwood, R. G., "Arthur's Battles." *Antiquity* III (1929).

Crichton-Stuart, John Patrick. *Scottish Coronations*. Edinburgh: A. Gardner, 1902; (Nat. Lib. Scot., LS R.232.b & BCL.C1065).

Drummond, Peter. *Placenames of the Monklands*. Monklands Library Services Dept., 1987.

Dumville, D. N. *Historia Brittonum : iii. The Vatican Recension.* Cambridge: Kessinger Publishing, 1985.

Duncan, A. A. M. *Scotland: The Making of the Kingdom, The Edinburgh History of Scotland,* Volume 1. Edinburgh: Oliver & Boyd, 1995.

Ellis, Peter Berresford. *The Celts.* London, Constable & Robinson, 2003.

Ellis, Peter Berresford. *Celt and Greek.* London, Constable & Robinson,1997.

The English Historical Review, No. CLXIV, Oct.1926.x

Finlay, Ian. *Columba.* Glasgow: Richard Drew Pub., 1979.

Forsyth Harwood, H. W., ed. *The Genealogist New Series,* Vol. XXXVIII. London: G. Bell & Sons Ltd; and Exeter: Wm. Pollard & Co. Ltd; 1922.

Foster, R. F. *Modern Ireland 1600–1972.* London: Allen Lane, Penguin, 1988.

Foster, S. M. *Picts, Gaels and Scots.* Historic Scotland / Batsford, England, 2004.

Froissart. *Oeuvres.* Edited by Kervyn de Lettenhove. Brussels, 1867.

Gerber, Pat. *The Search for the Stone of Destiny.* Edinburgh: Canongate Press, 1992.

Geoffrey of Monmouth. *Vita Merlini, The Life of Merlin.* Translated by Basil Clarke. Cardiff: UWP, 1973.

Geoffrey of Monmouth. *Vita Merlini Silvestris.* Translated by J. and W. MacQueen, *Scottish Studies* 29, 1989.

Gibbon, Edward. *The Decline and Fall of the Roman Empire, Volume I.*

Gidlaw, Christopher. *The Reign of Arthur.* Stroud, Gloustershire, England: Sutton Publishing, 2004.

Giles, J. A. *Six old English Chronicles.* 1808–1884. London: G. Bell & sons, 1891.

Giles, J. A., trans. *Historia Brittonum,* Nennius. Cambridge, Ontario: Parentheses Publications, Medieval Latin Series, 2000.

Gilles, H. Cameron. *The Place-Names of Argyll*. Bibliolife.

Green, Cynthia Whidden. *Saint Kentigern, Apostle to Strathclyde: A critical analysis of a northern saint*. Masters Thesis presented to The Faculty of the Department of English University of Houston, 1998.

Goodrich, Norma Lorre. *King Arthur*. New York: Harper Perennial, 1989.

Green, Miranda. *The Gods of the Celts*. Stroud, England: Sutton Publishing, 1986.

Green, Thomas. *A Gazetteer of Arthurian Onomastic and Topographic Folklore*. (NS879827).

Hardy, Stuart. *The Quest for the Nine Maidens*. Edinburgh: Luath Press, 2003.

Hennessy, W., ed. *Chronicon Scotorum*. London: Rolls Series 46, 1866.

Historical Manuscripts Commission, xiii, app.ii, Portland MSS, ii,56.

Jackson, Kenneth. "Once Again Arthur's Battles." *Modern Philology* 43 (1945–46), 44–57.

Jarman, A. O. H., ed. *The Black Book of Carmarthen*. Gwasg Prifysgol Cymru, 1982.

Lacy, Norris J., ed. *The Arthurian Encyclopedia*. New York: Garland, 1986.

Macleod, John. *Highlanders: A History of the Gaels*. London: Hodder & Stoughton, 1996.

MacLeod, John N. "Remarks on the Supposed Site of Delgon or Cindelgen, the seat of Conall, King of Dalriada. AD 563." In *Proceedings of the Society* (of Antiquarians), December 11, 1893.

MacKie, Euan W. *Scotland an Archeological Guide From Earliest Times to 12th Century AD*. London: Faber & Faber Ltd., 1947.

McKillop, James. *Oxford Dictionary of Celtic Mythology*. Oxford: OUP, 1998.

MacLean, Fitzroy. *Highlanders*. London: Penguin, 1995.

Moll, Richard J. *Before Malory, Reading Arthur in Late Medieval England.* Toronto: Univ. of Toronto Press, 2003.

Morris, John. *The Age of Arthur.* London: Phoenix, 1995.

Munby, Julian; Richard Barber; and Richard Brown. *Edward III's Round Table at Windsor.* Woodbridge, Suffolk, England: Boydell Press, 2007.

Nennius. *The History of the Britons.* Translated by J. A. Giles. Willitis, California: British American Books, 1986.

Nennius. *Historia Brittonum, British History and The Welsh Annals.* Edited and translated by John Morris. London and Chichester: Phillimore, 1980.

Nennius. *Historia Brittonum* from a manuscript discovered in the Library of the Vatican Palace at Rome, notes by the Rev. W. Gunn. London, printed for John and Arthur Arch, 1819.

Parry, Joseph D. "Following Malory out of Arthur's World." *Modern Philology.* 95.2 (1997), 717.

O'Brien, John. *Focalóir Gaoidhilge-Sax-Bhéarla: An Irish-English Dictionary.* Privately printed in Paris, 1768.

O'Rahilly, Thomas F. *Early Irish History and Mythology.* Dublin Institute for Advance Studies, 1946.

Ordnance Gazetteer of Scotland: A Survey of Scottish Topography, Statistical, Biographical and Historical. Edited by Francis H. Groome and Thomas C. Jack. Edinburgh: Grange Publishing Works, 1882–1885.

"Passenger & Immigration Lists." Filby & Meyer, Vol 1. A–G. Source Book 6220.

Graham Phillips and Martin Keatman. *King Arthur, The True Story.* HB Century, 1992.

Reid, Howard. *Arthur: The Dragon King.* London: Headline, 2001.

Renfrew, Colin. *Archaeology and Language: The Puzzle of Indo-European Origins.* London: Penguin, 1989.

Robinson, J. Armitage. *Two Glastonbury Legends: King Arthur & St. Joseph of Arimathea.* Cambridge: Cambridge UP, 1926.

Roy, General W. *The Military Antiquities of the Romans in Northern Britain*. 1793.

Scott, Archibald. *The Pictish Nation: Its People and Its Church*. Edinburgh: 1918.

Scottish Clans and Family Encyclopaedia. New York: HarperCollins, 1994.

Skene, W. F. *A History of Ancient Alban*. Edinburgh: David Douglas, 1886.

Skene, W. F. *Four Ancient Books of Wales*. Edinburgh: Edmonston & Douglas, 1868.

Skene, W. F. "Notes on the history and probable situation of the earlier establishments at Iona, prior to the foundation of the Benedictine Monastery in the end of the twelfth century." *Proceedings of the Society of Antiquaries of Scotland*. December 13, 1875.

Skene, W. F. *Arthur and the Britons of Wales and Scotland*. Felinfach: Llanerch Publishers, 1988.

Skene, W. F. *Chronicles of the Picts and Scots and Other Early Memorials*. Edinburgh: General Register House, 1867.

Skene, W. F. "Skene's Notes," Royal Scottish Academy. April 14, 1987.

Snowden, Keith. *King Arthur in the North*. Pickering, England: Castleden Publications, 2001,

Sri Aurobindo. "Árya—Its Significance." In *The Supramental Manifestation & Other Writings*. Wisconsin: Lotus Press, 1998.

Tatlock, J. S. P. *The Legendary History of Britain*. London: ~~1718~~. 1950?

Tennyson, Alfred. *Morte d'Arthur*. From *Poems*, 4th edition. London: Moxon, 1845.

Thomas, Charles. *The Early Christian Archaeology of North Britain*. The Hunter Marshall lectures delivered at the University of Glasgow in January 1968. London: Oxford University Press, 1971.

Wace and Lawman. *The Life of King Arthur*. Trans. J. Weiss and R. Allen. Dent, 1997.

Watson, William J. *The History of the Celtic Place Names of Scotland*. Edinburgh: Wm. Blackwood, 1926.

Webb, Albert E. *Glastonbury: Ynyswytryn; Isle of Avalon.* Glastonbury: Avalon, 1929.

Ziegler, Michelle. *Artúr mac Aedan of Dalriada.* From *The Heroic Age* Issue 1, (Spring/Summer 1999).

DICTIONARIES

MacBain, Alexander. *An Etymological Dictionary of the Gaelic Language.* Glasgow: Gairm Publications, 1896 & 1911.

MacFarlane, Malcolm. *The School Gaelic Dictionary.* Eneas Mckay Bookseller, 1912.

MacLennan, Malcolm. *Gaelic Dictionary.* Edinburgh: Mercat, 2001.

O'Brien, John, *Focalóir Gaoidhilge-Sax-Bhéarla: An Irish-English Dictionary.* Privately printed in Paris, 1768.

WEBSITES

Finding Merlin www.finding-merlin.com

Timothy Pont Maps http://maps.nls.uk/pont/

Blaeu Maps http://maps.nls.uk/atlas/blaeu/

List of Abbreviations

AC   *Annales Cambriae, The Welsh Annals*, History from the Sources, Arthurian Period Sources, Vol. 8, (London and Chichester: Phillimore & Co. Ltd, 1980).

CS   W. F. Skene, *Celtic Scotland, A History of Ancient Alban, History and Ethology* (Edinburgh: David Douglas, 1886).

DEB   Gildas, *De Excidio Britanniae, The Ruin of Britain*, History from the Sources, Arthurian Period Sources, Vol. 7 (London and Chichester, England: Phillimore & Co. Ltd,, 2002.

EHBP   Bede, *The Ecclesiastical History of the English People* (London: Penguin, revised edn. 1990).

FABW   W. F. Skene, *Four Ancient Books of Wales* (Edinburgh: Edmonston & Douglas, 1868).

HB   Nennius, *British History, Historia Brittonum*, History from the Sources, Arthurian Period Sources, Vol. 8, (London and Chichester, England, Phillimore & Co. Ltd, 1980).

HRB   Geoffrey of Monmouth, *History of the Kings of Britain* (London: Penguin, 1966).

LMDA   Thomas Malory, *Le Morte d'Arthur* (London: Penguin, 1969).

Notes

INTRODUCTION

1. Richard Barber, *The Figure of Arthur* (London: Longman, 1972), 20.

2. Lewis Thorpe, introduction to *HRB*, 10.

1. THE FOUR HORSEMEN OF HISTORY

1. See *Book of Aneurin* from *FABW*, trans. W. F. Skene (Edinburgh: Edmonston & Douglas, 1868).

2. *DEB*, 28.

3. Foreword to *DEB*, viii.

4. *EHBP* (London: Penguin, revised edn. 1990), 64.

5. Preface to *HB*, 9.

6. Richard Barber calls this religious passage "a glaring 9th c. addition." Barber, *Figure of Arthur*, 101.

7. *HB*, chap. 56; 35, 76. The names in brackets are the Latin originals.

8. Nennius, *The "Historia Brittonum," commonly attributed to Nennius; from a Manuscript Lately Discovered in the Library of the Vatican Palace at Rome; edited in the tenth century by Mark the Hermit*, translation and notes by the Rev. W. Gunn (London: Printed for John and Arthur Arch, 1819), 41–44.

9. *HB*, chap. 73; 42.

10. *AC*, 45.

11. Thorpe, introduction to *HRB*, 19.

12. *HRB*, book VII, chap. 1.

13. *HRB*, book XI, chap. 1.

14. Jocelyn of Furness, *Life of Kentigern*, trans. Cynthia Whiddon Green, as part of a Master's Thesis at the University of Houston, December 1998.

15. *LMDA*, bk.1, chap. V.

16. Alfred Tennyson, "Morte d'Arthur," from *Poems* (London: Moxon, 1845).

17. *LMDA*, bk. xxi, chap. 4.

18. *LMDA*, bk. xxi, chap. 5

2. THE WOULD-BE ARTHURS

1. Guy Halsall, *Worlds of Arthur* (Oxford: Oxford University Press, 2013), 152.

2. Ibid.

3. Geoffrey Ashe, *The Discovery of King Arthur* (Stroud, England: Sutton Publishing, 2005), 192.

4. Ibid, 120.

5. Leslie Alcock, *Arthur's Britain* (1971; reprint, London: Penguin, 2001), 4.

6. Ashe, *Discovery of King Arthur*, 129.

7. Thorpe, introduction to *HRB*, 10.

8. *LMDA*, bk. i, ch. 1.

9. Ashe, *Discovery of King Arthur*, 123.

10. Howard Reid, *Arthur, the Dragon King: the Barbarian Roots of Britain's Greatest Legend* (London: Headline Book Publishing, 2001), 47.

11. Chrétien de Troyes, *Arthurian Romances, Lancelot or the Knight of the Cart* (London: Penguin, 2004), 207.

12. Wace, *Roman de Brut: A History of the British*, trans. J. Weiss and R. Allen (University of Exeter Press, 1999).

13. *CS*, vol. I, 184.

14. Halsall, Guy, *Worlds of Arthur*, (Oxford, England:, OUP), 24.

15. Ashe, *Discovery of King Arthur*, 128.

16. Alcock, *Arthur's Britain*, 62.

17. *HB*, ch. 56, 35.

18. Alistair Moffat, *Arthur and the Lost Kingdoms* (London: Phoenix, 2000), 208.

19. See Gaelic-English Dictionaries by Alexander MacBain, Patrick MacFarlane, Malcolm MacLennan. Also see Howard Reid, *Arthur the Dragon King*, 58; Graham Phillips and Martin Keatman, *King Arthur: The True Story* (London: Arrow Books, 1993), 75; Keith Snowden, *King Arthur in the North* (Pickering, England: Castleden Publications, 2001), 23.

20. Goodrich, Norma Lorre, *King Arthur*. (New York: Harper & Row, 1989), 72.

21. Shakespeare's Stratford-upon-Avon is the most famous.

22. *HB*, 35, 76.

23. Morris, *Age of Arthur*, 112.

24. Alcock, *Arthur's Britain*, 66.

25. *HB*, 5.

26. Alcock, *Arthur's Britain*, 66.

27. *Harleian MS 3859* (c. 1100). *HB*, Introduction, 1–3.

28. *Vatican Reg. 1964* (11th century). c. 945 CE.

29. *British Library Cotton Caligula A VIII* (12th century).

30. *HRB*, 79.

31. Reid, *Arthur, the Dragon King*, 59.

32. Phillips and Keatman, *King Arthur, The True Story*, 164.

33. Morris, John, *The Age of Arthur*, 140, 513.

34. Phillips and Keatman, *King Arthur, The True Story*, 16.

35. Steve Blake and Scott Lloyd, *The Keys to Avalon* (England: Element Books, 2000).

36. David Francis Carroll, *Arturius: A Quest for Camelot* (privately printed, 1996).

37. James McKillop, *Oxford Dictionary of Celtic Mythology* (London: OUP, 1998), 29.

38. Albert E. Webb, *Glastonbury: Ynyswytryn; Isle of Avalon* (Glastonbury: Avalon, 1929), 11.

39. McKillop, *Oxford Dictionary*, 29.

40. MacBain, *Gaelic-English Dictionary*.

41. Norris J. Lacy, ed., *Arthurian Encyclopaedia*, 33.

42. Julian Munby, Richard Barber, and Richard Brown, *Edward III's Round Table at Windsor* (Woodbridge, Suffolk, England: Boydell Press, 2007).

43. Peter Berresford Ellis, *The Celts* (London: Constable & Robinson, 2004), 53.

3. WHY ARTHUR IS LOST TO HISTORY

1. *LMDA*, bk.1, ch. 5.

2. www.nls.uk/pont Go to "Specialist," then to map 14.

3. Letter to AA from Chris Fleet of National Library of Scotland, dated March 28, 2003. "Pont uses both small rectangles and circles (with points inside) to indicate the location of inhabited places, and sometimes both these types have vertical lines above. On Pont 14, along with several others in this area, the circles and squares merge . . . of the 37 Pont sheets with settlement symbols on them, 23 have rectangles, 12 have circular symbols, and 8 are combined. Do the combined symbols mean   anything different? Is it evidence of more than one hand on the map—such as Robert Gordon of Straloch—who we know added to and embellished Pont's maps? Is it simply inconsistency by Pont . . .?"

4. William J. Watson, *The History of the Celtic Place Names of Scotland* (Blackwood, Edinburgh: Blackwood, 1926), 394–5. Also see Adamnan, *Life of Columba* (London: Penguin, 1995), 291, note 136.

5. John O'Brien, *Focalóir Gaoidhilge-Sax-Bhéarla: An Irish-English Dictionary* (privately printed in Paris, France,1768), frontispiece.

6. *Dun Ard Righ*, "Hillfort of the High King," is always a possibility, but it does not fit as well as *Dun Ard Airigh* when considered with reference to all the other *Ard Airigh* names that run along the spine of Argyll, north to Ardnamurchan.

7. *DEB*, chap. 26, 28.

8. *HB*, chap. 56, 35.

9. *AC*, 45.

10. Introduction to *DEB*, 1.

11. Bibliographical foreword to *DEB*, viii.

12. *DEB*, 13.

13. *DEB*, 28. J. A. Giles, for no good reason except to place Arthur in the south, translates *Badonis* not as "Badon" but as "Bathhill": J. A. Giles, *Six old English chronicles*, London, G. Bell & sons, 1891.

14. Giles, *Six old English*.

15. *The English Historical Review*, No. CLXIV, Oct.1926, 497-503.

16. *DEB*, chap. 26, 28.

17. *EHBP*, 64.

18. J. A. Giles, *The Works of Gildas and Nennius* (James Bohm: London, 1841); and Giles, *Six old English*. "Saxons" was a catch-all term used, again by southern writers, to cover Angles, Saxons, and Anglo-Saxons.

19. *DEB*, 26.

20. Ibid.

21. Introduction to *DEB*, 5.

22. Michael Winterbottom, ed. and trans., *The Ruin of Britain and Other Documents*, (*Arthurian Period Sources*, Vol. 7, DEB), 29 and 99.

4. A FRAGMENTED KINGDOM

1. The efforts of that great Scot Ian Hamilton (and others) in 1950 to bring the stolen stone back to Scotland were no less gallant because the stone they took from Westminster was a fake. The film *Stone of Destiny* (2008) tells this story. I recommend it.

2. Peter Drummond, *Placenames of the Monklands* (Monklands Library Services Dept., 1987), 1 and 4; See also "Blaeu Maps" (National Library of Scotland website: http://maps.nls.uk/atlas/blaeu/).

3. Advocates' MS 72.1.1, Advocates Library, Edinburgh.

4. http://maps.nls.uk/atlas/blaeu/.

5. Ian Finlay, *Columba* (Glasgow, Richard Drew Pub., 1979), 8.

6. Adamnan, *Life of Columba*, I.7, 119.

7. *LMDA*, book III, chap.1, 92.

8. Peter Berresford Ellis, *The Celts*, 39.

9. 27th August 2011.

10. 22nd February 2011.

11. Béroul, The *Romance of Tristan* (London: Penguin Books, 1970).

5. LA NAISSANCE D'ARTHUR

1. *HRB*, part 7; ix.i.

2. Norma L. Goodrich, *King Arthur* (New York: Harper Perennial, 1989), 58.

3. *HRB*, 284.

4. J. S. P. Tatlock, *The Legendary History of Britain* (London, 1718), 423.

5. In 1871 the German explorer Karl Mauch rediscovered the magnificent ruins of Great Zimbabwe in southern Africa. Mauch refused to believe that the ancestors of the local people could have built this place and concluded that it must have been built by biblical characters from the time of Solomon(!). This was accepted for years until evidence came to light that proved Great Zimbabwe had been built by local people. I know how the local people must have felt.

6. *DEB*, 24/2, 27.

6. THE SWORD IN THE STONE

1. *AC*, 45.

2. Geoffrey of Monmouth, *The Life of Merlin*, *Vita Merlini*, trans. by John Jay Parry (1925).

3. "The Dialogue of Merlin and Taliesin" from *The Black Book of Carmarthen*, Peniarth MS 1 NLW.

4. Ibid.

5. Geoffrey of Monmouth, *Life of Merlin*.

6. *The Four Ancient Books of Wales*, ed. W. F. Skene, 1868, republished 2007 by Forgotten Books, www.forgotten books.org.

7. With thanks to Duncan Murray, Eugene, Oregon, USA, who made this point to me in an email on July 9, 2008.

8. Adamnan, *Life of Columba*, bk. II, 172.

9. Ibid, bk. II. para. 24, 173.

10. Ibid, bk. II, para. 22, 171.

11. Ibid, bk. III, para. 5.

12. Ibid.

13. Ian Finlay, *Columba* (Glasgow: Richard Drew Pub., 1979), 146.

14. Fitzroy MacLean, *Highlanders* (London: Penguin, 1995).

15. The Stone of Destiny should not be confused with the lump of Perthshire sandstone labeled "Stone of Destiny" in Edinburgh Castle.

16. J. Crichton-Stuart, *Scottish Coronations* (1902), NLS R.232.b & BCL.C1065.

17. John Macleod, *Highlanders* (London: Hodder & Stoughton, 1996), 81.

18. Thomas Malory, *LMDA*, book 1. chap. 5, 15.

19. Norma L. Goodrich, *King Arthur*, 54.

7. CAMELOT

1. *Annals of Tigernach*, my "translation." *Chirchind* is but another version of *Circenn*—see Bassas chapter.

2. Chrétien de Troyes, *Arthurian Romances, Lancelot or the Knight of the Cart*, note 4, 512.

3. There are different views about the order of words in Gaelic, but then there are different views about everything when there is no definitive evidence either way. Usually, in Gaelic, the noun comes first, so I am told, although there are exceptions—*Ard Righ* for one. Three years ago in Connel I asked an older woman, a native Gaelic speaker, about word orders with particular reference to *Ard Righ* and *Ard Airigh*. She laughed at my attempt to find formal answers to these questions and told me that when she was young it would be one way and then the other.

4. Chrétien de Troyes, *Arthurian Romances, Lancelot or the Knight of the Cart*, note 3, 511

8. THE SCOTTISH CIVIL WAR

1. *Annals of Tigernach* , 574.1

2. John N. McLeod "Remarks on the Supposed Site of Delgon or Cindelgen, the seat of Conall, King of Dalriada, AD 563," *Proceedings*

of the Society of Antiquarians of Scotland 28 (3rd S. 4), (December 11, 1893), 13–18.

3. *FABW*, trans. W. F. Skene (Edinburgh: Edmonston & Douglas, 1868), chap. IV, 52.

4. Leslie Alcock, *Arthur's Britain*, 66.

5. www.facesofarthur.org.uk.

6. Edward Gibbon, *The Decline and Fall of the Roman Empire*, vol.1, chap.6, part 1.

7. Caesar, *Gallic War*, vi, 9; Florus, i,45,15.

8. *CS*, vol. I, 85–91.

9. Too many historians in the north of Britain are too afraid of the opinion of the historians in the south of Britain to think of things in a Scottish light, and too many historians from the south of Britain are too insular, indeed, parochial to think of the north at all.

10. Probably the Cichican valley to which Gildas refers in *DEB, History*, chap. 19, 23.

11. Leslie Alcock, *Arthur's Britain*, 4.

12. *FABW*, chap. 6, 77.

9. THE GREAT ANGLE WAR

1. Taken from *Y Gododdin* by Aneirin, these lines apply to another battle but they reflect the atmosphere of the campaign of the time.

2. *HB*, 35.

3. Ibid.

4. *CS*, vol. I / 153 & 174.

5. D. N. Dumville, *Historia Brittonum* iii: *The Vatican Recension* (Cambridge, 1985); and *History of the Britons* (Kessinger Publishing's Rare Reprints: no date), 32.

6. Taken from *Y Gododdin* by Aneirin, these lines apply to another battle but they reflect the atmosphere at the time.

7. Taken from *Y Gododdin* by Aneirin, these lines apply to another battle but reflect the atmosphere of the campaign of the Caledonian Wood.

8. Ibid.

9. R. G. Collingwood, "Arthur's Battles," *Antiquity*, III (1929), 296. Traeth Trevroit, with *traeth* being Welsh for a "tidal estuary."

10. *HB*, chap. 6. Alternatively, "On the banks of the river Tral Treuroit."

11. *Black Book of Carmarthen.*

12. Ibid.

13. Translation by Robert Williams with a few lines from Patrick Sims-Williams.

14. Ibid.

15. British Library, *Harleian MS 3859* (c. 1100); and Introduction to *HB*, 1–3.

16. *Vatican Reg. 1964* (11th century). c.945CE.

17. British Library, *Cotton Caligula A VIII* (12th century).

18. J. A. Giles, translation of *HB*.

19. O'Brien, Introduction to *Dictionary*, xi.

20. *FABW*, 83.

21. Pat Gerber, *The Search for the Stone of Destiny* (Edinburgh: Canongate Press, 1992), 21.

22. *HB*, 35.

23. *AC*, 45. This entry has been given the date 516 CE.

24. *DEB*, chap. 26.

25. *DEB*, vol. 7, 28.

26. Preface to *DEB*, para 1.2, 13.

27. *DEB*, para. 26.2, 28.

28. *Monaidh* is the genitive singular of *monadh*. In MacBain's dictionary, *monadh* is a mountain range or mountain. And so Dun Monaidh, the hill fort of hills, the hill of hills. It was borrowed from the Picts and is rare in Argyll.

10. The Legend Is Born

1. *Finding Merlin.*

2. *Book of Aneurin* from *FABW*, trans. W. F. Skene.

3. *DEB*, 29 and99.

4. *LMDA*, book xxi, chap. 5, 517.

5. Ibid.

6. Ibid.

7. Ibid.

8. *HRB*, ix. 4, 217.

9. Glastonbury, according to Malory.

10. *LMDA*, bk. xxi, chap. 7; and Joseph D. Parry, "*Following Malory out of Arthur's World*," *Modern Philology*, 95.2 (1997) 717: 29–33 and 147. "Yet som men say in many partys of Inglonde that Kynge Arthure ys nat dede, but had by the wyll of oure Lorde Jesu into another place; and men say that he shall com agayne. . ."

11. *LMDA*, book xxi, chap. 7.

12. *LMDA*, book xxi. chap 6, 519.

13. *LMDA*, book xxi , chap. 5, 517.

14. The best exposition of the figure "Nine" in the Celtic world, with particular reference to Nine Women is Stuart McHardy's *The Quest for the Nine Maidens* (Edinburgh: Luath Press, 2003).

15. W. F. Skene, *Notes on the history and probable situation of the earlier establishments at Iona, prior to the foundation of the Benedictine Monastery in the end of the twelfth century* (Proceedings of the Society of Antiquaries of Scotland, 13 December 1875), 347.

16. *LMDA*, bk. 11, chap.6.

17. Adamnan, *Life of Columba*, book II, chap. 6.

18. Skene's *Notes* (RSA 14th April 1987), 204, see above.

19. Arthur died in 596. The first Archbishop of Canterbury, Augustine, arrived in the far south of Britain in 597.

20. Finlay, *Columba*, 182; Adamnan, *Life of Columba*, bk. 3, 228.

21. *Anglo Saxon Chronicle*, version E. Dawston, near Saughtree, a few miles north of the battlefield of *Arderydd*.

22. See *Finding Merlin*.

23. *DEB*, chap. 26, 29. Mungo's success did not please Gildas because they were not of the same Christian sect.

24. Ibid.

25. Geoffrey of Monmouth, *Vita Merlini Silvestris*, trans. by Winifred and John MacQueen, *Scottish Studies* 29 (1989): 77–93.

26. Ibid.

11. FINDING CAMLANN, THE LAST BATTLE

1. Thomas Green, *A Gazetteer of Arthurian Onomastic and Topographic Folklore* (NS879827).

2. *HRB*, bk. xi.2, 259.

3. The River Camel, according to the editor of the Penguin edition of Geoffrey's *History*.

4. *HRB*, bk. xi.2, 260 *et seq.*

5. *LMDA*, bk. xx., chap. 2. I have no idea what Malory meant by "love that time was not as is nowadays" but it sounds interesting.

6. *LMDA*, bk xxi, chap. 1.

7. Bamburgh, Northumberland.

8. *LMDA*, bk. xxi, chap. 2.

9. Ibid.

10. MacBain, *Etymological Gaelic-English Dictionary*.

11. "Canmore," RCAHMS website, *Archaeology Notes*, NMRS No. NS88SE 23.00. Falkirk, Camelon.

12. George Buchanan, *The History of Scotland*, (circa 1582); trans. James Aikman (1827).

13. *Historical Manuscripts Commission*, xiii, app.ii, Portland MSS, ii, 56.

14. RCAHMS website.

15. The same euphonic pressure that made Cam Lann into Camelon made Cam Loth into Camelot.

16. *Annals of Tigernach. Chirchind* is but another version of *Circenn*—see Bassas chapter.

17. *Annals of Ulster* 596.3. "The slaying of Aedán's sons," i.e. Bran and Domangart.

18. *Annals of Ulster* 596.4.

19. I read *Coraind* and *Corann* as corrupt versions of the same name.

20. Geoffrey Ashe, *Discovery of Arthur*, 130.

21. Adamnan, *Life of Columba*.

22. Ibid.

23. *The Red Book of Hergest* (c. 1425), col. 588–600.

24. *Triad 5*, trans. by J. Rhys and J. G. Evans (1887).

25. *HB*, chap. 63, 38.

26. Adamnan says Aedan, but only because Aedan was a king and so in titular charge of the army.

27. *The Four Ancient Books of Wales*, Peniarth MS 54.

EPILOGUE: ÁRYA

1. Sri Aurobindo, "Árya': Its Significance," in *The Supramental Manifestation & Other Writings*, (Wisconsin: Lotus Press, 1998).

2. *Länsmuseet På Gotland* website in 2009.

Acknowledgments

I WISH TO THANK EVERYONE AT OVERLOOK DUCKWORTH, PARTICU-
larly my editor, Dan Crissman, for his vision and decisiveness (things
we could do with more of in Scotland) and my copyeditor, Chantal
Clarke, for her expertise and care. Any mistakes that remain in this
book are entirely my responsibility. I also wish to thank my family,
Dorothy-Anne, Claudia, Kay, and Eliot, for their support and patience
over the years it took me to write *Finding Arthur*.

Index